From This Earth

FROM THIS EARTH

The Ancient Art of Pueblo Pottery

STEWART PECKHAM

Photographs by Mary Peck

Laboratory of Anthropology/
Museum of Indian Arts and Culture

Museum of New Mexico Press ♦ Santa Fe

Copyright © 1990 Museum of New Mexico Press. *All rights reserved*. No part of this book may be reproduced in any form or by any means, including electronic or mechanical, without the expressed written consent of the publishers, with the exception of brief passages embodied in critical reviews.

The Laboratory of Anthropology/Museum of Indian Arts and Culture and the Museum of New Mexico Press are units of the Museum of New Mexico, a division of the State Office of Cultural Affairs.

This publication is made possible through the generous support of funding from the National Endowment for the Arts and the Museum of New Mexico Foundation.

Printed in Japan.
Design: Eleanor Caponigro
Typography: Michael and Winifred Bixler
Project editor: Mary Wachs

LIBRARY OF CONGRESS CATALOGUING-IN-PUBLICATION DATA
Peckham, Stewart L.
　　From this earth : the ancient art of Pueblo pottery / by Stewart
　L. Peckham ; photographs by Mary Peck.
　　　p.　cm.
　　Includes bibliographical references; index.
　　ISBN 0-89013-204-6.　ISBN 0-89013-205-4 (pbk.)
　　1. Pueblo Indians—Pottery.　I. Peck, Mary, 1952-　　．II. Title.
E99.P9P37　1990
738.3'089'974—dc20　　　　　　　　　　　　　　　　　　　　90-30846
　　　　　　　　　　　　　　　　　　　　　　　　　　　　　　　CIP

Museum of New Mexico Press
P.O. Box 2087
Santa Fe, New Mexico 87504-2087

FRONTISPIECE: *Chaco Corrugated jar (bottom view showing coiling detail)*, A.D. 1075–1125. *Anasazi Utility Tradition, Chaco Province.*

CONTENTS

Foreword by J. J. Brody   VII

Preface   IX

Introduction   1

Chapter 1. Pottery and the Pioneer Archaeologists   6

Chapter 2. Coming to Terms with Pueblo Pottery   15

Chapter 3. Painted Pottery Traditions   57

Chapter 4. Pueblo Pottery Post–1600   120

Conclusion   135

Appendix of Pottery Vessel Data   138

Glossary   157

Selected Bibliography   162

Index   166

FOREWORD

In his long career as an archaeologist, Stewart Peckham certainly has studied hundreds of thousands of potsherds, a statement that sounds hyperbolic unless one has investigated Pueblo pottery with any degree of depth. The sheer quantity of pottery fragments at archaeological sites in the Southwest is staggering. At one place alone, familiar to Peckham, a fair estimate was made about twenty-five years ago that more than a million sherds were collected, washed, bagged, sorted, and classified over a five-year excavation period. Not all sites have quantities of that magnitude, thank goodness, but considering that during the better part of his thirty years as a professional Stew was a field archaeologist working primarily at ceramic sites, he must have examined millions of potsherds, sorting, classifying, and pondering the significance of the little buggers.

Little buggers. The phrase implies vitality—living, scurrying things—and well it should. The taxonomic system used by Southwestern archaeologists to classify pottery originated with the artificial classification system developed by the eighteenth-century Swedish botanist Linneaus and invented to organize organisms. I don't know whether or not it is the syntax that does it, but I have heard archaeologists talk of pottery types as though of their own volition moving from place to place and engaging in some sort of mating procedure so as to produce hybrid progeny. You could sell tickets to that one.

That absurd image is not entirely false, for pots and potsherds can bring us as close as we will ever come to sensing the personalities of the living and breathing people who made and used the pottery recovered from the ancient sites. The further back in time archaeologists take us, the more difficult it becomes to realize the humanity of people known to us only through archaeology. So it may be reasonable and appropriate to have pottery stand for those who made it, to think of a potsherd as a metaphor for a person, to pretend that pots are people. And it is a fact that in the Southwest, where all pottery was hand-built (and much of it still is), each pot contains human traces, is unique, and was made by an individual belonging to a tradition that is the sum of his or her own ancestry. Consideration of ceramic traditions provides the central focus of this book.

At one level (that of the "lumpers," as Peckham puts it) all of the products of a tradition look alike. That is when we concentrate on points of similarity and classify a pot or potsherd as representing a social person conforming as closely as possible to the mores and values of his or her own group. At another level (that of the "splitters") each product of a tradition is unique. That is when we concentrate on the large and small differences that allow us to classify that very same pot or potsherd as representing an individual personality independently asserting and perhaps even testing the mores and values of his or her own group. Both are right, but each only tells half the story.

Stew Peckham, who is neither a lumper nor a splitter, is probably amongst the world's two or three most knowledgeable typologists of Southwestern pottery. Thus he knows, appreciates, and understands the work of the splitters as few do. And as is evident in this broadly based synthesis, he also knows, understands, and is philosophically comfortable with the lumpers. He tells the long and complex history of the ceramic traditions of the Anasazi and Pueblo people of New Mexico as only a person familiar with millions of potsherds and the minutiae of ceramic typology can. Then, with rare skill, he selects from a very large inventory superb examples of whole vessels to illustrate that history. There is hardly a piece illustrated that is not precisely right, that cannot be referenced back and forth through time and space to demonstrate how a particular artistic tradition is the sum of myriad parts, each one a unique product of a creative human intelligence. Words and pictures, lumpers and splitters, tradition and creativity. As in the Pueblo world, oppositions make the whole.

J. J. Brody

PREFACE

Hardly a day goes by in Santa Fe, New Mexico, when Pueblo Indians are not selling their pottery under the portal of the Palace of the Governors. However, few of the tourists who buy the pottery—and probably not many of the Indians—realize that antecedents of even the simplest of these pottery trinkets can be found in prehistoric fragments that lay buried beneath the streets and buildings of downtown Santa Fe, and that the Southwestern heritage of them all can be traced back, without interruption, at least eighteen hundred years.

For many years, interested visitors have not too subtly pointed out that the large and varied collections of prehistoric and historic Pueblo Indian pottery in the Museum of New Mexico have been largely inaccessible to a general public whose interest in collecting Pueblo pottery extends to gaining some knowledge of the craft, its creators, its long heritage, and what its future may be. Although this major collection until recently has not enjoyed the benefit of an exhibition space in which to show itself off, it actually has been accessible to researchers and interested visitors by appointment, and always to Native American craftspeople.

This cultural void has been filled thanks to strong legislative support that enabled the construction of a new exhibit facility, the Museum of New Mexico's Museum of Indian Arts and Culture. With its opening in 1987, and the attendant renovation of the storage and research areas of the adjacent Laboratory of Anthropology, the care and use of the museum's pottery and other collections have been brought up to contemporary museum standards. New exhibits and other educational programs designed to ready the collections for public viewing have already been inaugurated and will enable the Museum of Indian Arts and Culture to fulfill the functions for which it was intended.

Many specimens in the collections are aesthetically choice ones that have been exhibited many times both in the Museum of New Mexico and in other museums and traveling exhibits around the country, as well as illustrated in topical publications. However, if only the finest specimens were available for study, our knowledge of the introduction and development of Pueblo Indian pottery might forever be incomplete. Actually, whole pottery vessels account for less than one-sixth of the cataloged collections of the Museum of New Mexico—a major resource, to be sure, but not always fully representative of the diversity of an art form whose history extends two thousand years.

In truth, from the hundreds of prehistoric and historic sites excavated throughout New Mexico relatively few exhibit-quality pottery vessels may surface. Consequently, these few specimens must speak for the thousands upon thousands of pottery fragments (potsherds) and other artifacts recovered by archaeologists. Although any museum would like to have all of its specimens in mint condition, archaeologists consider even fragmentary vessels to be as valuable as the whole ones. Pots, partially restored pots, and potsherds come alive and offer equal enjoyment and investigative opportunity to those who study them. These fragments are preserved in the Museum of New Mexico's Archaeological Repository Collections.

Archaeologists, ethnographers, and art historians have shown that pottery making has been an uninterrupted tradition in the Southwest for some two thousand years. The times and places of its introduction into the Southwest have begun to be identified; the areas in which it has been made over the centuries have been delimited; its technological variations have become increasingly well documented; and many variations in pottery have been tied to population shifts, cultural stability and upheaval, and environmental change.

For the sake of manageability of information, these are often treated as if they were totally separate, independent events, only remotely influenced by ceramic developments in other southwestern areas. However, such events often follow increasingly predictable tracks that imply the existence of long-established traditional links between prehistoric Pueblo groups.

This essay will rely on the established standards of pottery classification as a tool to articulate the concept of the Pueblo pottery tradition, an idea dealt with somewhat by archaeologists in the past, but seemingly overlooked by them in more recent years. The pottery tradition concept offers opportunities to reexamine some archaeological rationales that prevailed several generations ago when pioneer archaeologists had lots of enthusiasm but too little data on which to base their interpretations.

It is impossible to avoid the use of some of the basic integrative terminologies that are useful in organizing Southwestern archaeological data and interpretations, for example, "Anasazi Mineral-Paint Tradition." Culture names: Anasazi, Mogollon, Hohokam, and Hakataya; designated provinces, branches, or divisions of these cultures; and the named pottery types and wares associated with them often connote degrees of certainty or validity, however, that, even at this late date, continue to be subject to debate. Pottery traditions cross-cut many of the established terminologies. While combining such terms with the descriptive names of the pottery traditions discussed here may help readers see some of the basic linkages, it does not always indicate that the author is satisfied with these associations.

Almost since the first archaeological fieldwork was done in the Southwest, pottery has served as a framework on which subsequent analyses and interpretations have been constructed. It is virtually impossible to cope with the field of Southwestern archaeology without taking time to gain some familiarity with prehistoric Pueblo pottery. And yet, to begin to become familiar with a subject that encompasses the attributes of between one thousand and fifteen hundred pottery types recognized throughout the Southwest requires training, research, extensive practical experience, and, particularly, some actual exposure to Pueblo pottery making.

Following such a ceramic trail has led me on a thirty-five-year excursion during which I have met and "talked pottery" with many professional and nonprofessional archaeologists, teachers, museum curators, collectors, ceramicists, and interested members of the general public who, in one way or another, have shared with me their interest in and knowledge about Pueblo Indian pottery. Their contributions in my behalf have come in classrooms, seminars, conferences, meetings, workshops, field projects, correspondence, and informal conversations. They know who they are, and to all of them I express my thanks. I do not expect that they will always agree entirely with my views on the subject, nor I theirs, but they have all helped me gain perspectives on Pueblo pottery and, in doing so, have continued to encourage me in my ongoing assessment of Pueblo ceramics.

As an archaeologist, curator, and administrator at the Museum of New Mexico, I have enjoyed working in various capacities with former and present members of the Museum of New Mexico staff. Without their help this book might never have developed. I am indebted to Alfred E. Dittert, Jr., Steven Becker, Bruce Bernstein, Kenneth M. Chapman, Bertha P. Dutton, Frank W. Eddy, Bruce T. Ellis, Nancy L. Fox, Laura Holt, Steven Horvath, Marsha F. Jackson, Curtis F. Schaafsma, Stanley A. Stubbs, Rosemary Talley, Betty T. Toulouse, John A. Ware, A. Helene Warren, John P. Wilson, Louise Stiver, and Regge N. Wiseman.

Additionally, I want to acknowledge the fruitful conversations concerning prehistoric pottery that I have had with Dr. Nathan W. Bower, of the Colorado College Department of Chemistry; Dr. Bart Olinger, of Los Alamos National Laboratory; and Dr. Albert H. Schroeder, formerly of the National Park Service.

In particular, I want to acknowledge the constant interest and help of Dr. Florence Hawley Ellis who, as a teacher at the University of New Mexico, introduced me to prehistoric Pueblo pottery and, subsequently, has remained a most stimulating and valued colleague and friend.

All of the pottery illustrated herein has been selected from the collections of the Museum of New Mexico's Museum of Indian Arts and Culture and Laboratory of Anthropology in Santa Fe. While the pots exhibit varying degrees of photogenic quality, they nonetheless represent the creativity of a hundred generations of potters who made, used, broke, discarded, and abandoned almost twenty centuries' worth of pottery vessels that in one way or another culminate in the glistening treasures produced by present-day Pueblo potters.

Among the illustrated specimens are many that were acquired during a partnership of the Museum of New Mexico and the School of American Research which operated as a unit for almost fifty years. Separation of these two institutions in 1959 led to an agreement between them whereby collections acquired specifically by the SAR should be so acknowledged in exhibits and publications of the museum. Thus, where applicable, illustrations and accompanying catalog data refer to "School of American Research Collections in the Museum of New Mexico."

The pottery photographs in this volume represent the artistry, skill, and labor of Mary Peck. Each of her photographs is worth far more than the proverbial "thousand words." Deborah Reade is responsible for the fine map work.

The final form of the book is the work of two very special individuals who persevered while I made last-minute changes and additions and then took over to convert the manuscript and plates into the fine publication now available. For their support, patience, and labors, sincere thanks are due Eleanor Caponigro, of Santa Fe, who designed this book, and Mary Wachs, Editorial Director of the Museum of New Mexico Press, who performed wonders with a complex manuscript.

This publication was made possible through the generous support of funding from the National Endowment for the Arts.

INTRODUCTION

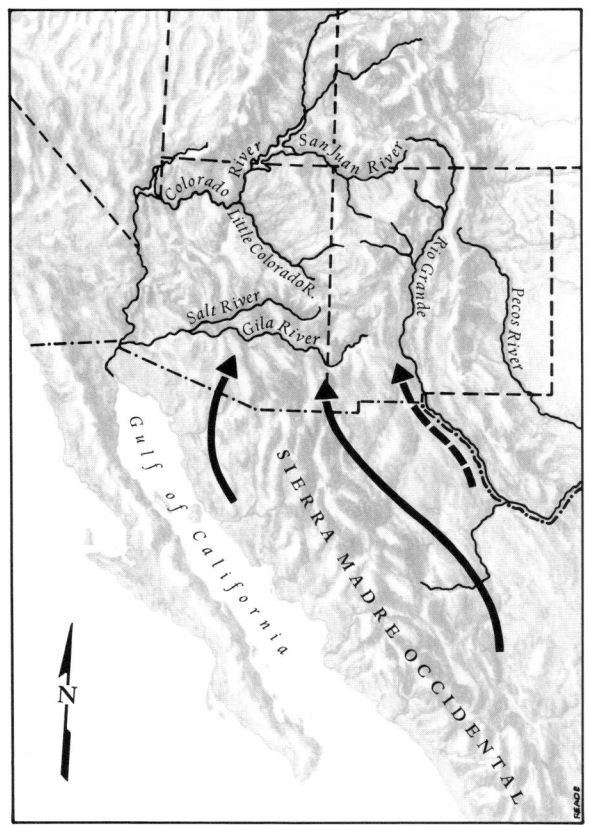

General routes of the diffusion of pottery into the Southwest. (Easternmost route is postulated).

Pueblo Indian pottery making is the most distinctive, versatile, and long-lived craft found among any North American Indian group. Almost two thousand years old, the Pueblo pottery tradition makes our three-hundred-year-old national traditions look youthful by comparison. However, in the early twentieth century, those who had begun collecting and studying this ancient craft, and perhaps even some Pueblo potters who were making it, lamented that, like many other aspects of Pueblo Indian culture, pottery making was on the verge of extinction. They feared that the potters would be subverted by the materialistic society that surrounded them and that their pottery would cease to be the pure native craft that it had been for centuries.

While at that time it was reasonable to predict the increasing attrition of almost all aspects of Pueblo Indian culture, no one could know the future course of its pottery development. To what stimuli Pueblo potters would react, or at what pace changes would take place, were impossible to identify. Today, as we approach the final decade of our century, we can look back on those rueful forecasts and see that some seem to have proven correct in a very general way. And yet Pueblo pottery survives and flourishes, gaining regional, national, and international recognition. Marked changes have indeed taken place, but Pueblo pottery making remains a vital national treasure.

Pueblo pottery making continues to undergo a major metamorphosis. Until about one hundred years ago, pottery was primarily a household craft; today, it is not. Since the time when ancestors of the Pueblos first learned to make pottery, millions of pots have been created for cooking and storing food in, holding water and ritual use, and to be sold, given away or traded, to be worn out, broken, and discarded—very much like our modern "throw-away culture." Modern pottery is only occasionally utilitarian and, when made for use within the pueblos, mainly for ceremonial purposes. A few fine old water jars, dough bowls, and food bowls may still be found as heirlooms in Pueblo households, but most have long since been sold and reside in museums and the homes of private collectors. Irrespective of its historical value, much of contemporary Pueblo pottery is valued purely on the basis of aesthetics, produced by one culture largely for the appreciation of another that collects it.

We should not be too judgmental about these current developments and what brought them about. As with changes in prehistoric pottery, if there are causes that led to the revolution in modern Pueblo pottery, they have only occasionally been recognized and documented, and usually long after the fact.

Published accounts about Pueblo pottery have scrutinized the works of individual potters and their families, described the pottery of specific pueblos, and given trait-by-trait descriptions of pottery types. Reports of archaeological excavations have presented pages of tables listing frequencies and percentages of pottery types.

As archaeologists have found, the pace at which Pueblo culture developed and the directions it took were regulated primarily by the Indians' ideas of how they got to be who and where they were. A term for that regulatory mechanism is *tradition*. Generally, we think we know what constitutes a tradition and things traditional. Sports rivalries like those between the Yankees and the Dodgers or Yale and Harvard are traditions of a sort. The observation of holidays, singing "Auld Lang Syne" on New Year's Eve, and christening a ship with a bottle of champagne are traditions not likely to become extinct in our culture.

Traditions, whether by definition or in fact, should not be taken casually. Our mobile, rapidly changing American culture is often complacent about traditions, perhaps because not everyone thinks of tradition in the same way. As a dynamic nation of people often only loosely tied to ethnic origins and values, we have tended to become more permissive and individualistic, free to observe traditions or not. Often we are only vaguely aware of how long-standing traditions began and how they affect our daily lives, especially when we don't actively participate in them. No single definition of tradition will ever suffice to explain what it means to different people, but there are many characteristics that traditions have in common.

Traditions are persistent. Persistence is basic to a tradition, and even though traditions do change, it is the steady slowness of that change, against all odds, that gives them an aura of durability and respectability that far outlasts the lives of those who fostered the traditions in the first place. People who take traditions seriously are likely to be conservative, and in tradition-oriented, nonindustrialized society there is a reluctance to upset the equilibrium a tradition affords, especially if the result of noncompliance is unpredictable.

When we speak about the persistence of a tradition, what we know about a tradition is at the "now" end of its existence. Before it could persist or continue, it had to have a beginning, but unless we have a historical document, a person's recollection, perhaps a diagnostic artifact, or a combination of these, we may not know precisely how and when the tradition began and why it is perpetuated.

Traditions help to maintain order. A defense of this maxim is offered simply by, "We do it this way because we have always done it this way." If one follows the dictates of one's forebears, action for action and word for word, a happy outcome is virtually guaranteed, but if something goes wrong, it somehow can be blamed on not achieving rote replication of the traditional model. Discovery of who or what, real or fictional, was out of order or caused the deviation from the norm further serves to point out that trust should be placed in traditional ways. In a close-knit society, such as among Southwestern Pueblos even up to the recent past, a person's nontraditional behavior may be blamed for the misfortunes experienced by the group, sometimes resulting in that person being targeted for malicious gossip, ostracism, and elimination through expulsion from the group (or worse).

Traditions have continuity. Differing somewhat from persistence is the continuity of observance of many traditions. Although the antiquity of a tradition may be spoken of in terms of having been done since time immemorial, it carries no less force than if it was a written document with names, places, dates, and specified procedures. Without continuous conscientious observance (daily, monthly, yearly, every Sabbath, or some other calendric cycle within prescribed limits) a tradition could fall into disuse and atrophy.

In largely nonliterate societies, those chosen to be community leaders are in essence the keepers of tradition and may have been selected not only because they had leadership qualities but also because they had received instruction in traditional knowledge. They have memorized all aspects of traditions important to the group: their origins and history, their material requirements, and the step-by-step procedures to be followed to ensure their exact replication. In passing on these traditions to their successors, these leaders are the guarantors of continuity. True traditionalists, without coercion, abide by the mandates of tradition and, in a self-reinforcing way, exert pressure on others to follow the rules of the tradition to the letter.

Traditions change through time. Although there may be some acceptable latitude in form and practice, traditions of nonliterate groups have been repeatedly validated to the point that there may never have been a time when members were aware that changes were taking place in their tradition. Controls may exist that help to perpetuate traditions. By their nature traditions are resistant to change (or those who perpetuate them are), but many acts of resistance that at first seem inconsequential may ultimately work to the detriment of those traditions being protected. For various reasons, people may be ignorant of all the requirements of a tradition. A few may know the rules but bend them or even reject them. Failure or refusal to follow the tradition to the letter may ultimately render it incomplete and ineffective, in essence resulting in disorder rather than order.

Not all traditions are unanimously accepted, and individuals may attempt to test how far they can stray from the norm before being chastised for antisocial behavior. Conflict or competition between pro-traditionalists and anti-traditionalists may disrupt the intent of the tradition. Not many years ago, objection by a single member of the governing council in many Pueblos was sufficient to quash any proposal that might lead to undesired change, such as further encroachment into Pueblo affairs by non-Indian governments and individuals. Thus, a lone dissenter could force the maintenance of a tradition. In many of today's council decisions, the rule of the majority is all that is required, thereby placing Pueblo traditions in greater jeopardy. Today's Pueblo elders still hold considerable influence, but as they die they will be replaced by younger members of the village who, through college education and jobs in nearby and distant cities, often vote according to new perspectives of their world, virtually assuring that some traditional values will gradually change. Still other traditions may disappear abruptly as catastrophic incidents destroy some critical component. A ceremonial tradition may become extinct when a key ritual practitioner dies, leaving no trained successor.

Traditions occupy definable space. A tradition may be in the form of an artifact, action, or idea. It may be a pottery vessel, a ritual dance, or a prohibition. Whether the tradition is material or nonmaterial, its bearer—a tribe, community, or even an archaeological culture—occupies a definable space that can be located on a map. The tradition will remain identifiable even though its spatial distribution may change through time.

A tradition persists even more widely when it is recognized and complied with as a collective response of many people. However, the larger or more dispersed a group, the greater the chance that individual interpretations of a tradition may bring about its alteration by new technology or modern substitutions. Change would be accepted until the consensus of the community allows that a new plateau of tradition observance has been reached.

Traditions may be altered by individuals. To some extent, observance of a tradition is a personal matter, and individual action is the ultimate basis for its persistence. A person may interpret the tradition and bring about its alteration through inventiveness, experimentation, or just testing it to see what degree of divergence from the norm will still be acceptable. At such times, individuals may seek a degree of freedom beyond that allowed by tradition. If adherence to the tradition is crucial to the wellbeing of the group, those who choose to set themselves apart from the group may be encouraged or permitted to leave—or they may be disposed of in some other manner.

Similar traditions are rarely identical. Outside observers may mistakenly think that all Pueblo people share a common culture, traditions, and language. On the contrary, a wealth of detail distinguishes the individual Pueblos from one another. The bases for these distinctions, which are themselves traditions, may be very old, perhaps ones that initially led people to establish and maintain separate villages centuries ago. Subsequent events may have led to the merging of Pueblo groups that, for various reasons, were forced to give up some of their old traditions abruptly or gradually as they adapted to new surroundings.

Extinct traditions are never really revived. Traditions die out when people no longer can or are willing to make an effort to observe them. Later, or even periodically, attempts may be made to revive traditions as remembered by members of the group or perhaps as "borrowed" from a neighboring group, but the revivals often involve only selected elements of the earlier tradition. The revival may bear only a superficial resemblance to the original, but this does not necessarily prevent it from being accepted and effective.

Traditions can be intrusive in time or space. Each attribute of culture can be thought of as a tradition, since each has continuity and persists, no matter how briefly. But whether a tradition is introduced to or developed within a group, to those most affected by it the tradition may often seem like a living anachronism. If it is a longstanding tradition, chances are its participants had no part in making the original judgments that initiated it. Whether followed since time immemorial or of relatively contemporary vintage, and regardless of whether the tradition reflects historical concerns or simply modern-day commercialism, such observances ultimately gain acceptance and respect by the collective.

A tradition is a thing of value. A tradition starts because a person, or a group of people, made a conscious or unconscious choice in adopting a thing or action on the basis of its merits. Initially, a tradition may begin as the result of trial and error, with someone making what seem to be innocuous decisions or choices among several alternatives. If the outcome works to the satisfaction of all concerned, the decision is validated and reinforced, and an effort may be made to make the identical decision whenever a similar need or occasion arises. Thus, the tradition is established and is perceived as something intrinsically valuable.

In addition to all the other attributes, a tradition is a thing of value that may incidentally require a person to make a choice between two or more alternatives that will be compatible with existing traditions and current or anticipated needs.

When pottery was introduced into the Southwest, it is likely that its values far outweighed any sentiments for rejecting it. It didn't replace basketry as a container, since baskets continued to be made. In terms of its relative ease of manufacture, durability, and versatility, pottery making was a revolutionary development in the Southwest. Its tremendous impact on the Indians of the region was to become a dominant theme of study by twentieth-century archaeologists.

1. POTTERY AND THE PIONEER ARCHAEOLOGISTS

There is no doubt that Spanish, Mexican, and Anglo explorers and occupiers of the Southwest were well aware of the utility of Pueblo Indian pottery. The Camino Real was the only route by which Mexican glazed earthenware (majolica) and a few European-made utensils could reach the Spanish and, later, Mexican colonials in northern New Mexico. It wasn't until the Santa Fe Trail was opened in 1821 that commercially made utensils of glazed earthenware, ironstone china, and porcelain reached colonial settlements from the United States. Pueblo potters supplied settlers' needs for these important household utensils for almost two hundred years.

By the mid-1800s participants in American military expeditions were making brief reference to Pueblo pottery, but it was later investigators, such as William H. Holmes in southwestern Colorado in 1878, who described the architecture and associated pottery of ancient ruins. William H. Jackson, in 1876 and 1878, did likewise for that area and Chaco Canyon. In the late 1870s, an early southwesternist, James Stevenson, recognized the distinctiveness of prehistoric and historic Pueblo pottery in the northern Rio Grande Valley of New Mexico and at the Hopi village of Walpi in northeastern Arizona and described and illustrated the pottery in a publication of the Smithsonian Institution (1883, 1884). By the time Stevenson's descriptions of Pueblo pottery appeared in print, Adolph F. Bandelier, a Swiss naturalist, had begun his survey of the ruins and Pueblos of the Rio Grande region (Bandelier 1880–1892). Called upon by the Archaeological Institute of America to conduct the survey, Bandelier made a trail-blazing reconnaissance that was quickly followed by similar ambitious investigations by a new breed of explorers from the East. By the turn of the century, Frank H. Cushing had excavated at Casa Grande in Central Arizona; George Pepper, of the American Museum of Natural History, had dug at Pueblo Bonito in Chaco Canyon; and J. Walter Fewkes, of the Smithsonian Institution, had dug Cliff Palace and Spruce Tree House at Mesa Verde.

Prompted by Bandelier's reports of spectacular cliff dwellings on the mesas and in the canyons of the Jémez Mountains west of Santa Fe, a schoolteacher from Greeley, Colorado, Edgar Lee Hewett, spent his summers in the middle to late 1890s prowling around an area he first called the Jémez Plateau. Exploring and probably digging in the cavate ruins and pueblos of that area, Hewett was so intrigued by the ancient remains and the beauty of the area that he managed to get a job as the first president of New Mexico Normal School (now New Mexico Highlands University) at Las Vegas, New Mexico, so he could be closer to the Pajarito Plateau, as he later named it.

Hewett was not one to let grass grow under his feet or people stand in the way of his research. He soon left Las Vegas and began promoting the establishment of a permanent research organization, the School of American Archaeology, as a western adjunct of the Archaeological Institute of America. Established in 1907, the Santa Fe–based organization was renamed the School of American Research about a decade later. Naturally, Hewett became its first director, a position he held for forty years.

Early on, Hewett realized that the archaeological resources of the Southwest were already being plundered by pothunters and Sunday antiquarians and were too significant and valuable as national treasures to continue unprotected. During the early 1900s, he lobbied forcefully for Congress to pass legislation to preserve archaeological sites on federally controlled lands. Hewett drafted much of the language of the Federal Act for the Preservation of American Antiquities (1906). It became the basis for administering thousands of archaeological sites on federal lands throughout the United States. In turn, the act became the primary justification for most, if not all, of the subsequent historic preservation legislation at both federal and state levels.

By 1907, Hewett had persuaded the legislature of the Territory of New Mexico that it should establish a Museum of New Mexico in Santa Fe, designating him as its first director, a position paralleling that which he held at the School of American Archaeology. Surprisingly, he still had time to conduct further explorations in the mesa and canyon ruins, and between 1909 and 1912 he dug part of the great Community House at Puyé, as well as the ruin of Tyuonyi and nearby cavate dwellings in Frijoles Canyon.

Hewett did not concern himself overly with details, preferring to leave such things to his assistants. One of these was a Harvard graduate student, Alfred V. Kidder, who got his start in archaeology in the first decade of the 1900s. He participated in Hewett's excavations at Puyé and Frijoles Canyon and in pioneering archaeological reconnaissances in the Four Corners area west of Mesa Verde. Kidder's work in the Pajarito ultimately led him to conduct a decade-long excavation of the great historic pueblo of Pecos beginning in 1915.

To these pioneers it was readily apparent that pottery constituted the most abundant artifact to be found at the majority of archaeological sites in the Southwest and, further, that not all pottery looked the same. The most obvious differences in pottery lay in color and surface treatment. Much pottery in the northern Southwest was dull gray to almost white, but within this range were both well-smoothed pots that had painted decoration and seemed not to have been used for cooking and those that were rough, unpainted, and encrusted with soot from cooking fires. The distinctions between "painted pots" and "cooking pots" were easily understood by the early investigators, but today's archaeologists are not at home with these delineations. They instead speak of the painted "service" pottery versus the crude-looking, rough "culinary" or "utility" pottery as the fundamental distinction common to most prehistoric pottery regardless of where it is found in the Southwest.

As pioneers in a totally new discipline, the first-generation archaeologists' published attempts to place their pottery finds into somewhat more rigorous categories were inadequate by present standards. Such types as "Pre-Pueblo Ware," "Blue-gray type," "Black-and-red Ware," and "Crackled Black-on-white" may seem naive to today's archaeologists, but with little or no previous experience in the Southwest and no libraries full of books containing comparative data and interpretations, the early archaeologists usually coined their own terms as their work progressed or adopted new terms learned from colleagues working in other parts of the region.

A. V. Kidder apparently was the first to name and formally describe a pottery type in detail. This was "Biscuit Ware" (Kidder 1915), a conspicuous painted pottery abundant at ruins such as Puyé, Otowi, and Tsirege on the Pajarito Plateau. Such were the details for which Hewett had no time, and though it took many years before other archaeologists followed Kidder's lead, systematic descriptions of the ubiquitous artifact were to become traditional in the study of Southwestern archaeology.

Generally, each pottery type was provided with a convenient given name, usually a place-name (a town, a river, an archaeological site) in the area where the pottery type was most commonly found. Either Spanish or English place-names were most common, but some archaeologists borrowed intriguing Indian place-names (often misspelled or mispronounced) that added to the mystique of the developing field of Southwestern archaeology. The given name was usually followed by a two- or three-word description of the color or surface treatment of the pottery. Thus, we find such pottery type names as "Mesa Verde Black-on-white," "Wingate Black-on-red," "Heshotauthla Polychrome," "Reserve Indented Corrugated," and "Potsuwi'i Incised."

Between 1912 and 1915, Nels C. Nelson (1914), of the American Museum of Natural History, conducted intensive excavations at over twenty major ruins mainly in the Galisteo Basin, within fifty kilometers (thirty-one miles) of Santa Fe. Using the stratigraphic technique of excavation for the first time in North America, Nelson showed that changes in the frequencies of potsherds of different colors and styles in a refuse mound could be used to establish relative ages of occupation levels at the ruined pueblo of San Cristobal.

At the same time, pottery provided the bases on which the major archaeological areas (Chaco, Mesa Verde, Pajarito, Pecos, Tiguex, Jémez, Zuni, Salinas, Mimbres) became better defined (map). Early fieldwork concentrated particularly on large Pueblo ruins that, except for those in the Chaco, Mesa Verde, and Mimbres provinces, we now know were occupied since A.D. 1300. The widespread occurrence of sites with monumental architecture and diversity and abundance of pottery and other artifacts seemed to confirm hypotheses that they and the modern Pueblos were somehow related. However, it would be decades before enough information had been gathered to draw such conclusions with certainty.

The archaeologists seemed to have been operating under basic assumptions that prehistoric Pueblo potters of a specific area and given time range made pottery that reflected the accessibility of suitable pottery-making resources and perhaps according to some agreed upon rules, or values, concerning what were acceptable forms, finishes, and designs. As an example, the potters at Chaco Canyon Province in the eleventh century A.D. obtained their gray-firing clays, tempering materials, slip clays, and pigments from nearby rock outcrops. The pottery they produced duplicated the same general forms, painted decoration, and surface treatment common to the Basketmaker-Pueblo people. These would contrast, at least in part, with those preferred by potters of the same time in the Mesa Verde Province. The consistent association of pottery attributes provided the bases for the modern system of *pottery types*. Overlapping distributions of the dominant pottery types suggested both cultural links between the same archaeological areas and cultural distinctions.

By the 1920s, the pioneer archaeologists had already learned a great deal about the Southwest and, in general, were aware of what their colleagues were finding in the field. However, they found that each area prompted the recognition of its own

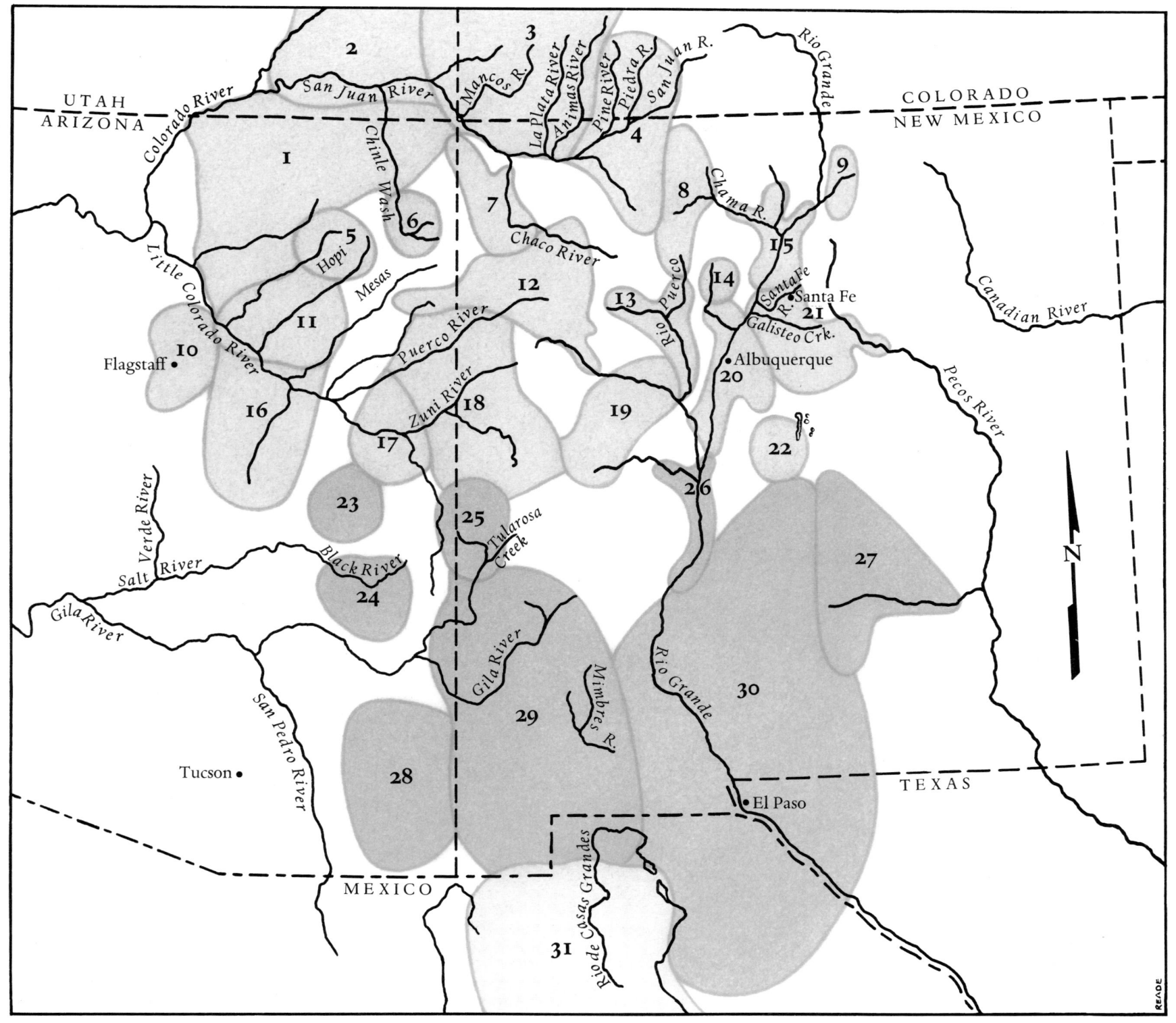

Prehistoric provinces of the Southwest.

ANASAZI PROVINCES: 1 Kayenta or Navajo Mountain; 2 Cedar Mesa; 3 Mesa Verde; 4 Upper San Juan; 5 Black Mesa; 6 De Chelly-Chinle; 7 Chuska; 8 Gallina; 9 Taos; 10 Flagstaff; 11 Hopi Buttes; 12 Chaco; 13 Middle Rio Puerco; 14 Jémez; 15 Tewa Basin; 16 Chevelon-Chavez; 17 Upper Little Colorado; 18 Cíbola or Zuni; 19 Acoma; 20 Middle Rio Grande; 21 Tano; 22 Salinas. MOGOLLON PROVINCES: 23 Forestdale; 24 Black River; 25 Southern Cíbola or Cíbola-Mimbres Transition; 26 Rio Abajo; 27 Northern or Upland Jornada; 28 San Simon; 29 Mimbres; 30 Southern or Lowland Jornada. NORTHERN MEXICAN PROVINCE: 31 Casas Grandes.

artifact assemblages and often the development of its own archaeological terminology. There was no common archaeological syntax that would render the findings in one area applicable to the others. In order to reconstruct the cultures of the prehistoric past, archaeologists would have to develop a system by which the results of past excavations could be compared and contrasted and subsequent fieldwork interpreted. Kidder, who had already spent twenty years at fieldwork in the Southwest and was one of the leaders in the profession, proposed an informal conference at which archaeologists could pool knowledge of their respective study areas, assess what they had learned so far, and establish some common ground on which to base their future research.

In 1927, Kidder convened a Conference of Southwestern Anthropologists (later an almost annual gathering to be known as the Pecos Conference), which met at the ruins of Pecos Pueblo, near Santa Fe. Its participants proposed and discussed a sequence of periods in the cultural evolution of what was then called Basketmaker-Pueblo Culture. This Pecos Classification (table) enumerated in approximate dates the stages of the development of Pueblo culture in a step-by-step, easily understood system, allowing each researcher to relate his findings to a conceptual framework that seemed applicable throughout much of the Southwest.

Not all archaeologists unanimously endorsed the system, and both modifications and outright alternative systems were proposed during the next few years. Some felt that important diagnostic traits were omitted; others said it allowed no room for insertion of additional periods within the numbered sequence, or it was not easily applied to all areas of the Southwest, especially the Rio Grande provinces, or it began with a hypothesized period that had not yet been found in the field (Roberts 1935; Wendorf and Reed 1955).

Perhaps because even its critics saw it as a way to bring order to the growing mass of archaeological data, the Pecos Classification was accepted with at least restrained enthusiasm. For the next thirty years, a primary goal of most Southwestern archaeologists was attempting to fit the data from their respective research areas into the system. They found that the original scheme developed at Pecos in 1927 had flaws that required revision as new or contradicting data were found. Originally, they thought that changes in the shapes of skulls from round to oval between Basketmaker III and Pueblo I were due to the arrival of a migrant population. Eventually, archaeologists concluded that a change in the type of cradleboard to which prehistoric infants were bound could account for the differing skull shapes.

Apparently archaeologists grew weary of referring to the "Basketmaker-Pueblo Culture" and yearned for a concise, Indian-sounding name that could convey the same meaning and which would serve as a counterpart to the previously named Hohokam Culture whose range was in the lowland deserts of southern Arizona. J. O. Brew, of the Peabody Museum at Harvard, queried local Navajo in the Four Corners area as to what was the Navajo word for the ancient Indians who had inhabited the thousands of ruins on the Navajo Reservation. Something sounding like "Anasazi" was the reply. The term *Anasazi Culture* was quickly adopted and ever since has been used to refer to the prehistoric Pueblo-building, pottery-making, agricultural Indians who once lived in the northern Southwest, as well as in other parts of the region.

Not until much later did linguists inform archaeologists that, to the Navajo,

	PECOS CLASSIFICATION	ROBERTS CLASSIFICATION	RIO GRANDE CLASSIFICATION	MIMBRES CLASSIFICATION	MOGOLLON CLASSIFICATION	
2000						2000
1900						1900
1800	PUEBLO V	HISTORIC PUEBLO	HISTORIC PERIOD			1800
1700						1700
1600						1600
1500	PUEBLO IV	REGRESSIVE PUEBLO	CLASSIC PERIOD			1500
1400						1400
1300	PUEBLO III	GREAT PUEBLO	COALITION PERIOD	POST-CLASSIC PERIOD	MOGOLLON 5	1300
1200						1200
1100				CLASSIC PERIOD	MOGOLLON 4	1100
1000	PUEBLO II					1000
900		DEVELOPMENTAL PUEBLO	DEVELOPMENTAL PERIOD		MOGOLLON 3	900
800	PUEBLO I			LATE PITHOUSE PERIOD	MOGOLLON 2	800
700						700
600	BASKETMAKER III	MODIFIED BASKETMAKER				600
500						500
400						400
300				EARLY PITHOUSE PERIOD	MOGOLLON 1	300
200	BASKETMAKER II	BASKETMAKER				200
100						100
A.D. B.C.						A.D. B.C.

"Anasazi" translated as "enemy ancestors." Since the Navajo may not have arrived in the Southwest until the 1400s or 1500s and were linguistically and culturally unrelated to the Pueblo Indians, the name "Anasazi" might be appropriate for the Navajo to use, but not entirely proper when used by Pueblo people or non-Indians.

Even when "Anasazi" was first adopted, it was obvious to Southwesternists that the various modern Pueblo Indians spoke a number of distinct languages (Kiowa-Tanoan, Keres, and Zuni, in New Mexico; and Hopi in northeastern Arizona) which presumably evolved and became differentiated during the prehistoric period being studied. To lump the ancestors of these diverse groups under a single generic name is comparable to saying that the Queen of England is a European.

Since the 1950s, archaeologists have repeatedly found that Anasazi people in some provinces built pithouses well into the 1300s (early Pueblo IV), long after the Pecos Classification's evolutionary sequence considered them to have been an extinct form of dwelling. New data will almost always require some changes, but, as a tradition itself, the Pecos Classification remains the only viable system that summarizes the general stages of development of prehistoric Indian cultures in the northern Southwest.

As more sites were dated by dendrochronology (tree-ring dating), general time ranges for the periods of the Pecos Classification gave the system added value. Today's archaeologists realize that there is far more observable variability in archaeological remains than was being recorded sixty years ago, and to attempt to fit all data into the neat little pigeonholes of the Pecos Classification often is to reduce them to insignificance. While the general evolutionary aspect of the Pecos Classification continues to be recognized to some extent, the system has become less and less important as other research interests have broadened, leaving behind many of the concerns of earlier generations of archaeologists.

In the mid-1930s, another major prehistoric group—the Mogollon Culture of southern New Mexico, southeastern Arizona, and parts of northern Mexico—was defined (Haury 1936), bringing with it its share of controversy. In the 1950s, Joe Ben Wheat (1955) proposed a classification comparable to the Pecos for the Mogollon Culture. It drew on a much greater amount of detailed data and referred to an arabic-numbered sequence based on an extensive list of basic attributes: traditions of village layout, dwelling construction, ceremonial chambers, burial practices, pottery, small artifacts of stone and bone, and other materials and practices. For the most part, however, the system is too complex and came at a time when more important archaeological issues were being raised. Recently, Steven LeBlanc (1983: 172) has condensed the Mimbres sequence of the Mogollon Culture into a more manageable size and scope.

As a dynamic discipline, Southwestern archaeology is constantly changing. Archaeologists today are less interested in fitting their data into rigid evolutionary sequences than were their predecessors. Some archaeologists of the last two decades have justifiably criticized the apparent earlier preoccupation with listing "typical" or "normative" aspects of prehistoric culture, stating that they allow no room for variations of culture and contribute little to explaining why they vary. While the original qualifying attributes of the Pecos Classification are out of date, however, many archaeologists still find its generalizing nature to be a useful point of departure and often speak of its periods (usually abbreviated, as BMIII, PI, PII, etc.). Today, however, the periods connote chronology rather than strict evolutionary development.

Archaeology Without Excavation

By the 1920s Southwestern archaeology was barely over forty years old. The big spectacular ruins had been dug. Exhibit cases and storage shelves in eastern museums and universities were packed high with artifacts. What more was there to learn?

Slow in coming, answers to this question emerged from an unexpected source and as a result of a curious career change. In 1922, Harry P. Mera, M.D., was a Santa Fe County Health Department physician who conducted clinic calls at outlying communities throughout the county. En route to these settlements, Dr. Mera was intrigued by the potsherds that littered the surfaces of the prehistoric ruins he passed. Perhaps because he had attended spellbinding lectures on archaeology by Hewett and others and had read newspaper articles and reports of some of the archaeological excavations of the day, Mera understood that potsherds could be as useful for research as whole pots. Their different colors, designs, and textures seemed regionally distinctive and could help identify the cultures of the ruins on which they were found and perhaps their relative ages.

Thus, Dr. Mera began a hobby that one day would elevate him among the region's most remarkable archaeologists. He began by marking on a road map the location of each site he discovered and collecting a small sample of potsherds, storing them together with slips of paper that identified where they had been found. From those small beginnings, his pastime developed over the next few years, and by 1931 his reputation as an avocational researcher in archaeology led to his being invited to formalize his hobby as the Curator of Archaeological Survey at the newly founded Laboratory of Anthropology in Santa Fe. As one of Southwestern archaeology's unsung heroes, Dr. Mera spent the next three years amassing records that located and briefly described some eleven hundred archaeological sites scattered for over 250 kilometers (155 miles) along the Upper and Middle Rio Grande drainage, supplemented by an index-card system that correlated sherd collections with site descriptive data and large-scale, skillfully hand-drawn relief maps on which he could show site locations. U.S. Geological Survey maps of those days lacked the detail he required.

Much of the initial research value of Mera's survey catalog came from the samples of potsherds he collected from the sites, some of which yielded over one hundred pieces, while others, barely a handful. After the sherds were washed, numbered, sorted, and neatly stored in cabinets, Mera was able to document the distributions of dozens of diagnostic pottery types and coincidentally show how the prehistoric configurations of cultures changed over time. While Mera never used the specific term *pottery tradition* in his concise publications, the way in which he presented his data, summarized them in distribution maps, organized his site survey collections, and hypothesized cultural development and population movements shows that his research was based on such a concept. Mera's published reports (1933, 1934, 1935, 1940) were brief and of limited distribution, but they continue to be relied upon as bases for the archaeological interpretation of many parts of New Mexico.

Mera continued to compile information on additional site locations until the mid-1940s, and during that time sherd collections came from many of the same pioneer archaeologists who had inspired him in the first place. In succeeding years, the Museum of New Mexico administered the survey catalog, adding data and sherd collections from many thousands of additional sites. Not solely a museum undertaking, data on many more sites were submitted by archaeologists with other public and private institutions and agencies. In the 1970s public interest in its prehistoric and historic heritage increased, and administration of New Mexico's archaeological survey record was assumed by the State's Historic Preservation Division. Today, it plays an increasingly important role as an inventory of over eighty thousand prehistoric and historic sites.

2. COMING TO TERMS WITH PUEBLO POTTERY

The recognition and description of pottery types often aids the archaeologist in understanding the day-to-day behavior of the people who produced and used it. By studying this most abundant and best preserved artifact of prehistoric Pueblo Indian culture, we can begin to answer such questions as: Who were the ancestors of the modern Pueblo people? When and where did they establish their settlements? How long did they stay in one place, and why did they eventually move elsewhere? What explains the Pueblo populations' gradual consolidation into larger and larger settlements? Were they influenced by other cultures, and did they influence neighboring groups? Answers to such questions are seldom easily obtained.

Pottery classification has long been used to distinguish regions or provinces of apparent cultural uniformity, such as Mesa Verde, Chaco Canyon, Middle and Northern Rio Grande, and Mimbres areas. However, the most convincing validation of this approach can be found in the relative ease with which most pottery of the historic Pueblos lends itself to classification into the system of wares, types, series, and varieties that the archaeologist applies to prehistoric pottery. Many of the descriptive attributes of Pueblo pottery—colors, finishes, paint types, designs, forms, and others—occur in such consistent configurations that it becomes relatively easy to distinguish the characteristic pottery of each of the pueblos. Reversing the rationalization, the consistency with which these traits occur together in contemporary Pueblo pottery suggests that prehistoric pottery should be equally distinguishable, perhaps revealing links between cultural groups when they were more populous and widely dispersed in western New Mexico and adjacent states during the period before A.D. 1300.

Mera and other early archaeologists identified those pottery attributes (or traditions) that gradually change through time, making it possible to distinguish certain ones that changed faster or more slowly than others or ceased to be perpetuated. Predominant association of a particular pottery type or group of types is considered an indication that they were made locally. However, in some areas and some periods evidence has been found that shows that not all groups made their own pottery, but imported it from other provinces or localities where there were pottery-making specialists whose pottery may have been of superior quality or desirable for other reasons.

Some archaeologists and most members of the public may feel intimidated by both the real and imagined complexities involved in the classification of prehistoric and historic Pueblo pottery.

Archaeologists and art historians have recognized now well over 1500 pottery types. It is no wonder some archaeologists choose to specialize in studying pottery-less cultures.

Pottery types and wares may never be comparable to a Rosetta stone that translates the cultures of the past into the languages of the present, but experience has shown that careful pottery classification offers many perspectives on the persistence of Pueblo Culture. This is not to say that all inferences made by archaeologists concerning prehistoric and historic Pueblo pottery are necessarily correct. In a number of instances such interpretations have been based on long-standing technological misconceptions that have been perpetuated as "archaeological folklore."

Although the pottery may be inflexible, pottery types are subject to all of the vagaries that are likely to occur as a result of being the products of human beings. As potters develop their own particular styles, so may archaeologists analyze, describe, and classify pottery according to their own concepts and experience. They may then be inclined either to limit or broaden the criteria that distinguish pottery types. Thus, individuals may disagree with the writer concerning whether a particular pottery vessel or potsherd is within the range that they accept as Kiatuthlanna Black-on-white, Gallup Black-on-white, Wingate Black-on-red, or some other type. They may subjectively see attributes that imply external influence on a pottery style. They may ignore microscopic attributes as being beyond the ability of a potter to control and prefer to base classification on the macroscopic ones, which are the most readily observed.

Essentially, the pottery types are research tools. They often show great sensitivity to resource conditions with which a potter must cope in a given province, and these conditions may be reflected in additional variability within Pueblo culture. Archaeologists may miss clues to significant differences in cultures unless they look for variability within the pottery recovered on many Southwestern sites. Uniformity in observing pottery enables archaeologists to produce data and interpretations that may be intelligible to others. At the same time, this in no way prevents archaeologists from looking at Pueblo pottery from many other specialized viewpoints.

Working from the academic side, archaeologists approach pottery descriptively and quantitatively. Ideally, each archaeologist must experience firsthand the routines of learning pottery classification, even though doing so may seem like reinventing the wheel. Each archaeologist may study a single pottery assemblage and arrive at either minor or major differences of opinion as to its cultural and chronological placement. Though it may seem that the intent is to show how scientific archaeology is by distinguishing minute differences in pottery attributes, unanimity in classification is hardly the ultimate goal.

There will always be friendly jousting between the "lumpers," who feel that there are already too many pottery types and that most can be lumped into fewer types and still be effective as research tools, and the "splitters," who favor distinguishing of even more pottery types in hopes of gaining greater precision of data.

Southwestern archaeologists often devote a major part of their research to detailed studies of pottery associated with prehistoric and historic Pueblo sites, and through this work it has become possible to document many developments in pottery, including its initial introduction, spread, regional differentiation, change through time, extinction, and revival. Older analytical methods relied on the unaided eye, but today's archaeologists are drawing on sophisticated analyses developed in the natural sciences, such as petrographic analysis, X-ray fluorescence microscopy, thermoluminescence analysis, and alpha recoil track dating.

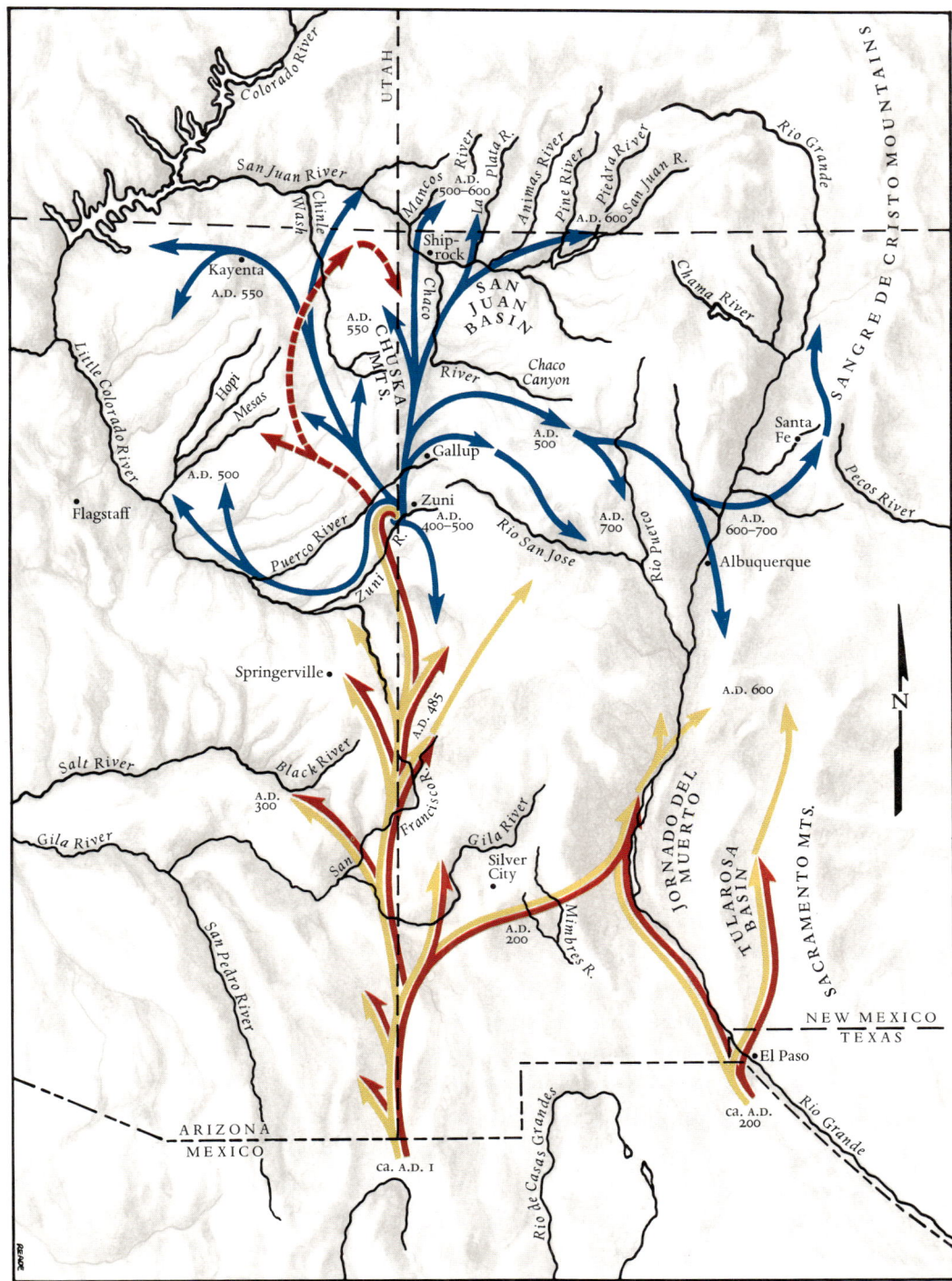

■ Red-pottery tradition
■ Brown-pottery tradition
■ Gray-and-white pottery tradition

Introduction of pottery making into the Puebloan Southwest

COMING TO TERMS WITH PUEBLO POTTERY 17

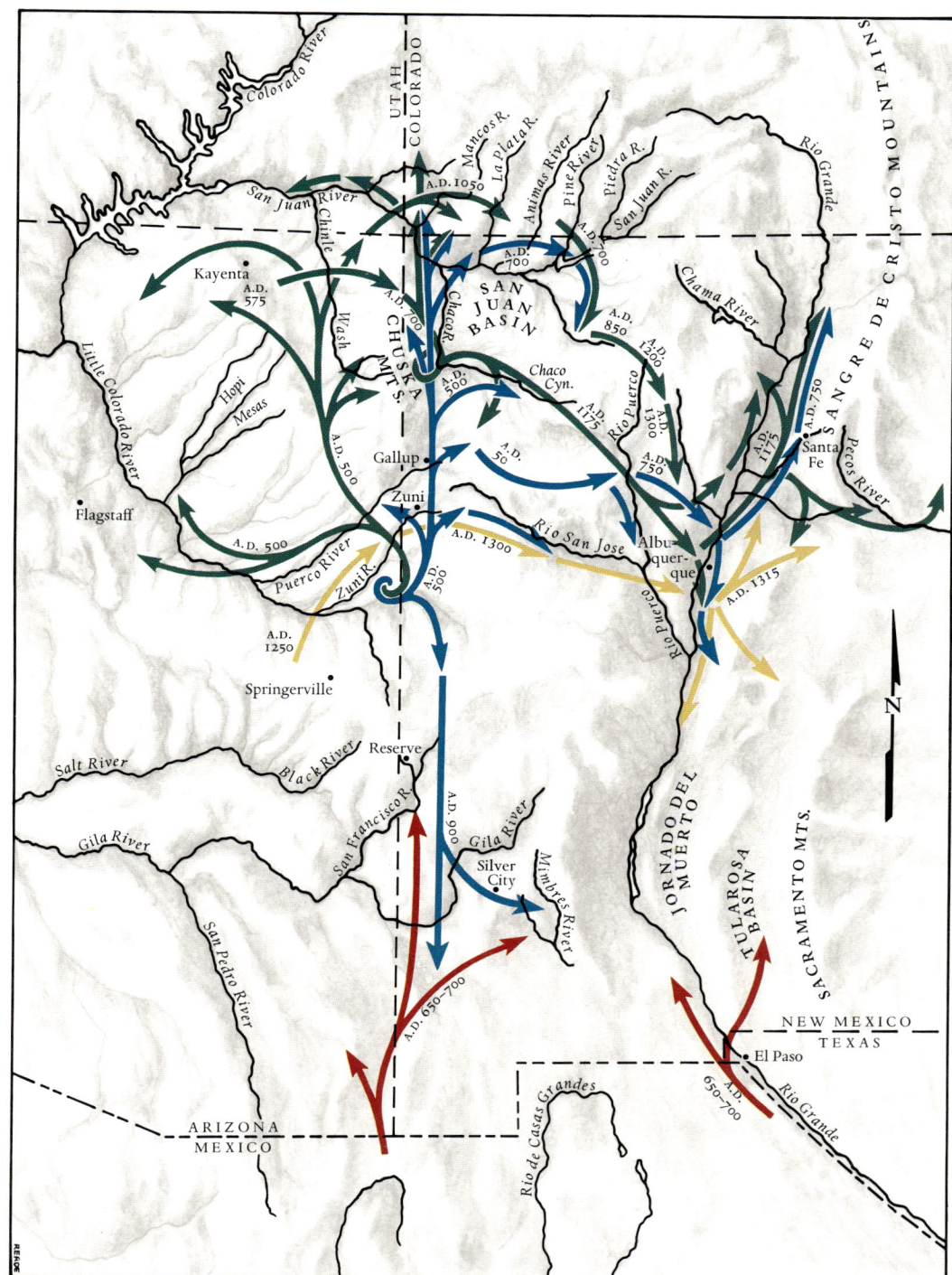

■ Vegetal-paint tradition
■ Red-paint tradition
■ Mineral-paint tradition
□ Glazes on redware

Painted pottery traditions

- Vegetal-paint tradition (A.D. 1175–1300)
- Boundary between principal vegetal- and glaze-paint traditions (A.D. 1315–1700)
- Initial introduction of glazes and red slipping from the west
- Local extensions of glaze-paint tradition (ca. A.D. 1520–1530)

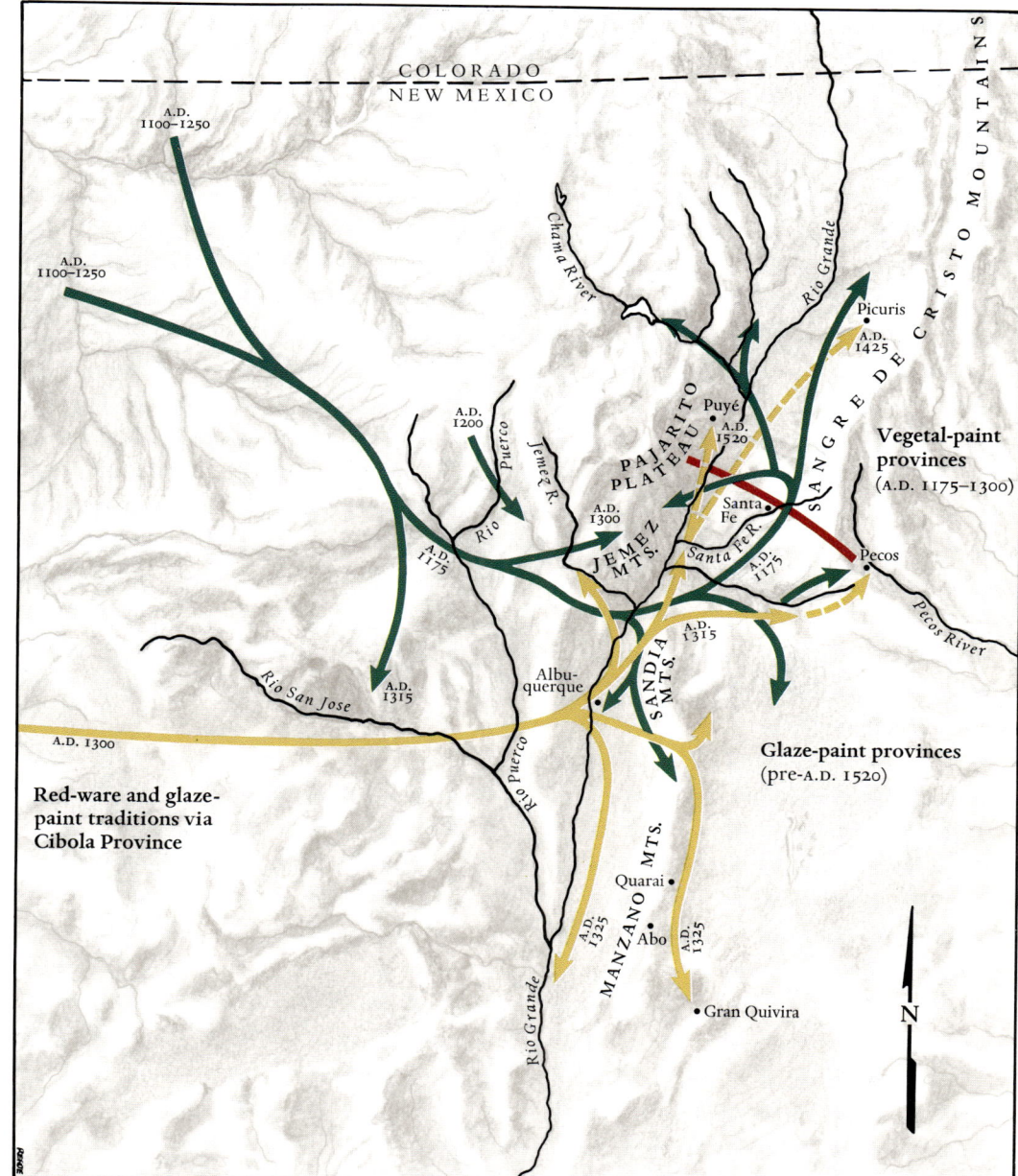

Vegetal- and glaze-paint traditions

Some of these offer real precision in reconstructing and explaining Southwestern prehistory. Without them, it would not be possible to remove ceramic analysis from the often subjective views of archaeologists. The relatively new and inexpensive analytical technique called "X-ray fluorescence (XRF) microscopy" yields a unique "fingerprint"—the spectrum of chemical elements derived when a pottery specimen has been excited by X-rays. At least one XRF procedure is nondestructive, and observations can be made on any of the constituents, temper, slip, and paint of a pottery vessel or potsherd. The resultant data can be plotted so as to record localized patterned occurrences of a broad range of parameters or the clustering of just a few elements to determine local versus nonlocal ceramics (Olinger 1988). Once local ceramics have been identified and segregated in this manner, the researcher can resort to standard archaeological classification methods involving technological and aesthetic attributes that are more likely to reflect some common features of traditions, i.e., persistence, change, and areal distribution.

Recognizing Traditions

Almost invariably, prehistoric Pueblo groups traditionally made or used two functional categories of pottery: rough or intentionally textured, coarse-tempered *utility ware* for cooking and storing foods; and more durable, well-finished, finer-textured painted *service ware* for serving foods, carrying water, and other specialized functions. In early periods in some provinces there was no apparent consistency of function, and surface color of pottery rarely varied over the course of many centuries; the same is true for the kinds of paint used for decoration. Exceptions to any of these observations can be cited. Identification of actual vessel functions is only occasionally possible, either when whole pots still contain identifiable food residues or because they have been found in association with certain features within a dwelling.

As traditional as making pottery itself is the fact that pottery vessels were offered as gifts or for exchange with other Pueblo and non-Pueblo groups. Archaeological reports frequently refer to "intrusive" or "trade" pottery for potsherds or whole vessels found in areas where it can be shown the pots were not made.

The frequency with which different trade pottery types appear on a site, even as tiny potsherds, helps to indicate the directions in which that site's occupants had contact, their distance from the source of the trade pottery, and the relative intensity of that contact. Although painted pottery seems to have been traded more commonly, utility pottery also was traded or given. If such pottery came from areas, periods, or traditions that have been reasonably well dated by dendrochronology or radiocarbon dating, such trade wares may be used for cross-dating of sites lacking wood or charcoal for dating.

To many observers, designs seem to be the most eye-catching and intriguing aspects of Pueblo pottery. Even on a crumb-sized potsherd lying in the weeds, a dense black decoration on a stark white background rarely fails to attract attention.

Designs tend to change more rapidly than any of the technological features, sometimes lasting only a generation or two before being replaced by others. Some designs, however, persisted for 150 to 200 years. Generally, they last long enough to serve as a major criterion of many pottery types. The influence of the potters that originated them often could spread far beyond the potters' home areas and usually long after they had ceased making pottery. Permanently fired onto a pottery vessel, a popular design could be copied many times over by other potters. It is generally not possible to identify the work of a particular prehistoric potter; lacking writing, individual potters did not sign their pots, and thousands of prehistoric Pueblo artists must remain forever anonymous. The practice of signing pottery is only about seventy-five years old. However, good potters today can easily recognize their own work and often that of relatives and friends, and the same may have been true for prehistoric potters, assuming they identified personally with their work.

In Pueblo pottery, we may see hundreds, even thousands, of traditions. Pottery types, though they may be partly the creations of the archaeologists who describe them, amply show both chronological and areal continuities. After almost one hundred years of archaeological observations on modern, early historic, and prehistoric Pueblo pottery, there is little doubt that many pottery types have validity as traditional expressions of specific Pueblo groups and, perhaps, of individual potters.

If we can recognize at least some of the basic attributes of a pottery type—ones that required that a potter make many choices—then we may also be able to discern some of the unspoken values the potter used in selecting the materials, procedures, forms, and designs in making the pottery. If her choices were influenced by her mother, relatives, and neighbors who taught her pottery making, then knowingly or unknowingly she may have been aiding in the perpetuation of traditions that began many years before she was born and may last long after she died.

This is an acceptable supposition if one considers the steps followed in pottery making and what sorts of technological and aesthetic alternatives there would be for the potter as she plans to make a pot or shows her daughter how to make a pot. Those alternatives may have been simple either/or questions such as, "Should I do it this way, or that way?" Later archaeologists may be re-phrasing such questions as they attempt to classify potsherds and whole pots: What will the function of the vessel be? What size of vessel shall I make? What temper should be used? What will its body and surface colors be? What should the surface treatment be? Is it to be slipped? Is it to be polished? Is it to be painted? What pigment should be used? Do I have a choice of decorative styles? How will I fire the vessel?

For the archaeologist, answers to as many of these questions as possible may permit localizing the source of the pottery in time and space. This is possible because, given where and when she lived, the potter typically had few alternatives available. As the archaeologist studies each pot or potsherd, the most commonly occurring attributes soon begin to indicate which pottery was locally made, with the less common traits suggesting those that were made elsewhere. The odds are against finding widely separated areas producing identical pottery, attribute for attribute. Of course, these differences will be most pronounced when there are different designs and colors to distinguish.

For the potter, the principal questions probably would have addressed the size and function of the proposed pot. Other issues, such as aesthetic considerations of surface texture and color, would have been predetermined by tradition. It would have been almost unthinkable for a potter to depart from tradition and create something totally new, not because the potter couldn't, but because she wouldn't. Other Pueblo traditions that supercede those relating to pottery making call for behavior that is in keeping with the collective benefit of the entire group. In such a social structure, individual assertiveness or nonconformity works contrary to the general well-being of the Pueblo and might even raise suspicions that the individual is working in other ways that are decidedly against the group. How, then, to account for change among the Pueblos? Most traditions involve some opposing forces that offer means for gradual change. Knowledge of some aspects of prehistoric pottery making can provide some of the principal technological alternatives on which members of a given culture made value judgments in the tradition.

Although contemporary Pueblo people increasingly have adapted to the dominant society around them, they have retained many important traditions that may be justified, at least in part, by the simple statement, "This is the way we have always done things." This isn't to suggest that their traditions are unchanging, but it is an indication that they change only gradually.

Pottery traditions are rarely neat, unilinear continuities. They may be separable into components or sub-traditions, as when a potter borrows some, but not all, aspects of another tradition. Traditions can merge, become extinct, or seem to develop out of nowhere for no apparent reason. A goal of modern archaeology is to explain such events through posing hypotheses to be tested systematically using statistics.

Early ethnographers studying turn-of-the-century aboriginal cultures realized that native traditions often had great antiquity, but by ethnographic descriptions of tribal life it is as if these traditions had no time dimension at all. These records reflect life as it occurred in the present, at a point on a continuum of unknown origin and longevity and expressed in the nearly timeless fashion of the native people who lived in the moment and whose memory recalled events and things of only the recent past.

Archaeologists have an advantage over ethnologists in being able to use data from archaeological surveys and stratigraphic excavations, supplemented by ethnographic data, to gain some relative time perspective for at least those few traditions whose existences are preserved in the fragments. Some traditions seen in the archaeological record may still be observed today, but others may have become extinct, whether recently or in the distant past.

The longer an attribute persisted, the stronger the evidence that potters were perpetuating a tradition, even though they might have been able to choose between some alternatives. The broader the area where the tradition can be noted, the stronger the evidence that the originating potters were making conscious choices between alternatives available to them. If we can match the relative constancy of certain pottery traditions over a large area through time, we can then consider the rate of change of other cultural attributes, such as subsistence pattern, village plans, house types, kiva forms, mano and metate forms, and stone ax types—shared attributes that are constituents of a single culture. The fewer the similarities, the greater the chance that the things observed are of different cultures, though degrees of similarity may be important for other reasons.

This essay will discuss only a few of the principal Pueblo pottery traditions observable in New Mexico. Though the prehistoric Pueblo people in all the southwestern states share these traditions, they are discussed here relative to the New Mexico Pueblos. Distinctions may be based on function, such as utility (usually unpainted) or service (painted) pottery; presence of a slip; or type of pigment used. Other criteria such as surface treatment (polishing, texturing, intentional blackening of vessel surfaces) may be important. Each of these may be part of its own exclusive tradition with its own time and areal ranges. Those chosen for discussion are not always the logical ones for an archaeologist trained to think in terms of wares, types, and varieties. Such classificatory approaches are clearly invaluable in archaeological research, but they are not the only ones that can be informative.

Before Pueblo Pottery

Nomadic peoples have lived in the Southwest for at least twelve thousand years. They arrived while the great glaciers of the Pleistocene still extended south of the modern International Boundary between the United States and Canada and while the cooler, moister Ice Age environment may have supported more widespread forests and woodlands in what are now prairie areas in the Southwest. During this early era —often called the Paleoindian period—populations were probably very small and dispersed over enormous areas.

From their arrival at least as early as 10,000 B.C., the Paleoindians of the Southwest appear to have subsisted on now-extinct species of wild game—particularly mammoths and giant bison. Of their early lifeways little evidence remains except for their chipped stone tools and the isolated or massed skeletons of the game animals that often contain projectile points lodged in the bones. Toward the end of the Pleistocene Period, Paleoindians probably varied their diets to include more plentiful species of smaller game, as well as wild plant foods such as seeds, nuts, berries, and leaves. With only stone tools and occasional pieces of worked animal bone to suggest this primitive existence, archaeologists are limited in their efforts to describe what these Indians might have used for containers. They may have made bags or packs from animal hides and possibly coarsely woven fiber netting, as were suggested by findings of such materials in areas outside of, though still near, the Southwest.

By about 7000 B.C., the great Ice Age mammals had died off, the environment had become increasingly arid, and, for the next five thousand years, small nomadic groups of Indians ranged over virtually every part of the Southwest as they continued to subsist by hunting and gathering. Their culture is often collectively called *Archaic*, a term that connotes the development and widespread existence of a great variety of shared lifeways, or traditions. As research on these early groups intensified, it became possible to distinguish two major divisions based on somewhat different types of settlement locations, assemblages of stone implements, and differences in the natural environment.

The first of these is the Cochise Culture, which ranged across southwestern New Mexico and southeastern Arizona and into northern Mexico. A northern group, the Oshara Tradition, had their hunting and gathering areas in the prairies and mesa and canyon woodlands of the Colorado Plateau of northwestern New Mexico and parts of Arizona, Utah, and Colorado. Both groups appear to have been at least seasonally nomadic, moving from place to place to avail themselves of wild plant foods as they matured and game animals wherever they might be found.

There is great likelihood that these groups had some sort of basketry and hide containers, although few remnants of such items have come to light. Perhaps as late as 1000 B.C., Indians from northern Mexico introduced the Cochise people to maize agriculture, and though it may have been many centuries before the grain could be counted on as a major food source, scattered farms sprang up throughout many parts of the Cochise and Oshara provinces. More or less concurrently, but perhaps more likely in the cooler northerly areas, small, roughly circular dwellings began to be constructed. They may have been permanent dwellings, but possibly they were used only during the coldest times of the year. Gradually, each of these groups began to take on more and more of the attributes of the settled life, and by A.D. 200 or so, the Cochise people again received a boon from Mexico, this time in the form of pottery.

The presence of pottery has enabled archaeologists to distinguish the nominally sedentary Cochise and Oshara farmers from their even more settled successors. Potsherds collected on the surface of a site render early settlements recognizable and lead archaeologists to search for inconspicuous dwellings and other evidence of settled life.

The generally held inference is that, upon learning to make pottery, the Cochise and Oshara become the Mogollon and Anasazi cultures, respectively, and that sedentary living led to the two cultures becoming much more differentiated, visible, and better preserved. Sedentism seems to have encouraged the adoption or development, elaboration and association of a greater variety of household and other useful items than were associated with the camps of hunter-gatherers. The concentration of a greater assemblage of stone and bone artifacts—whole, broken, recycled, or discarded—helps to delimit the actual settlement sites. Careful scrutiny of even seemingly simple items generally shows them to be complex and capable of conveying a variety of information about the maker's knowledge, skills, and traditions; sources of raw materials; tools, techniques, and places of manufacture; functions within the household, on the hunt, in the fields, or in ritual; and trade with other groups.

The Beginning Pottery Traditions

There is a remote possibility that even before fired pottery was introduced into the Southwest early sedentary Indians occasionally made what might be called "protopottery," or "pseudopottery." A few early dwelling sites in the northern and southern Southwest have yielded the remains of thick, shallow, tray-like bowls crudely made of clay to which had been added a binder of shredded plant fiber, possibly juniper bark (fig. 1). The clay appears to have been shaped into thick strips and pressed in coiling fashion into the interiors of shallow, coiled baskets. Some of these baskets appear to have been worn out, and the clay liner may have been a kind of patch to make the basket wear a little longer.

Examples of these basket liners in the Museum of New Mexico's collections bear clear impressions of basketry, show no evidence of interior polish, and appear to have been at least semi-fired or burned, possibly in an open campfire. It is possible that the basket liners may have been used as parching trays, wherein seeds were toasted with hot coals by swirling them around together. Ethnographic accounts of baskets being used for this purpose exist for some historic Great Basin Indian groups. Whatever their functions, the basket liners give the impression of being crude attempts to imitate the pottery that early Indians in the Southwest may have seen but did not know how to replicate. Two of these basket liners were found associated with polished brown pottery in a well-dated, fifth-century pithouse near Quemado, New Mexico. This suggests that, if their origins were in the pre-pottery period, the basket

Fig. 1. Semifired, fiber-tempered, basket-liner bowl, A.D. 400–600. Unknown Tradition, Mimbres Province.

liners continued to be used for a specific function long after the Indians were making true pottery.

The making of fired pottery seems to have reached the Southwest by at least two routes. One route followed the west coast of Mexico, bordering the Gulf of California, and entered southern or southwestern Arizona, the subsequent homelands of the Hohokam and Hakataya cultures. Another, more inland approach was along the eastern margins of the Sierra Madre Occidental into the general area of the Gila River Valley in southwestern New Mexico and adjacent Arizona. Pottery technology was transmitted rapidly, especially northward, climbing almost like a vine into the areas populated by the Cochise people, following what is now the New Mexico-Arizona boundary, and sending branches east and west into areas where Indians only a short time earlier had begun to practice farming. Within three hundred to five hundred years, the craft had spread as far north as southwestern Colorado and southern Utah and had been adopted almost everywhere between the Grand Canyon on the west and New Mexico's central mountain chain on the east. A possible third route may have entered from Mexico along the lower Rio Grande, downstream from El Paso.

Instruction on how to make pottery apparently came from unidentified, slightly more advanced (inasmuch as they already had pottery) Indians from northern

Mexico. At first, they may only have traded pottery to the early Cochise farmers, who, in turn, opted to learn the practice firsthand. To have rejected the option of learning to make pottery would have meant continuing to use baskets for almost all daily tasks requiring containers. There is no indication that any of them chose to reject. As a general-purpose container, pottery had advantages of easy manufacture, durability, and nominal portability. From a dietary point of view, it could be placed in a fire to cook food and, hence, make the food more digestible. Still, there is no evidence that the Indians ever gave up basketry, which, although labor intensive in the making, had its own special advantages of lightness and portability.

The Cochise Become the Mogollon

It is conceivable that some Cochise people may have seen pottery in southern Arizona among the Hohokam or Hakataya peoples, who may have learned the craft from another source along the west coast of Mexico. However, Mogollon pottery shows no indication that its makers copied the characteristic coil-paddle-and-anvil finishing techniques used by the southern Arizona groups. This would seem to reinforce the theory that the stimulus for Mogollon pottery came from the south rather than the west. It further suggests that east-west contact between Hohokam and Mogollon groups was not common enough to bring about Mogollon adoption of Hohokam pottery-making techniques. Even in later centuries, the New Mexico Mogollon people apparently saw no benefits in acquiring Hohokam pottery through trade. Very little coil-paddle-and-anvil pottery seems to have reached the sedentary farming Indians of New Mexico.

Only a few sites have been systematically investigated that appear to date from the time when pottery making arrived in the Southwest—roughly A.D. 200–250. Some sites have been dated quite accurately by dendrochronology, while others have been less precisely dated by Carbon-14 (radiocarbon method). Since all of these dated sites are located at least 100 kilometers north of the International Boundary, it is reasonable to assume that somewhere in the intervening area there may have been dwelling sites whose inhabitants were introduced to pottery even earlier—perhaps as early as A.D. 1.

On the other hand, the route or routes taken by the bearers of the first pottery cannot be determined with certainty. From the International Boundary northward for almost 160 kilometers (100 miles) to the southern extent of mountains of the Upper Gila drainage in New Mexico, there were few impediments to the spread of the craft east or west of the modern New Mexico-Arizona boundary. There is some suggestion that early, but not well-dated, sites of the San Simon Branch of the Mogollon Culture, in southeastern Arizona, may have been among the earliest recipients of the pottery-making craft.

The Mogollon Utility-Ware Tradition

One characteristic of the first pottery that, at first, seems not to have resulted from choice is its brown-firing color. Although the correlation is not always precise, brown-firing pottery was made primarily in the area of the Mogollon Culture, extending

Fig. 2. Alma Plain small jar, A.D. 400–600. Mogollon Brown Tradition, Mimbres Province.

Fig. 3. Alma Plain seed jar, A.D. 400–600. Mogollon Brown Tradition, Mimbres Province.

Fig. 4. Alma Plain seed jar, A.D. 400–600. Mogollon Brown Tradition, Mimbres Province.

from the states of Chihuahua and Sonora, Mexico, northward to near the current east-west route of U.S. Highway 60 (between Socorro, New Mexico, and Springerville, Arizona). Mogollon potters apparently had no difficulty finding suitable pottery clay. Soils in most Mogollon areas are shallow and are largely underlain with residual clays formed by disintegrating volcanic materials whose iron-rich minerals tended to fire to a brown-to-reddish color.

When it came to choosing a firing color for their pottery, Mogollon potters seem to have had no choice; in southern New Mexico potters could only make pottery that was brown. Pottery was apparently fired under conditions where air could circulate around it freely, causing the iron minerals in the clay to oxidize to a brown or red-brown color. There apparently were no easily reached deposits of clay that fired any other color. So dominant was this brown-firing pottery that it is generally considered to be the diagnostic attribute of the prehistoric Mogollon Culture that produced it, allowing us to refer to a *Mogollon Brown Tradition* which persisted from about A.D. 200–250 to approximately A.D. 1400–1450. However, not all pottery types that fire to a brown color are unquestionably of the Mogollon Brown Tradition. Pottery made from brown-firing clays containing iron minerals occur in many Anasazi provinces where Mogollon affiliation or influence seems unlikely.

Generally, the pottery the Mogollon people made was fine-grained and seems not to have been adversely affected by shrinkage. At sites near Reserve, in Catron County, New Mexico, archaeologists Paul S. Martin and John B. Rinaldo, of the Field Museum of Natural History, recovered brown ware whose dull surface seemed to have been simply scraped smooth, possibly representing the first pottery-making technology introduced to the Mogollon potters. The scientists named the pottery "Alma Rough" (Martin and Rinaldo 1940). Since most early Mogollon Brown Ware is moderately well polished, this may have been a slightly later local idiosyncrasy. The early brown pottery was generally fired at low temperature, and it is possible that it was polished. Its smooth surface is better explained by the underfiring method, which left its soft surfaces subject to erosion from normal wear and exposure to liquids. The most common early Mogollon brown utility pottery, Alma Plain, sometimes had a semi-dull luster (figs. 2–5), but before long, and perhaps after developing better firing methods, the pottery was reasonably hard and well polished inside and out.

Early decoration of the plain brown pottery was limited to simple incised lines, punching the surface with a reed stem to produce tiny circles, and occasional scoring of jar necks with a bunch of grass stems, thereby leading archaeologists to name these variations "Alma Incised," "Alma Punched," and "Alma Scored," respectively. For at least five centuries, these were the only kinds of decoration applied to pottery, and they were almost exclusively confined to the necks of jars. Once introduced, these texturing techniques generally remained in the repertoires of Mogollon potters until the fifteenth century.

While we know the general sources of Mogollon pottery clay, it is most perplexing that so little is known about where the prehistoric Indians fired their pottery. On occasion, archaeologists have discovered concentrations of pottery-making materials (worked sherd scrapers, polishing stones, and lumps of unfired clay) that suggest pottery-making sites. However, recognizable pottery-firing areas are not found on most archaeological excavations. They may lie just outside what the archaeologist feels are the limits of the typical prehistoric dwelling site.

Fig. 5. Alma Plain olla, A.D. 400–600. *Mogollon Brown Tradition, Mimbres Province.*

Mogollon brown pottery generally was not fired at a particularly high temperature—probably less than 900°C (1652°F). While firing locations have not been recognized, wood fires on the surface level of the ground would seem to have been most likely. Some historic potters tell of preparing a firing area by first sweeping it clean, which may explain why prehistoric firing areas have not been found within Pueblo sites.

For vessel shapes, the potters probably borrowed those utilized in their earlier basketry, and possibly gourd, containers. Round-bottomed bowls, *ollas* and seed jars, and dippers were typical. Some appear crude and uninspired (figs. 2–4), while others, like the splendidly symmetrical *olla* in figure 5, show that Mogollon potters developed their skills very early.

Succeeding potters in the Mogollon Brown Tradition concentrated on more variety in texturing the necks of jars. At first, Mogollon potters left a few broad neck coils,

Fig. 7. Tularosa Patterned, Corrugated Smudged Variety, bowl, A.D. 1050–1250. Mogollon Slipped Tradition, Mimbres Province.

producing a type known as "Alma Neckbanded." Later, coils were made narrower and left "plain" (unobliterated), as in the type "Three Circle Neck Corrugated" (fig. 6). The lowermost coil of this type was commonly pinched or indented to produce an attractive semi-sculpted fillet. Before long this "indented corrugated" treatment was applied to the entire neck of jars and finally to the entire exterior of the vessel, except for the top coils around the rim. Soon, potters were alternating the horizontal rows with plain and indented corrugated coils or, to even greater aesthetic appeal, selectively indenting parts of each coil to create rectilinear scrolls or lozenge-shaped figures around the vessel exteriors (fig. 7). During the period ca. A.D. 1000–1100s, Mogollon potters seem to have tried every conceivable exterior surface treatment on their utility pottery, including extremely narrow coils (fig. 8) or leaving several tiny rows of indented fillets around the rims of bowls (fig. 9). In A.D. 1200s–1300s, Mogollon potters in east-central Arizona carried this one step further by applying a thick white paint to the indented elements to accentuate them further. As we will see, the same general trends of exterior surface treatment were followed in the gray utility pottery made by Anasazi potters, though differences in clays and tempers, as well as regional preferences, led to conspicuous divergences.

Fig. 6 (OPPOSITE). Three Circle Neck Corrugated jar, smudged interior, A.D. 900–1000. Mogollon Brown/Mogollon Slipped(?) Traditions, Mimbres Province.

THE MOGOLLON UTILITY-WARE TRADITION 31

Fig. 8. Fine coil punctate with smudged interior bowl, A.D. 1100–1150. Mogollon Slipped Tradition, Mimbres Province.

The Mogollon Slipped Tradition

The best polished Mogollon pottery was usually a red ware. If not introduced together with plain brown pottery, it arrived very shortly thereafter when potters learned to apply a "slip," or fine-grained coating, of red-firing clay on the interior and exterior of bowls and on the outside of jars, producing the type known as "San Francisco Red." The red slip would take a higher polish than that achieved on the plain brown pottery, and it would also cover imperfections on a plain brown surface. Early versions of the red-slipped pottery often were not fired to a high enough temperature to guarantee that the slip would adhere well. Consequently, the red was often "fugitive" (i.e., it would partially rub or wash off); later red slips were quite permanent. Interestingly, it was another two or three centuries before an enterprising Mogollon potter thought to selectively apply the red slip clay to a vessel surface to produce simple painted decoration.

An unusual decorative treatment was particularly common to San Francisco Red. Evenly spaced finger indentations left on bowl exteriors during the coiling process were only partially obliterated by scraping. Then, both interior and exterior surfaces were well slipped and polished, leaving an attractive dimple effect on the bowl exterior. This treatment often is seen on the earliest painted pottery type, Mogollon Red-on-brown (figs. 10, 11). The paste color of the red ware was often a somewhat lighter brown than that of the Alma series, possibly reflecting different clay sources or firing techniques and perhaps leading to the application of lighter firing slips used with the first painted brown ware (LeBlanc 1982: 112). The relationship of slipping to painted pottery does not become evident until two or three centuries later, ca. A.D. 700, when Mogollon potters selectively applied a red slip clay to vessel surfaces to produce a simple painted decoration on a tan slip.

Fig. 9. Tularosa Fillet Rim bowl, A.D. 1100–1250. Mogollon Slipped(?) Tradition, Mimbres Province.

The use of a lighter slip, possibly together with the Mogollon potters' awareness that early Anasazi potters had discovered a showy white slip clay on which their designs could be painted, may have led to the appearance of a very handsome type, Three Circle Red-on-white, named after the cattle brand of a ranch near Silver City, New Mexico. The red-orange paint on a well-polished creamy white slip on bowl interiors was often complemented by a red-slipped, dimpled exterior. This variation on the *Mogollon Slipped Tradition* began about A.D. 750 (Withers 1985). Not all developments in a pottery tradition develop sequentially, and it appears that at more or less the same time that Three Circle Red-on-white began to be made, some potters adopted a pigment or firing technique that produced a brownish black painted decoration on a somewhat dirty white slip on the interiors of bowls. This was Mangas Black-on-white (fig. 12), formerly called "Mimbres Bold Face Black-on-white" because of the common use of broad, straight, or wavy lines and heavy solid elements. The illustrated specimen of this type is particularly interesting because of the occurrence of almost identical designs to a bowl of the Anasazi type, Kiatuthlanna Black-on-white (fig. 50). This suggests that, even though they lived almost 320 kilometers (200 miles) apart, the potters who decorated the two bowls may have been nearly contemporaries, about A.D. 700–900. Despite their distance, they had adopted the same popular quartered layout and use of barbed lines and wavy-line hatching.

Refinements in the decoration of the black-on-white pottery ultimately led in two directions, though under only one type name, Mimbres Black-on-white, sometimes called "Mimbres Classic Black-on-white." A predominantly geometric style consisted of fine-line black or sometimes red or red-brown designs of carefully balanced solid and hatch-filled elements, often appearing to have been drawn with a ruler (figs. 13, 16). Concurrently, painted pottery developed a pictorial style with depictions of animals, birds, fish, insects, and human forms in both static and action scenes of daily

Fig. 10. Mogollon Red-on-brown bowl, A.D. 700–900. Mogollon Slipped Tradition, Mimbres Province.

Fig. 11. Mogollon Red-on-brown bowl, A.D. 700–900. Mogollon Slipped Tradition, Mimbres Province.

Fig. 12 (OPPOSITE). Mangas Black-on-white bowl, A.D. 900–1000. Mogollon Slipped Tradition, Mimbres Province.

Fig. 13. Mimbres Black-on-white bowl, A.D. 1000–1150. Mogollon Slipped Tradition, Mimbres Province.

Fig. 14. Mimbres Black-on-white bowl, A.D. 1000–1150. Mogollon Slipped Tradition, Mimbres Province.

Fig. 15 (OPPOSITE). Mimbres Black-on-white jar, A.D. 1000–1150. Mogollon Slipped Tradition, Mimbres Province.

life. Some of these graphic representations involved composites of two or more forms in a single figure. Unquestionably the Mimbres Black-on-white comprises the most distinctive prehistoric ceramic art found anywhere on the North American continent.

Art historian J. J. Brody (1977:107), in an excellent discussion of Mimbres pottery, compares the white-slipped surfaces of Mimbres Black-on-white bowl interiors to an artist's canvas whose limits aptly frame the subject matter. The comparison is an intriguing one that applies especially well to the Mimbres pottery. Bowl exteriors were normally unslipped, or slipped only about one or two centimeters down from the rim, and it appears that Mimbres potters chose to use their creamy white slip and black framing lines around bowl rims to set off the "portraiture" on the vessel interior. Of course, to some degree we can make the same inference from almost all slipped or painted Southwestern pottery, since the surface painted, inside or out, always is framed and limited by the configurations of the vessel surface.

Except for a rare pictorial decoration on pre-Pueblo IV Anasazi pottery and congested masses of little pictorial elements on Hohokam pottery in southern Arizona, Mimbres potters were the only ones in the Southwest to have chosen this kind of painted decoration. The basis for this distinction may have been religious. One almost gets the impression that Anasazi potters may have strongly disapproved of the Mimbres practice of painting pictures on pottery—perhaps somewhat comparable to the absence of pictorial art in Moslem religious contexts. Mimbres pictorial pottery almost never was traded outside the Mimbres area, and only a few pieces of plain geometric pottery were transported north of what is now U.S. Highway 60. Since little

Fig. 16. Mimbres Black-on-white ring-shaped canteen, A.D. 1100–1200. Mogollon Slipped Tradition, Mimbres Province.

Fig. 17. Mimbres Black-on-white bowl, A.D. 1000–1150. Mogollon Slipped Tradition, Mimbres Province.

Anasazi pottery or other items seem to have been traded down into the Mimbres Province, one is led to the conclusion that the Anasazi preferred to have as little contact as possible with the Mimbres.

The ultimate function of many Mimbres Black-on-white bowls (very few jar forms of this type were ever made) was as "grave goods" placed with human burials. Placing personal belongings in the grave of the deceased is a practice noted in many, though not all, archaeological regions of the Southwest. The practice would seem to reflect some idea that the pottery, or its contents, should accompany the dead person's spirit to the afterworld. To carry this concept a bit further, the Mimbres people appear to have ritually "killed" such pottery by punching a hole in the bottom of the bowl, or simply by breaking the vessel, to allow its essence to go to the spirit world with its former user. There is ample evidence that most Mimbres painted pottery was first used as household utensils, as attested by abraded edges and bottoms of vessel interiors and exteriors. Some painted vessels, such as the two pictorial bowls from the Rock House Ruin, in the Mimbres Valley, have been found on the floors of dwelling rooms, indicating that they were still being used when that Pueblo was abandoned (figs. 22, 23).

Fig. 18. Cuyamungue Black-on-tan (Biscuit C) miniature medicine jar, A.D. 1475–1600. Anasazi Vegetal-Paint Tradition, Tewa Basin Province. CENTER: *Gallup Black-on-white miniature medicine jar, A.D. 1000–1100. Anasazi Mineral-Paint Tradition, Cibola or Chaco Province.* RIGHT: *Mimbres Black-on-white miniature medicine jar, A.D. 1000–1150. Mogollon Slipped Tradition, Mimbres Province.*

From Slipped to Polished Black

Potters discovered that a higher polish could be achieved on brown ware that was slipped. It was thus that red and tan slipping helped to foster another significant development in Pueblo pottery making. Many brown ware bowls and some jars made after A.D. 600 bear highly polished, often iridescent black interiors. Pottery types with this treatment continued to be made in much of west-central, southwestern, and south-central New Mexico until as late as about A.D. 1400.

Long thought to have been the result of carbon deposits achieved by exposing the pottery interiors to sooty smoke during the firing of the brown ware—a technique known as "smudging"—this highly polished effect has been shown to have been largely the result of reduction-firing, which converted the hematite in the clay to black magnetite (Lyon 1988). The same treatment applies to the striking black ware of the modern Tewa Pueblos of San Ildefonso and Santa Clara.

Probably because the constricted orifices of jars discouraged successful slipping and polishing, open bowls alone were the forms that most commonly received the "smudging" treatment. At first the *Polished Black Tradition* simply involved local reduction of the interiors of Alma Plain bowls, producing the type "Reserve Smudged." But as other texturing techniques were developed, Mogollon potters applied the glossy interiors to the whole gamut of utility types, including Reserve Plain Corrugated, Reserve Indented Corrugated, and Tularosa Patterned Corrugated.

In the southern part of the Cibola Province, in the vicinities of Reserve and Quemado, New Mexico, the Polished Black Tradition may have been a substitute for painted types of the Mogollon Slipped Tradition. Little or no painted pottery of any kind seems to have been produced here. Mangas Black-on-white and, rarely, Mimbres Black-on-white pottery occurs on eleventh- and twelfth-century sites in this province, but not in quantities one would expect were it made locally. The latter type, even as a trade ware, is very rare, possibly suggesting that north-south contact between the two provinces had been severed. The principal painted pottery found on pithouse and Pueblo sites here are Anasazi Mineral Paint black-on-white types, Reserve Black-on-

Fig. 19. Mimbres Black-on-white pictorial bowl, A.D. 1000–1150. Mogollon Slipped Tradition, Mimbres Province.

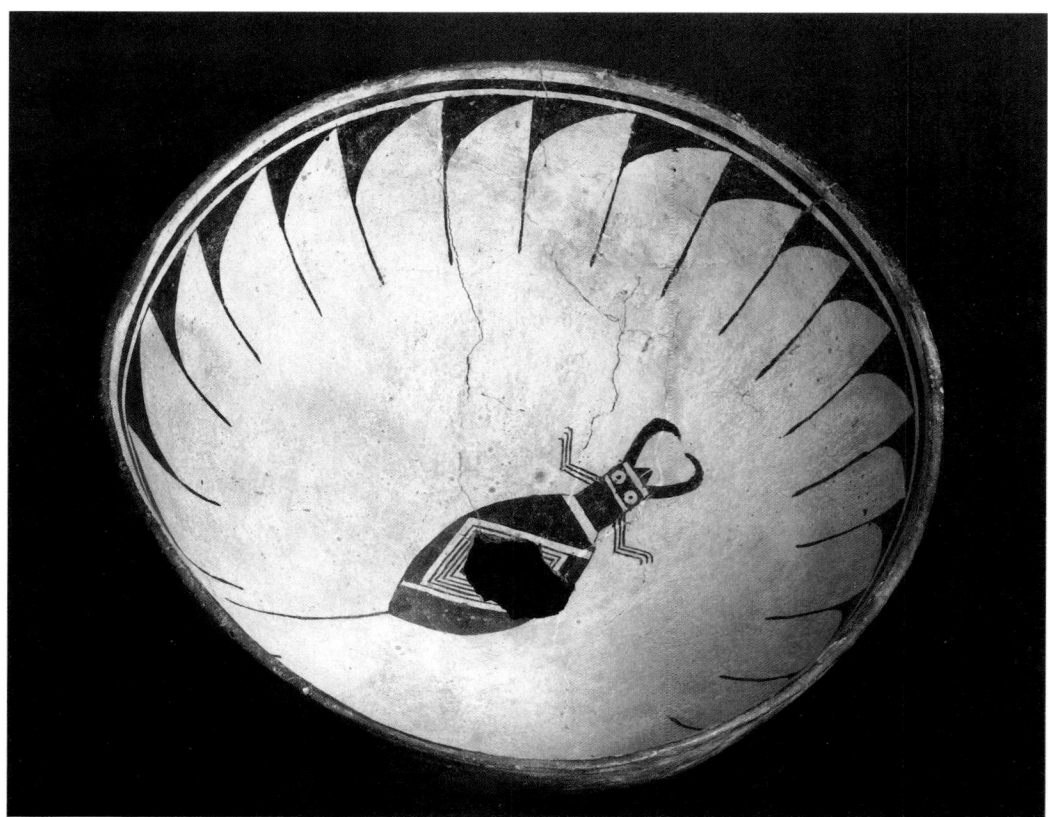

Fig. 20. Mimbres Black-on-white bowl, A.D. 1000–1150. Mogollon Slipped Tradition, Mimbres Province.

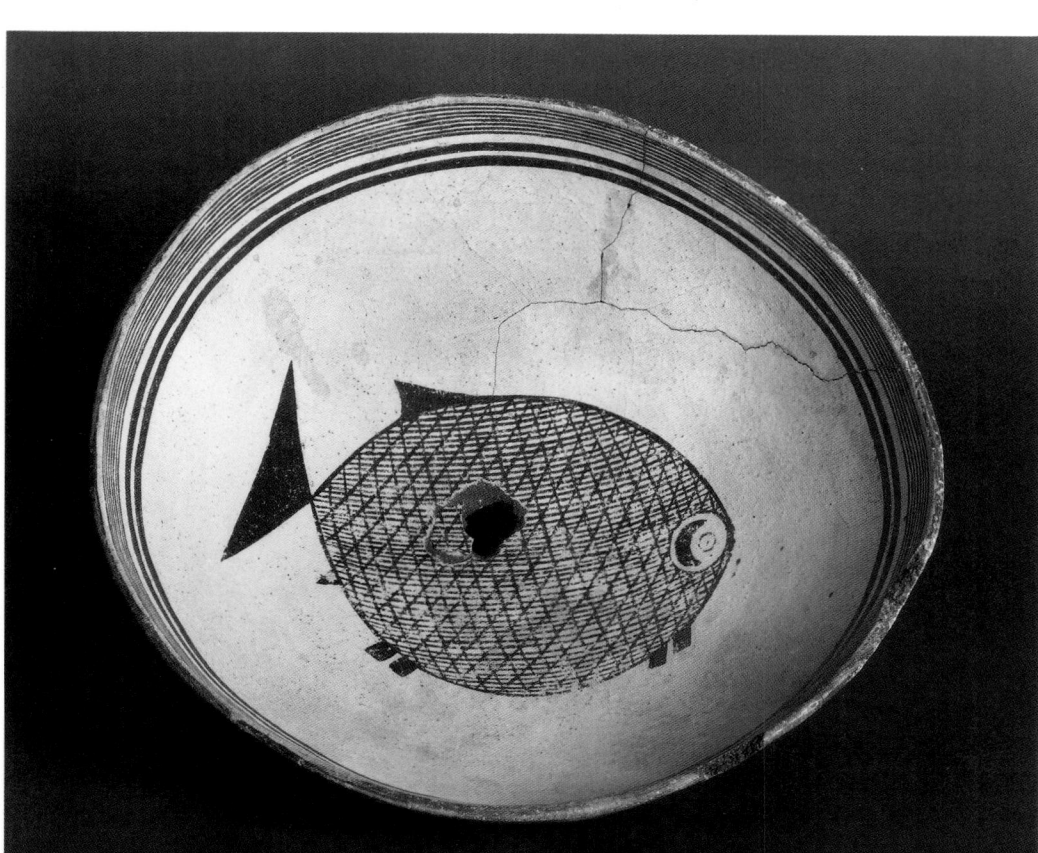

Fig. 21. Mimbres Black-on-white bowl, A.D. 1000–1150. Mogollon Slipped Tradition, Mimbres Province.

Fig. 22. Mimbres Black-on-white bowl, A.D. 1000–1150. Mogollon Slipped Tradition, Mimbres Province.

white (fig. 75) and its successor, Tularosa Black-on-white (figs. 76–78, 80). Even these types, however, typically occur in only small amounts, and Tularosa Black-on-white is predominantly in the form of small pitchers, suggesting that none of it was locally made, but rather was traded into the province.

The black ware with its fine interior finishes was superior to all but the latest Anasazi painted pottery, and bowls with polished black interiors appear to have been the only candidates for service pottery or table ware in much of the Mogollon area.

By about A.D. 1150 in the Mimbres Province and by the late 1200s in the Southern Cibola Province, the Mogollon pottery traditions had begun to fade. The Mimbres area fell on bad times from unknown causes and was abandoned; drought seems to have been a common reason for abandonments in many parts of the Southwest. Mogollon people may have survived in east-central Arizona and in south-central New Mexico, but the pictorial tradition of Mimbres Black-on-white disappeared without a trace, leaving archaeologists to guess where its makers went.

Some of the Mimbres people may have moved south into northern Chihuahua to merge with the people of Paquimé, the great ceremonial and trading center at Casas Grandes. In this migration, Mimbres identity was lost. Still others apparently moved eastward into the Rio Grande drainage and then, at least briefly, into the Tularosa Basin. Eventually, they seem to have joined upland Jornada people in the Sacramento Mountains and then headed northward toward the Gallinas Mountains, southeast of Gran Quivira, in the Salinas Province. One gets the impression that when migrants arrived in new areas, they gave up many of their old traditions, either because they wanted to be courteous to the people in their adopted homes or because their hosts required it.

It cannot be correctly said that the Mogollon Brown Tradition ceased to exist when the old Mogollon provinces were abandoned. Brown ware pottery was still made at substantial Pueblos farther north in parts of the northern Mimbres Province until the middle or late 1200s to the middle 1400s in east-central Arizona, when those villages, too, were abandoned. It is generally believed that at least some of their inhabitants moved northward to areas closer to modern Zuni Pueblo.

Nominally, brown—often more of a tan color—ware pottery continued to be made by some Pueblos throughout the early Historic Period and is still made right up to the present. However, this is not to say that the Mogollon Brown Tradition has survived or that the modern brown ware reflects latent Mogollon influence. Rather, many of the modern pottery-making Pueblos are in areas where extensive volcanic deposits contributed to the development of iron-rich clays that turned red under certain firing conditions.

Archaeologists may continue to try to demonstrate the survival of specific cultural attributes of the Mogollon Culture in post-A.D. 1300 architecture, pottery, and other artifacts. However, in most cases, the archaeological criteria that distinguished the Mogollon Culture in the first place are so exclusive that, when applied by subsequent generations of archaeologists, it is all but impossible to distinguish uniquely Mogollon attributes.

As migrants, the Mogollon people moved into different natural environments, leaving much of their material individuality behind them. Conditions for their being accepted in host areas very likely meant that they were expected to adopt the ways of the groups among whom they sought refuge. Maintaining many of their old ways—

Fig. 23. Mimbres Black-on-white small bowl, A.D. 1000–1150. Mogollon Slipped Tradition, Mimbres Province.

perhaps even their pottery traditions—might even have exposed them to accusations of trouble-making (a serious offense, at least among modern Pueblos) and, worse, their being ostracized from their adopted villages.

Elsewhere, plain brown and polished black pottery dating between A.D. 1300 and 1450 was still being made in parts of the Jornada Province, east of the Rio Grande, and into the 1600s in the Salinas Province. Isleta potters in the Middle Rio Grande Province were still making large brown-ware dough bowls with polished black interiors late in the nineteenth century (Bandelier 1966–1984, 2: 54) and Isleta Red-on-tan vessels into the 1920s (Batkin 1987: 191; Chapman and Ellis 1951: 261). Except for being larger than most prehistoric vessels, Isleta Red-on-tan bowls bear great similarity to eleventh-century Jornada Province expressions of red-slipped ware whose slip also extends only a centimeter or two below the rim on bowl exteriors. However, too little is known of the ancestry of Isleta Red-on-tan to verify its links to the Mogollon Slipped Tradition.

Pottery Comes to the Oshara People

There are, as yet, no archaeological data that pinpoint where and when the first Mogollon "seeds" of pottery making were planted among Indians of the Oshara Tradition. The most likely area lies in the upland areas between U.S. Highway 60, near Quemado, and Interstate 40, near Gallup. Identifying this intercultural boundary with greater precision is made difficult by the fact that groups of semi-nomadic Cochise and Oshara, as well as later Mogollon and Anasazi, were unimpeded in their wanderings and seem to have shifted north and south over the centuries. Sites with abundant brown ware pottery were sometimes occupied almost as far north as modern Gallup, whereas early sites with Anasazi ceramics have been found only a few miles north of Quemado.

In this area of cultural transition between Interstate 40 and U.S. 60, pottery clays usually come from sedimentary deposits often derived from volcanic areas or that were overlain by more recent lava flows. In one area west of Gallup, just across the border in Arizona, archaeologists found sites where the color traditions seemed to merge because outcrops of both brown-firing and gray-firing clays were locally available, albeit from different geological formations (Swarthout and Dulaney 1982: 95–101). The potters there really had a choice and made pottery of either color.

As pottery making spread northward and out into the San Juan Basin, it moved into areas where clay sources were largely those associated with sedimentary shales and sandstones that were laid down in ancient seas. These clays are generally low in iron content and contain greater amounts of carbon formed by the decay of plant materials when the deposits formed. In New Mexico and adjacent southwestern Colorado, pottery made from these clays almost invariably fired to a light- to dark-gray color, thereby serving as one of the diagnostic attributes of the Anasazi Culture that occupied this vast area.

The physical dissimilarity of early Mogollon and Anasazi pottery might be attributed to lack of communication between the groups, with resultant failures of the Anasazi in their attempts to copy surface color and finish of Mogollon pottery. However, the Mogollon may have been of little help in instructing the Anasazi beyond the basics of the craft, since they would probably have been unfamiliar with the unique, sometimes bothersome qualities of clays, tempers, and slip materials of the northern Southwest. The Anasazi may have needed to experiment with various of these materials and modify techniques before they could successfully replicate the Mogollon pottery they had seen.

There are no physiographic barriers that would have impeded sustained contact between the groups. Early Mogollon brown ware types are commonly found in Anasazi Basketmaker III settlements in west-central and northwestern New Mexico, a good indication that contact between the two groups was peaceful and conducive to easy exchange of information and the continued rapid spread of pottery-making technology.

Anasazi Utility Tradition

The oldest, most widespread, and most recognizable of the pottery traditions in the northern Southwest is the *Anasazi Utility Tradition*, the general category of rough-surfaced, plain gray pottery that was primarily used for cooking and general storage of food. Although there are exceptions, such as scoops, canteens, and smoking pipes, most Anasazi utility vessels are in the form of cooking pots, storage jars, and small pitchers. Utility bowls were only occasionally made.

As with the earliest plain brown pottery in the Mogollon area, the first one hundred years in the development of Anasazi pottery yielded few distinguishing characteristics. Called "Lino Gray" by archaeologists, it varies from light to dark gray in color, has coarse sand temper, and has a notably rough surface (figs. 24–26). Its gray color has led archaeologists to the conclusion that Anasazi potters had developed and mastered reduction firing. In this process oxygen was, at first, allowed to reach vessel surfaces to burn out the carbon by converting it to carbon dioxide. For the remainder of the firing, air (oxygen) was excluded—a reducing atmosphere—thereby avoiding the oxidation of any residual iron in the clay that would produce brown, buff, or red color. However, a leading authority on the study of prehistoric pottery technology, Anna O. Shepard, advises against making such broad inferences—even though they may be true—without first thoroughly testing clays available to the Anasazi to determine their actual firing qualities, preferably under aboriginal firing conditions. Lacking such tests, she suggests simply referring to "gray-firing clay" or "white-firing clay" (Shepard 1980: 217–222). However, more recent observations show that, to a considerable extent, some clays used to produce gray or white pottery will oxidize to a red or orange color in an oxidizing atmosphere. From this we can deduce that Anasazi potters did discover how to control the firing atmosphere.

While Anasazi utility pottery was almost invariably gray to gray-black in color, repeated placement in cooking fires has often left thick encrustations of soot on vessel exteriors, sometimes making it hard to tell what the original color was.

Potters in the Anasazi provinces did experiment with tempers to counteract the severe shrinkage of the clays available. Without the temper, their pottery would have cracked and shattered in the drying and firing processes. There was still shrinkage that caused the sand grains to protrude on utility pottery (figs. 24–41), often leaving a markedly rough surface. Potters south of the San Juan River relied on what some archaeologists have simply called "sand temper." It is quite possible that loose sand of the desired quality was added to temper the clay, but some provinces relied

consistently on crushed sandstone. Whether sand or sandstone, it involved a traditional practice. For the archaeologist analyzing the pottery, not all sand tempers are considered to be identical. With magnification, sand grains can be described objectively in terms of *material*: quartz, basalt, earthy ores (like hematite or limonite); *opacity*: clear, frosted, or opaque; *shape of particles*: rounded, subangular, or angular; *grain size*; *color of staining minerals*: hematite (red), limonite (yellow); and *adhering minerals*: calcium carbonate and opal, which were sometimes the cementing agents for the sandstone. Anyone traveling around the Anasazi area on foot becomes aware that there are many kinds of sandstones. Some of them would be suitable for temper; others would not. For the Anasazi potters, knowledge of local geology was a necessity. Although they might travel considerable distances for their clay, slip, and paint materials, there is little evidence that they carried heavy, bulky lumps of sandstone very far. They almost always selected from tempering material from nearby sources.

North of the San Juan, in the Mesa Verde Province, potters originally tempered much of their pottery with a light- and-dark-colored igneous rock, variously identified as diorite, andesite, or dacite. Although localization of these temper types may simply relate to their greater availability in the alluvial gravels along the San Juan River, some archaeologists have hypothesized that the different temper types may also reflect linguistic—and thereby cultural—differentiation, with Keres speakers to the south and Tewas to the north.

By late Pueblo I or early Pueblo II (ca. A.D. 900), Mesa Verde potters had adopted a new tempering material for their painted pottery—crushed potsherds. Apparently first used by potters in the Chaco and Chuska provinces to the south, sherd temper would have required scavenging old refuse heaps for potsherds which could be ground. Though light gray or white and often ground fine, sherd temper is easily recognized, since, under magnification, tiny grains of the igneous rock are still visible in the sherd temper. Mesa Verde potters continued to use crushed igneous rock for their utility pottery, however.

South of the San Juan River, midway between Gallup and Shiprock, New Mexico, Anasazi potters of the Chuska Province first used sand or crushed sandstone during Basketmaker III (ca. A.D. 450–750). After that time, they switched to using the crushed fragments of another distinctive igneous rock, trachyte (sometimes called sanidine basalt), found in one or two places in the Chuska Mountains to the west and along some of the arroyos that drain them. This igneous rock temper contains minute crystals of olivine and biotite mica. Whether ground coarse or fine, these minerals are easily recognized, often without magnification, even when found in trade pottery far from the Chuska Province. Utility pottery tempered with trachyte often comprises over half of the pottery found at Chaco Canyon, even though the Chuska Valley source is over seventy kilometers (forty-five miles) to the west. Trachyte continued to be the preferred temper for utility pottery in the Chuska Province until the San Juan Basin was abandoned in the late 1200s. Like their Mesa Verde neighbors, Chuska potters then switched to crushed sherd temper for painted pottery.

As in the Mogollon area, few, if any, Anasazi firing areas have been uncovered in archaeological excavations. However, near Yellowjacket, in southwestern Colorado, archaeologists have been intrigued by the discovery of a number of fairly large, shallow, stone-filled pits containing charcoal and Mesa Verde pottery fragments and thought to have been kilns (Fuller 1984). Located in the heart of the Mesa Verde

Fig. 24. Lino Gray pitcher, A.D. 600–800. Anasazi Utility Tradition, Cibola Province.

Fig. 25. *Lino Gray, Fugitive Red variant, bowl,* A.D. 700–800. *Mogollon Slipped/Anasazi Utility Traditions, Cibola Province.*

Fig. 26. LEFT: *Lino Gray ring-shaped canteen,* A.D. 600–800. *Anasazi Utility Tradition, Chaco Province.* RIGHT: *Lino Gray trilobed pitcher,* A.D. 600–800. *Anasazi Utility Tradition, Cibola Province.*

Fig. 27. *Kana-a Gray pitcher,* A.D. 800–875. *Anasazi Utility Tradition, Cibola Province.*

Province but a kilometer or two from the nearest contemporary dwelling sites, these pits appear to have been used during a period of great population growth in the Mesa Verde area when wood consumption for construction, cooking, and heating dwellings was so great that there were no longer adequate fuel sources located close to the villages. This would have required that potters haul wood great distances to the Pueblos, or carry the pottery to the wood source. Archaeologists infer the latter.

Although modern Pueblo potters will use wood to start their kiln fire, the preferred fuel is animal dung, which burns readily and fast. Cow dung for such purposes is abundant and can be dried and stockpiled with ease. Prehistoric potters would not have had the advantages of cow dung, since they had no domesticated animals other than the dog and the turkey. However, wood would have been reasonably plentiful near most settled areas, and lesser materials such as shrubs and grasses might also have been used. Although outside the area being discussed, Hopi potters in northeastern Arizona from the 1400s onward often fired their pottery with coal, sometimes adjacent to the outcrops of coal seams that are near or underlying the mesas on which their villages were built. Although coal can be found near many Anasazi settlement areas in northwestern New Mexico, there is no indication that the Anasazi were aware of its value as a fuel. The San Juan Basin had already been abandoned by the time that coal began to be used by the Hopi. Nor is there evidence that prehistoric potters in the Rio Grande region of central and northern New Mexico used coal for pottery firing.

The exterior surface of Basketmaker III to early Pueblo I utility vessels were smoothed but usually not polished (figs. 24–27). This lack of polish seems to have been due in part to extreme shrinkage of clays during drying and firing. Some archaeologists have also cited a possible desirability of having a rough exterior surface to make it easier to grasp and carry a vessel or to facilitate either heat transfer when cooking or evaporation when used for storing water.

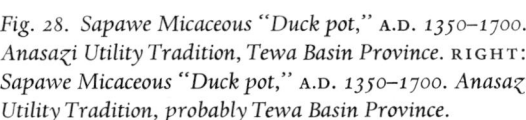

Fig. 28. Sapawe Micaceous "Duck pot," A.D. *1350–1700. Anasazi Utility Tradition, Tewa Basin Province.* RIGHT: *Sapawe Micaceous "Duck pot,"* A.D. *1350–1700. Anasazi Utility Tradition, probably Tewa Basin Province.*

Fig. 29. Mesa Verde Corrugated jar, A.D. *1200–1300. Anasazi Utility Tradition, Mesa Verde Province.*

By the middle 700s, Anasazi potters were making a pottery type named "Lino Gray, Fugitive Red Variety," achieved by applying a slip of red iron oxide (hematite) pigment to vessel exteriors, apparently after the vessel had been fired (fig. 25). This treatment may have been a faulty Anasazi attempt to replicate the red-slipped pottery as made by their Mogollon contemporaries. The slip may have been poorly fired or not fired at all, since the pigment was impermanent, would wash or brush off easily, and often left a faint rosy hue adhering to the vessel surface. It was obviously a poor substitute for the Mogollon type, though even San Francisco Red sometimes had a fugitive red slip. Whether this red slip was a simple pigment-and-water mixture or a pigment-water-and-vegetal extract solution is unknown. Fugitive red slips are commonly found on exteriors of some late Basketmaker III painted types, especially bowls, but the practice was generally not continued thereafter.

By late Basketmaker III (ca. A.D. 675), some Anasazi potters in northeastern Arizona had begun making Tallahogan Red, a gray pottery with a reasonably durable red slip applied before firing. This may have been an outgrowth of the utilization of the Fugitive Red slip applied to Lino Gray and some contemporary black-on-white painted types. The distribution of Tallahogan Red is not well documented, but it may have fostered the development of oxidized orange ware or red ware in northeastern Arizona and part of the Mesa Verde Province in the Four Corners area. From the latter area, two pottery types, Abajo Black-on-orange and, later, La Plata (or Deadmans) Black-on-red, were especially popular trade or gift wares that reached the eastern Anasazi provinces of Chaco Canyon, Chuska, Upper San Juan, and occasionally into the Middle Rio Grande.

From late Basketmaker III or Pueblo I through early Pueblo IV (A.D. 800–1400), Anasazi utility pottery continued to show intentional accentuation of the coils. The coil treatments went through a progression of neck banding, neck corrugating, overall indented corrugating, and, ultimately, a gradual return to obliteration of coils. Early in this period, traditions apparently died hardest in the Upper San Juan Province where plain, rough-surfaced gray ware was still being produced as much as a century after neck banding had begun to be done elsewhere (figs. 35–38).

Fig. 30. Coolidge Corrugated jar, A.D. 1000–1075. Anasazi Utility Tradition, Chaco or Cibola Province.

Fig. 31. Chaco Corrugated jar, A.D. 1000–1075. Anasazi Utility Tradition, Chaco Province.

As in the Central Anasazi area, early pottery types of the Anasazi Utility Tradition in the Eastern Anasazi area characteristically were made with gray-firing clay and coarse temper. All vessels—jars and pitchers, primarily—have surfaces that appear to have been left intentionally rough or were only perfunctorily smoothed. At this early stage, it is not really possible to distinguish with certainty between some vessels that had serving functions from those for cooking and storing.

Beyond these few essential qualities, the Anasazi Utility Tradition followed roughly the same evolutionary sequence of surface treatments that the Mogollon Utility Tradition did, and at about the same time. It is likely that some of the early developments also had their beginnings in Mexico. Once the idea of surface texturing had been widely accepted, Anasazi potters began to develop their own regional traditions within the Anasazi area.

During Basketmaker III, Anasazi potters in several provinces tried to produce plain gray serving vessels with polished surfaces and even polished black interiors, such as those produced in the Mogollon area. Though nominally successful, the advent of slips that easily could be polished seems to have encouraged further differentiation between utility wares for storage and cooking and slipped, polished, and painted pottery for food service and specialized uses. During late Pueblo III, some potters in the Zuni area introduced polished interiors on some gray utility pottery. These artisans may have been migrants from nearby Mogollon provinces who yearned for the slick finishes of fine-paste brown-ware utility pottery of their native areas.

Occasionally, especially during Pueblo II, potters in a number of Anasazi provinces made slipped and painted bowl forms with corrugated exteriors. Normally, slipping of Anasazi utility pottery was generally not practiced until Pueblo IV and V, when potters in Rio Grande provinces applied glistening micaceous clay slips to a variety of vessel forms (fig. 28).

Perhaps more than in other provinces, Basketmaker III potters of the Upper San Juan Province commonly started their utility vessels in a coiled basket, firing the pot without obliterating the basket impression (fig. 35). This practice may mark the beginning use of what in the Tewa Basin Province is called a "puki," referring to a kind of platform, often made from a recycled jar neck or bottom, that serves as a supporting mold to facilitate starting and rotating pottery vessels as they are being formed. The link between the Upper San Juan and the Rio Grande provinces in this respect is less than clear-cut. Although vaguely suggestive of a potter's wheel, the puki could not be turned rapidly enough to produce wheel-thrown pottery. That type of pottery making was never used by prehistoric Indians in the New World.

The puki became an important potter's tool particularly for the production of painted pottery during Pueblo IV (beginning ca. A.D. 1325) and in present-day Pueblos. Contemporary Pueblo potters seem to resist using any pottery-making technique that might result in their giving up their coil-scrape tradition of forming pottery. Prehistoric pukis have also been found in the Casas Grandes Province in northern Chihuahua.

From the introduction of pottery right up to the present, pottery used for cooking and general storage remained essentially the same in its principal attributes. The only major differences occurred after about A.D. 700 or 750 and involved some choice by the potters to texture the exterior surfaces, make slight modifications in the general shape of the vessel, and occasionally add handles or lugs.

Fig. 32. Coolidge Corrugated jar, A.D. 1000–1075. Anasazi Utility Tradition, Chaco or Cibola Province.

As with Mogollon pottery, the Anasazi utility ware began with broad neck coils that were sometimes almost an inch wide. As time passed, widths of neck coils were reduced to produce narrow, somewhat everted bands of plain corrugation with greater surface relief than seen earlier. This trend was especially evident in pottery of the southern and western provinces of the San Juan Basin and also eastward near the Rio Grande, where potters made deeply indented neck coils in a surface texturing treatment called "exuberant" corrugation (fig. 42). Eventually, the indented corrugations became smaller, though still quite deep, and were applied over all but the rims of vessels (figs. 30–32). The trend continued with a gradual flattening (figs. 34) and incipient obliteration of the indented coils during Pueblo III (figs. 29, 33) until, by Pueblo IV, the indentations had become merely ripples on the exterior (fig. 28). By the beginning of the Historic Period (Pueblo V) around A.D. 1600, the surface treatment of Anasazi Utility Tradition pottery had come full circle to the smoothed, but otherwise untextured, style of the earliest plain gray pottery of Basketmaker III.

The Anasazi Utility Tradition persisted throughout most of the Historic Period, surviving at some of the modern Pueblos until late in the nineteenth century and even, at some Pueblos, well into the twentieth. During this time a trend developed toward larger, thicker-walled, unpainted, and primitive-looking vessels that have rarely survived to reach museums or collectors.

Fig. 33. Chaco Corrugated storage jar, A.D. 1075–1125. Anasazi Utility Tradition, Chaco Province.

Fig. 34 (LEFT). *Chaco Corrugated jar (side view), A.D. 1075–1125. Anasazi Utility Tradition, Chaco Province.*

Fig. 35. Rosa Gray seed jar, A.D. 700–850. Anasazi Utility Tradition, Upper San Juan Province.

Fig. 36. Piedra Gray large bowl, A.D. 850–950. Anasazi Utility Tradition, Upper San Juan Province.

Fig. 37. *Piedra Gray jar*, A.D. *850–950. Anasazi Utility Tradition, Upper San Juan Province.*

Fig. 38. *Piedra Gray pitcher*, A.D. *850–950. Anasazi Utility Tradition, Upper San Juan Province.*

Fig. 39. Gallina Banded Utility beaker, A.D. *1200–1275. Anasazi Utility Tradition, Gallina Province.*

Fig. 40 (LEFT). *"Pojoaque Neckbanded" (provisional name) jar,* A.D. *850–950. Anasazi Utility Tradition, Tewa Basin Province.*

Fig. 41. Piedra Neckbanded tripod pitcher, A.D. *850–950. Anasazi Utility Tradition, Upper San Juan Province.*

Fig. 42 (OVERLEAF). *"Pojoaque Corrugated" (provisional name) jar,* A.D. *900–1000. Anasazi Utility Tradition, Tewa Basin Province.*

3. PAINTED POTTERY TRADITIONS

The Mogollon were making pottery for some four hundred years before they felt compelled to produce more than plain brown or red pottery. Emil W. Haury, of the University of Arizona, who provided the original description of the Mogollon Culture and has been studying both it and the Hohokam Culture since the early 1930s, places the earliest painted pottery in the Southwest as early as A.D. 1, when the Hohokam Culture potters started decorating their buff-colored pottery with a red-firing pigment in simple designs of broad parallel lines and chevrons in quartered layouts. It is conceivable that Mogollon potters, who began to apply a red slip to their pottery from perhaps as early as A.D. 250 or 300 (LeBlanc 1982:110) might have copied their Hohokam neighbors and selectively applied the red clay slip in a simple design. However, they don't seem to have begun painting their pottery until much later—about A.D. 700 (Withers 1985).

The first Mogollon painted pottery, Mogollon Red-on-brown (figs. 10, 11), bears a basic similarity in style and layout to the earliest Hohokam painted pottery but none at all to the busy hatch-filled curvilinear designs and repetitious zoomorphic figures the Hohokam were putting on their pottery around A.D. 700. The earliest Mogollon painted pottery is so out of synchronization with both Hohokam and Anasazi painted pottery development that it is more likely that Mogollon potters learned painting from some other source. Conceivably, it was a relatively late introduction from some unknown group in northern Mexico or perhaps neighboring groups along the Lower Rio Grande near El Paso.

There seems to have been no single tradition of painted pottery that came in at the beginning of Pueblo pottery making and continued up to the present. As a matter of fact, painted pottery in the Pueblo tradition may have developed twice. Almost as soon as pottery making was adopted, Anasazi painted pottery developed and divided into two traditions distinguished by the pigment used: in northern Arizona, a Western Anasazi tradition which used a vegetal pigment for their painted pottery, and, mainly in northwestern New Mexico, a Central and Eastern Anasazi tradition that used a mineral (usually an iron oxide) pigment. Anasazi potters in the Mesa Verde and Upper San Juan provinces occasionally used both types of pigments, though mineral paint was more common among the former (fig. 74) and vegetal paint typical among the latter. These garbled paint traditions may have resulted from Anasazi groups being out on the northern fringes of the Anasazi world, where they learned about pottery paints from two different sources: mineral paint from the San Juan Basin and vegetal paint from the Kayenta Province in northeastern Arizona. Regardless of the

Fig. 43. La Plata/White Mound Black-on-white bowl, A.D. 600–700. Anasazi Mineral-Paint Tradition, Cibola Province.

Fig. 44. La Plata/White Mound Black-on-white seed jar, A.D. 600–700. Anasazi Mineral-Paint Tradition, Cibola Province.

type of paint used by the Anasazi, its blackish color seems to have first depended on another Anasazi ceramic development: firing in a reducing atmosphere. Some archaeologists suggest that, because some Mesa Verde and Upper San Juan Anasazi chose to use vegetal paint, there may have been two different language groups in those areas. Thought-provoking as they are, attempts to correlate language spoken with paint type, temper, design, and other ceramic attributes are risky undertakings unless other supporting data exist.

Whether the Western or Central Anasazi discovered pottery painting first is difficult to say. Each had essentially the same naturally occurring resources that would have enabled the development or use of either kind of pigment. However, the predominance of vegetal paint among the Western Anasazi area, and the simpler "recipe" for preparing it, raise the possibility that the Western Anasazi may have developed their paint first.

If, as most archaeologists generally believe, the Anasazi chose to decorate their earliest painted pottery with designs reminiscent of ones they had woven into their basketry, they also may have chosen as pottery pigments some of the same vegetal and mineral materials they used for dying neutral-colored basketry splints. (Vegetal Paint is discussed later.)

In the Four Corners area, another, somewhat different paint tradition also developed involving a lustrous reddish black or maroon pigment. It was also an iron oxide, possibly containing traces of a manganese mineral. This pigment was applied to pottery whose clay apparently contained ferric oxide that, when fired in an oxidizing atmosphere, yielded an orange background color. This tradition may have been either an outgrowth of the Lino Gray, Fugitive Red pottery discussed earlier or perhaps a local development caused by the nature of the available

Fig. 45. White Mound Black-on-white double bowl, A.D. 700–800. Anasazi Mineral-Paint Tradition, Cibola Province.

Fig. 46. San Marcial Black-on-white bowl, A.D. 750–875. Anasazi Mineral-Paint Tradition, Middle Rio Grande Province.

Fig. 47. La Plata/White Mound Black-on-white bowl, A.D. 600–750. Anasazi Mineral-Paint Tradition, Cibola Province.

clays and mineral pigments used in the western Mesa Verde Province. Within a century or two of its first use, however, the potters who developed this paint tradition moved southwestward into northeastern Arizona and seem to have had little influence on later Central and Eastern Anasazi pottery traditions. We will therefore limit our focus here to the two principal Anasazi pigment distinctions in black-on-white pottery: the *Anasazi Mineral-Paint Tradition* and the *Anasazi Vegetal-Paint Tradition*.

While well-dated specimens of the earliest Anasazi painted pottery are rare, it is evident that its makers didn't learn their craft from the Mogollon, though there may have been some very indirect influence from the Hohokam. This leaves the likelihood that painted pottery was an outgrowth of Anasazi creativity, taking place perhaps as early as A.D. 550–575. Their first painting was applied to their rough gray utility pottery (figs. 43–48, 117) and shared few, if any, styles of contemporary Hohokam pottery. But consistent with their basketry design, their early painted ware featured almost free-form isolated figures and graceful curving elements (fig. 46).

PAINTED POTTERY TRADITIONS   59

Anasazi Mineral-Paint Tradition

Anasazi mineral-paint black-on-white pottery was made throughout a huge area, from as far south as near Quemado to north of Cortez, Colorado, and from the Chuska Mountains and Petrified Forest on the west to the Sangre de Cristo and Sandia mountains on the east, with local extensions even farther east. It was the prevailing paint tradition in the Central Anasazi area until potters in the San Juan River drainage (Chuska, Chaco, and Mesa Verde provinces) gradually switched over to vegetal paint between A.D. 1050 and 1150. The more southerly of the Eastern and Central Anasazi provinces (Puerco-Zuni, Acoma-Laguna, Salinas, and parts of the Middle Rio Puerco and Middle Rio Grande provinces) continued the mineral-paint tradition up into the Historic Period, and some even up to the present.

The earliest Basketmaker III mineral-paint black-on-white pottery type was La Plata Black-on-white (fig. 43). It is similar in form, finish, and design to its vegetal-paint counterpart in northeastern Arizona, Lino Black-on-gray (fig. 116). In transitional versions, it is often difficult to distinguish La Plata Black-on-white from its late Basketmaker III successor, White Mound Black-on-white. Both types have the characteristic rough surfaces of the Basketmaker III period, though there is a tendency for

Fig. 48 (OPPOSITE). White Mound Black-on-white bowl, A.D. 700–800. Anasazi Mineral-Paint Tradition, province unknown.

Fig. 49. Crozier Black-on-white bowl, A.D. 800–875. Anasazi Mineral-Paint Tradition, Chuska Province.

Fig. 50. Kiatuthlanna Black-on-white bowl, A.D. 800–875. Anasazi Mineral-Paint Tradition, Cibola Province. Compare with Fig. 12, Mangas Black-on-white bowl of Mogollon Slipped Tradition.

Fig. 51. Kiatuthlanna Black-on-white bowl, A.D. 800–875. Anasazi Mineral-Paint Tradition, Cibola Province.

Fig. 52 (OPPOSITE). Kiatuthlanna Black-on-white bowl, A.D. 800–875. Anasazi Mineral-Paint Tradition, Cibola Province.

ANASAZI MINERAL-PAINT TRADITION 63

Fig. 53. *Piedra Black-on-white effigy jar*, A.D. 850–950. Anasazi Mineral-Paint Tradition, Mesa Verde or Upper San Juan Province.

the latter type to be not quite as rough. This allows for some subjectivity—and probably inaccuracy—in classification. In such cases, a commonly used means of avoiding misclassification is to hyphenate or insert a slash between the type names, e.g., La Plata-White Mound Black-on-white or La Plata/White Mound Black-on-white.

As early as Basketmaker III, near the northern extent of the Central Anasazi area—the Mesa Verde Province—a few potters occasionally chose a vegetal pigment, though the majority favored a mineral pigment, generally an iron oxide. For a short time in an area near Durango, Colorado, some early Anasazi potters decorated with a mineral pigment that produced a glaze.

In contrast with the somewhat shinier-surfaced, fuzzy-edged vegetal paint of the west, mineral or "iron" paint had a matte surface that contrasted with the usually slipped and polished surface of the vessel, quite consistently produced sharp-edged lines, and usually fired to a dense black to reddish-brown color. Apparently troubled by the same clay shrinkage that caused the surface in the pottery of the

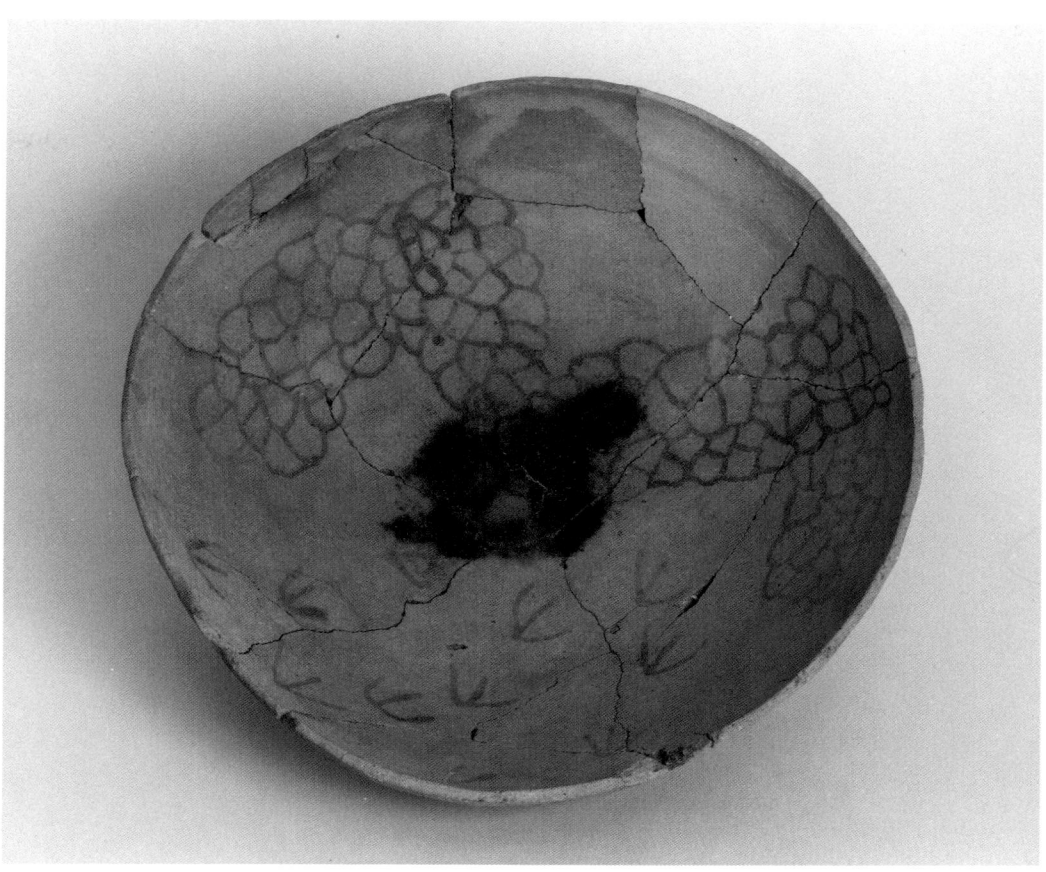

Fig. 54. Piedra Black-on-white bowl, A.D. 850–950. Anasazi Mineral-Paint Tradition, Upper San Juan Province.

Anasazi Utility Tradition to be rough from the protruding temper, potters soon learned to use finer sand tempers, or even crushed potsherds, which, in combination with a thin white slip, provided a relatively shrink-proof surface on which to paint.

Potters of the Central Anasazi area—primarily the San Juan Basin and Continental Divide areas—initially chose designs that seem to have copied the graceful, sometimes asymmetrical designs of basketry, such as on the San Marcial Black-on-white bowl (fig. 46). Then, a little over a century later, black-on-white decoration turned to increasingly busy elements combining relatively fine lines and solid rectilinear shapes, such as on the late Basketmaker III type, White Mound Black-on-white (figs. 45–48).

In the Puerco River drainage, northwest of present-day Zuni Pueblo, Frank H. H. Roberts, Jr., of the Smithsonian Institution, excavated several Pueblo I (A.D. 750–875) villages whose potters produced an especially well-made pottery type, Kiatuthlanna Black-on-white (Roberts 1931: 114–149; 1940: 3–109). With fine, sand-tempered, gray-white paste, ultra-smooth surfaces, and carefully executed decoration, it was unmatched by any other contemporary Anasazi painted pottery (figs. 50–52). In its use of moderately wide parallel lines, some with attached solid, pennant-like triangles, interlocking scrolls, and widely spaced wavy line hatching at right angles to framing lines, the type has occasionally been confused with roughly contemporary iron-paint pottery found over a much wider area extending far north to the Chuska and Chaco Canyon provinces (figs. 46, 49) and as far east as the Acoma Province. However, Kiatuthlanna Black-on-white seems to have had a much more limited distribution centering in a small area southwest of Gallup.

Fig. 55 (OPPOSITE). *Red Mesa Black-on-white pitcher, A.D. 875–1000. Anasazi Mineral-Paint Tradition, Cibola Province.*

Fig. 56. Red Mesa Black-on-white bowl, A.D. 875–1000. Anasazi Mineral-Paint Tradition, Chaco Province.

Red Mesa Black-on-white (figs. 55–63), the successor to Kiatuthlanna Black-on-white, was made over a much wider area, though it was rarely of the same quality. It ranged from the Chaco Canyon and Chuska provinces on the north down to the fringes of the Mogollon area on the south, and from near Holbrook and Ganado, Arizona, eastward to the Rio Grande. Made during Pueblo I and much of Pueblo II (A.D. 875–1000), the long-lived type was commonly associated with the gray neck banded type, Kana-a Gray, at the early end of its time range, and later with early and middle versions of gray plain and indented corrugated utility pottery.

Red Mesa Black-on-white bowl forms had a stark white slip polished inside and out, but the polish was spotty, sometimes leaving an irregular surface. Once seen, its decorative style is easily recognized: solid triangles, interlocking scrolls, and relatively

ANASAZI MINERAL-PAINT TRADITION   67

Fig. 57. Red Mesa Black-on-white bowl, A.D. 875–1000. Anasazi Mineral-Paint Tradition, Cibola Province.

fine, parallel lines or ticked parallel lines following zigzag fashion around the inner circumference of bowls and the exterior body of jars.

The significance of the abundance of Red Mesa Black-on-white at Chaco Canyon remains to be fully explained, but there is little doubt of its predominance in the lower strata and rooms of the "great houses" there. It seems to have been a harbinger of the growth of that area, as well as a companion of the florescence of the "Chaco Phenomenon" during the tenth and eleventh centuries. Some archaeologists believe that the actual area of manufacture of Red Mesa Black-on-white and its successors was much more limited and that it was traded widely, accompanying whatever exported goods that come under the general category of "Chaco influence."

Chaco Canyon has preoccupied many Southwestern archaeologists, especially during the past fifteen years when the National Park Service and other agencies and institutions have conducted extensive archaeological studies there, all in hopes of learning more about the causes and effects of its spectacular growth from the middle 800s to the early 1100s. Its unique concentration of a dozen or so massive masonry pueblos suggests to archaeologists that it had been a very special place at a time of cultural expansion experienced by all Anasazi communities within a radius of 200 kilometers (125 miles). Outlier communities typically consist of concentrations of dozens of small pueblos built within a mile or two of a large pueblo having Chaco-style

Fig. 58. Red Mesa Black-on-white pitcher, A.D. 875–1050. Anasazi Mineral-Paint Tradition, Middle Rio Grande Province.

Fig. 59. Red Mesa (or early Gallup) Black-on-white bowl, A.D. 950–1000. Anasazi Mineral-Paint Tradition, Chaco or Cibola Province.

architecture, usually including a *great kiva*, or community ceremonial chamber. Many outliers have been shown to be linked to Chaco Canyon by a series of formal road systems.

Whether or not the Central Anasazi made full-time use of the area, various archaeologists have hypothesized that Chaco Canyon may have been the seat of a complex trade network emanating out of Mexico, or a center for redistributing surplus food to needy Anasazi in other provinces, or the focus of flourishing, regionwide religious fervor, and more. When one sees even the remnants of what was there, any of these somewhat grandiose hypotheses seem reasonable.

ANASAZI MINERAL-PAINT TRADITION 69

Fig. 60. Red Mesa Black-on-white bowl, A.D. 850–1050. Anasazi Mineral-Paint Tradition, Middle Rio Grande Province.

Fig. 61. Red Mesa Black-on-white seed jar with pierced lug handles, A.D. 875–1050. Anasazi Mineral-Paint Tradition, Middle Rio Grande Province.

Fig. 62. Red Mesa Black-on-white beaker, A.D. 950–1050. Anasazi Mineral-Paint Tradition, Chaco(?) Province.

Fig. 63. Red Mesa Black-on-white bowl, A.D. 900–1025. Anasazi Mineral-Paint Tradition, Chaco Province.

The development of the monumental structures at Chaco Canyon entailed marshaling both material and human resources on a scale previously unmatched in the Anasazi region. Although there were several separate building episodes at Chaco Canyon over the course of some three hundred years, some aspect of building probably was going on at all times. This would have included quarrying stone; cutting and transporting thousands of timbers from mountain forests sixty-five to one hundred kilometers (forty to sixty miles) away; gathering adobe; hauling water for mortar; and building the structures.

The major buildings at Chaco Canyon were used seasonally as ceremonial structures for initiations, "rain-making" ritual, trade fairs, "new fire" ceremonies, curing,

Fig. 64. Gallup Black-on-white bowl, A.D. 1000–1100. Anasazi Mineral-Paint Tradition, Chaco Province.

and other activities that might best be accomplished when the greatest spiritual help could be achieved by congregating a large part of the populace. The many smaller pueblos in the vicinity may have housed a succession of individual and extended families whose members performed all stages of "great house" construction and participated in the ritual events they housed. Presumably, other family members had to work in nearby agricultural areas to feed and clothe those workers. The undertaking would have required the organization and dedication of thousands of the populace of the San Juan Basin, whether they worked at Chaco Canyon or at one of many areas that contributed construction timber, food (perhaps even water), pottery, labor, and ritual support.

Participants in the Chaco Phenomenon apparently were also the perpetuators of much of the Anasazi Mineral-Paint Tradition throughout the region, as indicated by the abundance and wide distribution of Red Mesa Black-on-white and its equally abundant successor, Gallup Black-on-white (figs. 64–68).

Gallup Black-on-white seems to have been the model on which a technologically finer and partly contemporary version, Chaco Black-on-white, was made (fig. 69). The latter rarely accounts for more than one or two percent of sherds recovered from Chaco Canyon sites and may have been made by a few superior potters. Since a great deal of pottery was brought to Chaco Canyon from outlying settlements, it is even possible that a potter or group of potters elsewhere made the type for export to Chaco Canyon.

Fig. 65. Gallup Black-on-white seed jar, A.D. 1000–1100. Anasazi Mineral-Paint Tradition, Chaco or Cibola Province.

Fig. 66. Gallup/Puerco Black-on-white seed jar, A.D. 1000–1100. Anasazi Mineral-Paint Tradition, Chaco or Cibola Province.

Fig. 67. Gallup Black-on-white bowl, A.D. 1000–1100. Anasazi Mineral-Paint Tradition, Acoma Province.

Regional and even local varieties of Gallup Black-on-white apparently were being produced in almost all provinces of northwestern New Mexico, adjacent parts of Colorado, Utah, and Arizona, and even eleventh-century settlements in the Middle Rio Grande, Tewa Basin, and Taos provinces. These were often distinguishable on the basis of the use of their own traditional local materials and techniques: tempers, paste colors and textures, presence or absence of slips, polish, qualities of paints, and, in the Chuska Province, the use of vegetal paint.

Just how all these renditions of essentially the same style relate to one another has been the cause of much consternation for archaeologists working with them. In the development of a tradition of pottery classification, not all researchers working with mineral-paint pottery have based their type determinations on the same diagnostic criteria. Some consider design to be most significant; others emphasize surface finish; and still others stress the tempering material used. This has created considerable confusion, as it has led to assigning the same type names to combinations of attributes different from those established by earlier research. In published accounts, there is generally no way of knowing whether all researchers do or do not replicate the classifications developed by earlier workers.

Early descriptions of Escavada Black-on-white, another type conspicuous at Chaco Canyon, distinguish it from Gallup Black-on-white in its painted surfaces, which were left unpolished and often rough. In design, Escavada Black-on-white tends to bolder black lines and solids and less of the hatching so common to its contemporaries.

Fig. 68. Gallup/Chaco Black-on-white olla, A.D. 1000–1100. Anasazi Mineral-Paint Tradition, Chaco Province.

Fig. 69. *Chaco Black-on-white pitcher*, A.D. 1075–1130. Anasazi Mineral-Paint Tradition, Chaco Province.

Fig. 71. *Escavada Black-on-white bowl*, A.D. 1000–1100. Anasazi Mineral-Paint Tradition, Chaco Province.

Fig. 70. *Puerco Black-on-white jar*, A.D. 1000–1100. Anasazi Mineral-Paint Tradition, Cibola Province.

Almost one hundred kilometers (sixty miles) away, in the Puerco-Zuni Province, near Gallup and Zuni, the same cluster of decorative styles (overall hatched designs, overall solid designs, and mixed hatched and solid designs) prevails, but with a difference. The vessel walls are often thicker, the paste is chalkier, the surfaces are moderately well polished, and the paints tend to be more red-brown than black. From the point of view of pottery classification, the distinctions between the contemporary Chaco and Puerco-Zuni technologies suggest that we should recognize that their developments followed separate tracks, at least intermittently.

In the Chuska Province mineral-paint black-on-white pottery predominated in Basketmaker III, yet a tradition of painting pottery with a vegetal pigment had become dominant, except for two or three mineral-paint enclaves, throughout the province by the end of Pueblo I.

ANASAZI MINERAL-PAINT TRADITION 75

Fig. 72. Gallup/Escavada Black-on-white bird effigy pitcher, A.D. *1000–1100. Anasazi Mineral-Paint Tradition, Cibola Province.*

Fig. 73. Escavada Black-on-white bowl, A.D. *1000–1100. Anasazi Mineral-Paint Tradition, province unknown.*

Fig. 74. Mancos Black-on-white bowl, A.D. *1000–1075. Anasazi Mineral-Paint Tradition, Chaco Province.*

Fig. 75 (OPPOSITE). *Reserve Black-on-white pitcher,* A.D. *1000–1125. (Note masked figure painted on handle.) Anasazi Mineral-Paint Tradition, Cibola Province.*

From the middle 800s until the early 1100s, the potters in these mineral-paint enclaves seemed to follow a sequence of decorative styles that appeared to emanate from Chaco Canyon. However, a Chaco origin for these decorative styles just might be a misconception. Even the followers of the Anasazi Vegetal-Paint Tradition rendered their own vegetal versions of the imputed Chacoan styles. Actually, these styles can be found dominant on sites within one hundred kilometers (sixty miles) of Chaco Canyon, in almost any direction, and the original stimuli for them have not been identified with any certainty. However, until more accurate determinations are made, it is not unreasonable to consider Chaco Canyon to have been a major focus of attention for thousands of Central and Eastern Anasazi people—potters included—from the ninth century until about the third decade of the twelfth century.

Significant construction activity at Chaco Canyon ended shortly after A.D. 1130. The Chaco Phenomenon appears to have collapsed, and the province was largely abandoned, its influence on the San Juan Basin ended. Some hypotheses dealing with the collapse suggest that drought or breakdown of an economic system involving the Chaco roads and outlier settlements may have led to the large-scale abandonment of the province. Other hypotheses include a lapse of cultural stimuli from Mesoamerica; ineffectiveness of the ceremonial activities conducted at Chaco Canyon; and the rise of a competing socioreligious complex of sites in the Montezuma Valley, northwest of Mesa Verde. The Anasazi Mineral-Paint Tradition came to an abrupt end in the northern provinces of the Central Anasazi, including the Chuska Valley, but it continued in the Cibola and Acoma provinces, surviving up to the present day.

Red-Ware and Glaze-Paint Traditions

A relatively early development in the Anasazi Mineral-Paint Tradition was its merger with a tradition of applying a red slip to one or both surfaces of a vessel. The oldest slipping tradition was that which began with the red-slipped Mogollon brown pottery type, San Francisco Red, which seems to have been introduced almost simultaneously or at least very shortly after the original introduction of pottery. For some reason, red ware was never very common even in the Mogollon region, except in its earliest years. Whether color had some special significance, or red-ware vessels some special function, is not known, but it seems to have been popular for gifts or as trade items, often reaching provinces far from its point of manufacture. Even though the Anasazi Puerco-Zuni Province is close to some Mogollon provinces, solid evidence is lacking that would show that the Mogollon type, San Francisco Red, was ancestral to the highly polished White Mountain Red Ware (Carlson 1970) that developed in the general Zuni area and east-central Arizona in the eleventh century.

Fig. 76. Tularosa Black-on-white pitcher, A.D. 1125–1250. Anasazi Mineral-Paint Tradition, Cibola Province.

Fig. 77. Tularosa Black-on-white dipper, A.D. 1125–1250. Anasazi Mineral-Paint Tradition, Cibola Province.

Fig. 78. Tularosa Black-on-white pitcher, A.D. 1125–1250. Anasazi Mineral-Paint Tradition, Cibola Province.

Mineral pigments containing iron, manganese, and copper were used on the earliest White Mountain Red Ware types, Puerco Black-on-red (A.D. 1000–1200) and Wingate Black-on-red (A.D. 1050–1200; fig. 87). The latter often bears designs identical to the contemporary Cibola White Ware type, Reserve Black-on-white (A.D. 1000–1100; fig. 75), which is perhaps best known for its occurrence in the southern Cibola Province in the vicinity of Reserve, New Mexico. However, the relative infrequency of Reserve Black-on-white in that area suggests that it probably was not locally made but was produced somewhat farther north and northwest, probably in the home area for Wingate Black-on-red.

Fig. 79. Klagetoh Black-on-white stirrup-shaped canteen, A.D. 1125–1250 or 1300. Anasazi Mineral-Paint Tradition, Cibola Province.

Wingate Black-on-red always seems to have been an immensely popular and widely exchanged type among the Anasazi in the San Juan Basin, many provinces of the Middle and Northern Rio Grande, and into northern Mogollon provinces. It was succeeded in the 1200s by an even more colorful and popular trade type, St. Johns Polychrome. Occurring most commonly in bowl forms, with a red-orange slip, St. Johns Polychrome is decorated in black or brownish designs in what is known as Tularosa Style similar to that on Tularosa Black-on-white vessels (figs. 76–78), the successor to Reserve Black-on-white. However, St. Johns Polychrome was further embellished on bowl exteriors by bold, white, broad-line decoration.

Fig. 80 (OPPOSITE). *Tularosa Black-on-white pitcher with parrot effigy handle,* A.D. *1125–1300. Anasazi Mineral-Paint Tradition, Cibola Province.*

Fig. 81. Cebolleta/Tularosa Black-on-white bird effigy jar, A.D. *1100–1225(?). Anasazi Mineral-Paint Tradition, Acoma(?) Province.*

As an alternative origin for the red wares in the Puerco-Zuni Province, we might consider the periodic friendly contact between the Hopi and Zuni during the Historic Period, well recorded in oral histories. It is possible that earlier cordial contact between the two groups in the eleventh century might have introduced the red-slipping technique of San Juan Red Ware to the Zuni, perhaps initiating the White Mountain Red Ware Tradition. Coincidentally, the potters who made black-on-red pottery in the western Mesa Verde Province discontinued its production in the late tenth century. This left a red-ware void that was quickly filled by pieces of the colorful White Mountain Red Ware types (Carlson 1970), which were widely traded in Central and Eastern Anasazi provinces.

Worthy of repeating, but only coincidentally related to the development of red wares, was the early appearance of glaze-paint decoration on Basketmaker III pottery in southwestern Colorado. Apparently, potters accidentally discovered a pigment containing a small amount of a lead mineral that would produce a greenish-black, maroon, or blue-black glaze. Based on the relative abundance of pottery decorated with the glaze pigment, the Durango district may have been its center of production (Carlson 1963: 34; Breternitz, Rohn, and Morris 1974: 25, 29). At least a small amount of the glaze-decorated pottery reached Mesa Verde during Late Basketmaker III and early Pueblo I, but its makers in the source area either chose to abandon the pigment or move away from its source. This brief glaze tradition became extinct before A.D. 900, and it was to be more than three hundred years before lead-glaze pigment was again used by the Anasazi.

Other mineral pigments used on black-on-white painted pottery in the Mesa Verde, Chaco-Puerco, and Cibola provinces show only a slight tendency to produce a glaze, but these seem to be silica glazes rather than ones containing lead. Though

Fig. 82. Socorro Black-on-white olla, A.D. 1050–1275. Anasazi Mineral-Paint Tradition, Acoma Province.

Fig. 83. Chupadero Black-on-white bowl, A.D. 1200–1375. Anasazi Mineral-Paint Tradition, Northern Jornada Province.

widespread, they never were very common. Such glazes must be considered fortuitous and not really part of a continuing glaze-paint tradition.

Glaze decoration reappeared in the late thirteenth century, in the White Mountain Red Ware type, St. Johns Polychrome, which was occasionally painted with a black mineral paint that tended to produce a sub-glaze, i.e., a slight tendency to flow and fuse without forming a shiny glaze. Some of this glaze may have been fused silica, but the iron-mineral pigment also contained impurities of copper, manganese, and traces of lead, the latter being the essential fluxing agent that lowered the melting point of the other minerals sufficiently to cause them to fuse.

Although most St. Johns Polychrome was made in the west, at least one potter, almost certainly a migrant, was producing the type at a pueblo near modern Santo Domingo Pueblo in the Rio Grande drainage and tempering it with crushed local igneous rock instead of the traditional crushed sherd temper of the Zuni area. This early appearance of the western-style red ware may have presaged the slightly later introduction of glaze decoration in the Middle Rio Grande provinces.

Fig. 84. *Socorro Black-on-white bowl*, A.D. 1050–1275. Anasazi Mineral-Paint Tradition, Acoma Province.

Fig. 85. *Chupadero Black-on-white olla*, A.D. 1100–1200. Anasazi Mineral-Paint Tradition, Northern Jornada Province.

Fig. 86 (OPPOSITE). *Socorro Black-on-white olla*, A.D. 1050–1275. *Anasazi Mineral-Paint Tradition, Acoma Province.*

Fig. 87. Wingate Black-on-red bowl, A.D. 1050–1200. *Mogollon Slipped/Anasazi Mineral-Paint Traditions, Cibola Province.*

Fig. 88. Agua Fria Glaze-on-red (Glaze A) bowl, A.D. 1315–1425. Mogollon Slipped/Anasazi Mineral-Paint Traditions, Middle Rio Grande Province.

Influence from Mesoamerica, or even northern Mexico, is often suggested to account for many prehistoric socioeconomic or technological advances among the Pueblos, and at least some mineral-painted pottery from the Casas Grandes Province in Chihuahua, Mexico, exhibits some tendency to glaze. However, the occurrence of glaze paint in that area seems to have been more accidental than by intent and shows no evidence of being perpetuated to the degree that was in the Southwest. Thus, discovery of the glaze-producing pigment seems to have been indigenous to the Southwest, perhaps by accident, as it was in Basketmaker III, or experimentation, bringing to an end the long tradition of nonglazing iron paint.

The glaze tradition gained strength in the west during the time of the Great Drought when more northerly Anasazi abandoned all areas of the San Juan Basin. Many of the San Juan Basin migrants resettled in the Middle Rio Grande provinces, northeastern Arizona, and possibly the Zuni area. With old trading patterns into the San Juan Basin disrupted, Zuni traders appear to have made their way eastward first to Acoma and then on to the Middle Rio Grande, introducing a new glaze-decorated red ware type with thin-line white exterior decoration, to which archaeologists gave an almost unpronounceable name, "Heshotauthla Polychrome."

By the early fourteenth century, both Acoma and Middle Rio Grande potters were forsaking their drab vegetal-paint black-on-white pottery for the Rio Grande equivalent of Heshotauthla Polychrome. This was a short-lived type, Los Padillas Glaze Polychrome, whose principal difference was the use of crushed-rock temper rather than the traditional crushed-potsherd temper of the Zuni area. The Los Padillas type bore the typical white decoration on red or red-orange bowl exteriors, but the white paint was soon abandoned, perhaps because it tended not to adhere well to the red slip. Rio Grande potters soon developed and preferred their own type, Agua Fria Glaze-on-red (fig. 88), whose band and paneled designs in shiny black-glaze paint applied over a deep red slip was very popular throughout most of the fourteenth century.

It is possible that some of the early glaze-decorated pottery in the Middle Rio Grande was painted with pigments acquired from the Zuni, but before long, Rio Grande potters had located their own lead minerals, at least one of which was in the general vicinity of Cerrillos, about twenty-five kilometers (fifteen miles) south of Santa Fe. This heavily mineralized zone probably was known earlier, since it was also a source of hematite and limonite pigments, as well as turquoise.

Rim forms on Rio Grande glaze-decorated pottery underwent gradual change over a four-hundred-year period. Shapes of bowl rims progressed from a simple "direct" rim with parallel inner and outer surfaces and flat top (figs. 88, 89) through a sequence of beveled (figs. 90, 91), thickened, thinned, and angled rims. The rim configurations have been divided into six groups—Glaze A through F, in the Rio Grande drainage, and Glaze I through VI at Pecos Pueblo—and chronologically established at pueblos where glaze-decorated pottery was associated with datable timbers of piñon, ponderosa pine, and Douglas fir. Unfortunately, not all Middle Rio Grande localities were located close to woodlands and forests where datable construction timber was available. Dendrochronology is of no use for construction cottonwood, the principal building wood at many pueblos close to the Rio Grande.

Fig. 89. Cieneguilla Glaze-on-yellow (Glaze A) bowl, A.D. 1325–1425. Anasazi Mineral-Paint/Anasazi Vegetal-Paint/Mogollon Slipped(?) Traditions, Galisteo Province.

While the Rio Grande Anasazi were still recovering from the disastrous years following the Great Drought—building new homes, clearing land for farming, and

Fig. 90. Espinoso Glaze-polychrome (Glaze C) bowl, A.D. 1425–1490. Mogollon Slipped/Anasazi Mineral-Paint Traditions, Middle Rio Grande Province.

otherwise adjusting to a totally new environment—they may have been introduced to yet another major change in their traditions. The religious practices of the Middle Rio Grande and nearby provinces may have begun to involve personification of their old deities or the introduction of new ones in the form of masked figures—kachinas—abundantly depicted in rock art (petroglyphs) on boulders and cliffs along the Rio Grande and eastward into the Galisteo Basin. Kachina figures and symbols of this religious renaissance were painted on the walls of kivas and, less frequently, as pottery decoration. For reasons that will probably never be known, the Anasazi of the Tewa Basin, north of Santa Fe, seem to have clung to far older religious traditions that made little use of the masked figures, or at least made less use of their imagery on their painted pottery.

Decorative styles don't necessarily change simultaneously with new technological developments. An atypical bowl of Galisteo Black-on-white (fig. 134), found at Pecos, and one of Cieneguilla Glaze-on-yellow (fig. 89), also recovered at Pecos, have almost identical designs—a popular one in early Pueblo IV. However, the latter was executed in a mineral glaze characteristic of the Early Pueblo IV type. As such, this particular bowl may have been one of the last vessels made using the Middle Rio Grande expression of the Anasazi Vegetal Paint Tradition while simultaneously being one of the first to adopt the new style of the glaze wares. The vegetal-paint tradition, however, did continue in the Northern Rio Grande, among the Tewa Basin, Pajarito Plateau, and Taos-Picuris provinces, possibly reflecting their conservatism and belief that adoption of glaze-paint pottery was too much of a break with the far older vegetal-paint tradition.

Fig. 91. Puaray Glaze-polychrome (Glaze E) bowl, A.D. 1515–1650. Mogollon Slipped/Anasazi Mineral-Paint Traditions, Salinas Province.

Fig. 92. Puaray Glaze-polychrome (Glaze E) olla, A.D. 1515–1600. Mogollon Slipped/Anasazi Mineral-Paint Traditions, Galisteo Province.

Petrographic studies of Pecos pottery by Anna O. Shepard, a pioneer in the microscopic analysis of Pueblo ceramics, have shown that glaze-decorated pottery apparently was not made at Pecos until the early 1400s (Shepard 1936:520). While both of the above-mentioned vessels were recovered at the ruins of Pecos Pueblo, it is quite possible that both were made at pueblos in the Galisteo Basin farther west. It appears most Pueblos in the Rio Grande provinces made their own utility pottery, but the painted wares were often obtained by trade from other villages whose potters had skills and perhaps better pottery clays for making the glaze wares.

Midway between the Rio Grande and Pecos Pueblo is a broad basin—the Galisteo Basin—that was the homeland of the Tano, or Southern Tewa. Originally, the Tano may have lived in pueblos in and around what is now Santa Fe. However, between A.D. 1250 and 1325 they moved away from the Tewa Basin to settle along several of the major drainages of the Galisteo Basin and westward along the base of La Bajada (the abrupt descent in elevation that separates the Middle Rio Grande from the uplands south of Santa Fe) to the Rio Grande near modern Cochiti and Santo Domingo pueblos. At first, Tano potters followed the Anasazi Vegetal-Paint Tradition, but they abandoned this tradition when Pueblos in the Middle Rio Grande Province switched to glaze decoration in the early 1300s. The Tano adopted the new paint and its colorful pottery, possibly breaking with more northerly Tewa, whose views on tradition may have been more conservative.

Although the Tano may have chosen to adopt the glaze-paint tradition, theirs was often painted on a creamy yellow slip that seems to have become a Tano trademark.

Fig. 93. Kotyiti Glaze-on-yellow (Glaze F) shouldered bowl, 1650–1700. Mogollon Slipped/Anasazi Mineral-Paint Traditions, Middle Rio Grande Province.

Fig. 94. Puaray Glaze-polychrome (Glaze E) olla, A.D. 1515–1600. Mogollon Slipped/Anasazi Mineral-Paint Traditions, Middle Rio Grande Province.

Like White Mountain Red Ware, Tano yellow ware was traded far beyond the area where it was made, mainly into the general Rio Grande region, but some possibly even down into Mexico. By the middle 1400s the Tano potters had abandoned this yellow trademark, adopting a red or pinkish slip for their glaze-decorated pottery.

Although Tano people may have remained in the Galisteo Basin, in the 1520s or 1530s some of the western Tano villagers apparently moved northward from the vicinity of Cochiti Pueblo onto the Pajarito Plateau to settle in parts of the great Community House at Puyé. Many of the original inhabitants of Puyé, who had made and used Biscuit Ware, had abandoned Puyé, possibly due to drought, and moved down to the village of Kapo (now Santa Clara Pueblo) on the banks of the Rio Grande.

The arriving Tano migrants brought with them the pottery type San Lazaro Glaze-Polychrome of the Mineral-Paint Tradition, a glaze-decorated pottery having bold black and red-orange designs on a muddy red slip. Eventually, a severe drought during the 1580s also forced the Tano to abandon Puyé and join their Tewa kin at Kapo, bringing with them what remained of their glaze-pottery technology, most notably the red slip used on that pottery. Before long, Anasazi Vegetal-Paint Tradition bowls and jars were being partially slipped with a thin red slip especially around the exterior base, producing Sakona Polychrome (fig. 144), the first of a local tradition of Tewa polychrome pottery types.

Apparently, the Tewa had very conservative views concerning the value of vegetal paint in their pottery-making traditions. This is more understandable given that among the glaze-pottery makers were the migrant Keres, who, perhaps because they

Fig. 95. Kotyiti Glaze-polychrome (Glaze F) olla, 1650–1700. (A Tewa-style vessel with a "puki-bulge" around the middle.) Mogollon Slipped/Anasazi and Pueblo Mineral-Paint Traditions, Middle Rio Grande Province.

Fig. 96. Ashiwi Polychrome olla, 1710–1750. Mogollon Slipped/Anasazi and Historic Pueblo Mineral-Paint Traditions, Acoma(?) Province.

were encroaching on Tewa terrain in the Frijoles Canyon area, were for a time traditional enemies of the Tewa. Anything that smacked of Keres culture may have been anathema to the Tewa, whether it was pottery or more esoteric matters such as the Kachina Cult, which seems to have been well developed among the Keres and minimally present among the Tewa.

Too little is known about post-1700 pottery making in the Middle Rio Grande region. Unlike potters at Zia Pueblo, those at Cochiti and Santo Domingo pueblos chose not to revert to iron-oxide pigments and instead adopted the vegetal-paint tradition of their Tewa neighbors (figs. 154–162). With occasional exceptions, the Middle Rio Grande Keres retained the red-slip feature of earlier glaze-decorated pottery, though often only as a decorative band below the painted design and

Fig. 97. Zuni Polychrome stew bowl, 1850–1890. Mogollon Slipped/Anasazi and Historic Pueblo Mineral-Paint Traditions, Cibola Province.

on the interiors of bowls. In this way, they appear to have selectively and indirectly perpetuated a part of the original Mogollon Slipped Tradition. With or without the use of red as part of their design or as an encircling band below the design, its use was definitely within the traditional repertoire of the Keres, just as it was among the Tewa. Sustained abandonment of red might have eventually constituted a true break in the tradition, but based on information collected, there still is a kind of continuity that can be recognized. Other Middle Rio Grande pueblos, such as Sandia and Isleta, appear to have abandoned painted pottery even before the Spanish reconquered the Pueblos in 1693–1694. Whatever painted pottery the Spaniards needed probably came from nearby Keres pueblos.

Since the middle 1970s, a revival of glaze-decorated pottery has been accomplished by Evelyn Vigil, of Jémez Pueblo. Aware that the last inhabitants of Pecos Pueblo moved to Jémez in 1838, Mrs. Vigil undertook experiments to reproduce Pecos glaze ware, achieving a well-fired pottery decorated in glaze paint and in forms and designs copied from specimens from Kidder's 1915–1927 excavations at Pecos Pueblo (fig. 174). Although modern Jémez people are the most vocal about their links to Pecos, other Middle Rio Grande pueblos, notably Cochiti and Santo Domingo, also received former Pecos residents in the years prior to its final abandonment.

Fig. 98. Zuni Polychrome olla, 1860–1875. Mogollon Slipped/Anasazi and Historic Pueblo Mineral-Paint Traditions, Cibola Province.

Fig. 100. *Acomita Polychrome, Laguna variant, olla, 1780–1820. Mogollon Slipped/Anasazi and Historic Pueblo Mineral-Paint Traditions, Acoma Province.*

Fig. 99. *Ako Polychrome (late) or Acomita Polychrome (early) olla, 1750–1800, Mogollon Slipped/Anasazi and Historic Pueblo Mineral-Paint Traditions, Acoma Province.*

RED-WARE AND GLAZE-PAINT TRADITIONS 93

Fig. 101. Acoma Polychrome olla, 1900–1920. Mogollon Slipped/Anasazi and Historic Pueblo Mineral-Paint Traditions, Acoma Province.

Fig. 102. Acoma Polychrome canteen or double-spouted water jar (or "wedding vase"), 1920–1940. Mogollon Slipped/Anasazi and Historic Pueblo Mineral-Paint Traditions, Acoma Province.

Fig. 103 (OPPOSITE). *Acoma Polychrome olla, ca. 1900. Mogollon Slipped/Anasazi and Historic Pueblo Mineral-Paint Traditions, Acoma Province.*

Fig. 104. Acoma Polychrome olla, 1951. Mogollon Slipped/ Anasazi and Historic Pueblo Mineral-Paint Traditions, Acoma Province.

Fig. 105. Acoma Black-on-white seed jar, 1961. Anasazi and Historic Pueblo Mineral-Paint Traditions, Acoma Province.

RED-WARE AND GLAZE-PAINT TRADITIONS

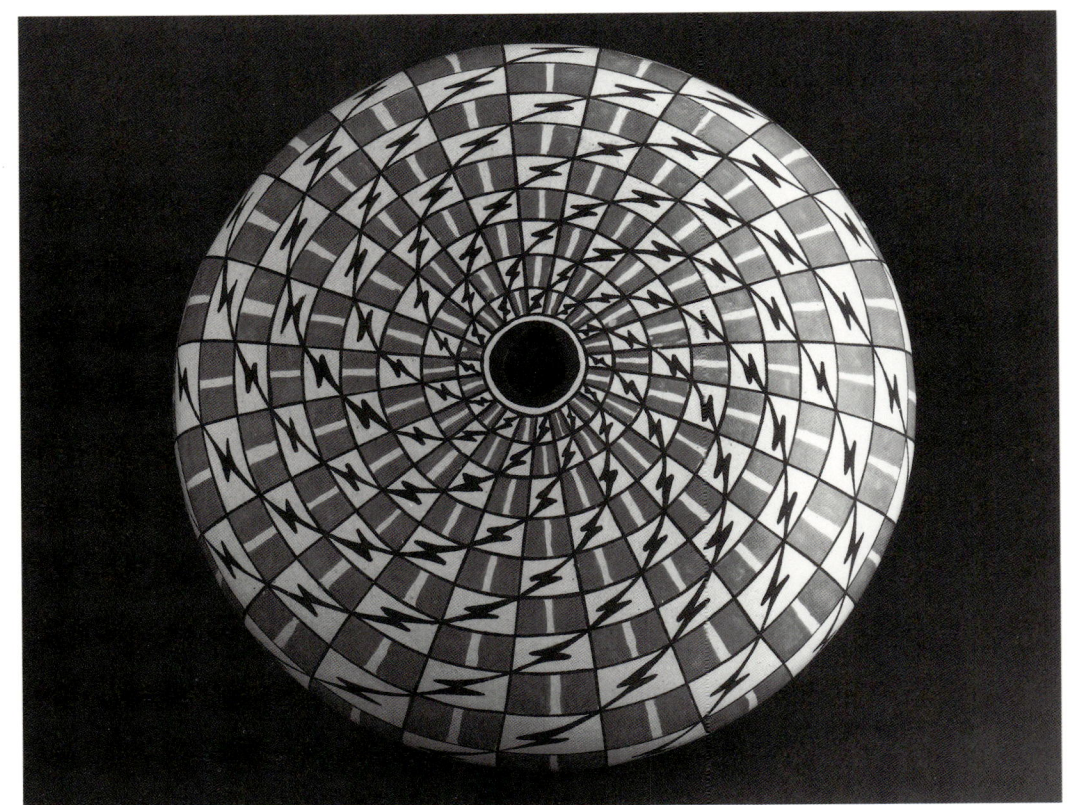

Fig. 106. Acoma Polychrome seed jar (top view), 1984. Mogollon Slipped/Anasazi and Historic Pueblo Mineral-Paint Traditions, Acoma Province.

Fig. 107. Acoma Polychrome seed jar (side view), 1984. Mogollon Slipped/Anasazi and Historic Pueblo Mineral-Paint Traditions, Acoma Province.

Fig. 108. *Acoma Black-on-white seed jar, 1961. Anasazi and Historic Pueblo Mineral-Paint Traditions, Acoma Province.*

Fig. 109. *Acoma Black-on-white seed jar or closed bowl, 1960s. Anasazi and Historic Pueblo Mineral-Paint Traditions, Acoma Province.*

Fig. 110. *Acoma White, Tooled, Corrugated jar, 1961. Anasazi and Historic Pueblo Mineral-Paint(?) Traditions, Acoma Province.*

Fig. 111. *Zuni Polychrome jar, 1984. Mogollon Slipped/ Anasazi and Historic Pueblo Mineral-Paint Traditions, Cibola Province.*

Fig. 112 (OPPOSITE). *Zia Polychrome olla, 1940. Mogollon Slipped/Anasazi and Historic Pueblo Mineral-Paint Traditions, Middle Rio Grande Province.*

Fig. 113. Laguna Polychrome olla, 1984. Mogollon Slipped/Anasazi and Historic Pueblo Mineral-Paint Traditions, Acoma Province.

Fig. 114. Puname Polychrome olla, 1710–1750. Anasazi and Historic Pueblo Mineral-Paint Traditions, Middle Rio Grande Province.

Fig. 115 (RIGHT). *Zia Polychrome dough bowl, 1951. Mogollon Slipped/Anasazi and Historic Pueblo Mineral-Paint Traditions, Middle Rio Grande Province.*

RED-WARE AND GLAZE-PAINT TRADITIONS

Fig. 116. Lino Black-on-gray pitcher, A.D. 600–700. Anasazi Vegetal-Paint Tradition, Cibola Province.

Fig. 117. Bancos Black-on-white fish effigy, A.D. 900–950. Anasazi Vegetal-Paint Tradition, Upper San Juan Province.

Anasazi Vegetal-Paint Tradition

Early in the development of a pottery classification system for the Southwest, archaeologists noted obvious differences between pigments in painted pottery found in the Central Anasazi provinces and those occurring in the Western Anasazi provinces. The former produced sharp, dense, matte-black to reddish designs that were made from nodules of iron oxide that could be found weathering out of sedimentary rocks throughout the Anasazi area.

The latter was characterized by more muted blacks and grays that tended to be blurry along the edges of lines. This pigment, the same used by modern Hopi potters, was made from a common native plant, tansy mustard (*Descurainia pinnata*), a rapidly growing early spring plant that has the added advantage of being an edible green. When used as a paint, the leaves and stems of the plant are boiled down to a black, gummy material that is mixed with water and applied to pottery with a brush made from the fibrous leaf of a yucca plant. The pigment fires to a brownish or light gray to gray-black, commonly appearing watery, with slight to marked blurring along the edges of lines (figs. 116–124). This is apparently caused by the pigment soaking into the vessel surface and bleeding outward slightly from the painted line. Vessel surfaces decorated with vegetal paint have a uniform sheen that gives the appearance of having been polished over the paint, but the paint was usually applied after polishing.

Potters in the Central and Eastern Anasazi provinces also used a plant-extract pigment, one that modern Tewa potters call *guaco*, but they chose a different edible wild plant, Rocky Mountain Beeplant (*Cleome serrulata*). Prepared in the same way as the tansy mustard paint, it too had a tendency to produce slightly blurred edges on painted designs, but in most modern pottery these are not noticeable.

In the traditional folklore of archaeological pottery classification the tansy mustard and beeplant paints were generally called "carbon paint." The rationale behind this term is the assumption that during firing the carbonaceous vegetal pigment charred to produce a black-painted design. Ethnographers recorded this process, and archaeologists accepted their conclusions. However, recent research has revealed that the black color of the paint resulted not so much from carbonizing the plant material but from organic iron compounds in the plant material (Blair and Blair 1986: 128). Any carbon in the so-called "carbon paint" would have burned off as carbon dioxide during the initial oxidation stage of firing and would have contributed little to the visible decoration. An organic iron compound in the vegetal paint might have become initially red-tinged by oxidation, but subsequent reduction firing would have turned it black. On red-slipped pottery, the oxidation of the iron-oxide pigment would have produced a red that would have been lost in the reds of the surface color. Exceptions to this may exist, but use of the term "carbon paint" is nonetheless clearly erroneous. Although the term will doubtless remain in use, another term—vegetal paint—herein replaces it.

When Basketmaker III Anasazi potters in northeastern Arizona provinces inaugurated what was to be a long-lived vegetal-paint tradition, ca. A.D. 575 (Breternitz 1966: 82), they simply painted the basic Anasazi Utility-Tradition pottery, Lino Gray, to produce Lino Black-on-gray. In subsequent periods, as ornamentation of utility

Fig. 118. McElmo Black-on-white bowl, A.D. 1100–1200. Anasazi Vegetal-Paint Tradition, San Juan Basin Province.

pottery developed with simple incised lines and various manipulations of the coils into bands and corrugations, the vegetal-painted pottery likewise advanced with the addition of a slip, polish, finer sand temper, and a progression of definable design styles.

Vegetal-painted pottery eventually was adopted in other areas of the Anasazi world, each with its unique combination of attributes. In archaeological contexts, each province produced its own "ware" and "types," though for the purposes of this discussion all of the vegetal-paint types and wares are considered as one long-lived tradition that had its beginnings in Basketmaker III and is traceable over many centuries and many kilometers to pottery that some Pueblo potters still make in the Rio Grande provinces today.

It is conceivable that a plant-extract pigment was "invented" to initiate this paint tradition. However, it is equally possible that the Western Anasazi used a plant-extract pigment that had been developed by their pre-pottery Oshara ancestors as either a pigment or a binder for mineral pigments on basketry or wood.

A somewhat arbitrary dividing line between the vegetal paint sub-traditions of northeastern Arizona and San Juan Basin can be drawn along the largely uninhabited mountains that straddle the New Mexico-Arizona boundary. During Basketmaker III and Pueblo I, the manufacture of vegetal-painted pottery in northeastern Arizona and northwestern New Mexico (mainly the Chuska Province) seems to have been a single tradition, with potters in the several provinces often choosing different tempers. By the ninth or tenth century, however, the Vegetal Paint Tradition can be seen gradually dividing into Central and Western Anasazi expressions. The use of vegetal paint continued in northern parts of the San Juan Basin until the area was abandoned ca. A.D. 1276–1299.

Fig. 119. Chaco-McElmo Black-on-white dipper, A.D. 1100–1200. Anasazi Vegetal-Paint Tradition, Southern San Juan Basin Province.

ANASAZI VEGETAL-PAINT TRADITION   103

Fig. 120. Chaco-McElmo Black-on-white triangular canteen, A.D. 1100–1200. Anasazi Vegetal-Paint Tradition, Chaco Province.

Fig. 121. McElmo or Mesa Verde Black-on-white pitcher, A.D. 1100–1300. Anasazi Vegetal-Paint Tradition, Mesa Verde Province. RIGHT: *McElmo Black-on-white pitcher, A.D. 1100–1200. Anasazi Vegetal-Paint Tradition, Middle San Juan Province.*

Fig. 122. *Mesa Verde Black-on-white bowl*, A.D. 1200–1300. *Anasazi Vegetal-Paint Tradition, Mesa Verde Province.*
RIGHT: *Mesa Verde Black-on-white bowl*, A.D. 1200–1300. *Anasazi Vegetal-Paint Tradition, Mesa Verde Province.*

Fig. 123. *Mesa Verde Black-on-white mug*, A.D. 1200–1300. *Anasazi Vegetal-Paint Tradition, Mesa Verde Province.*
RIGHT: *Mesa Verde Black-on-white mug*, A.D. 1200–1300. *Anasazi Vegetal-Paint Tradition, Mesa Verde Province.*

Fig. 124. *Mesa Verde Black-on-white mug*, A.D. 1200–1300. *Anasazi Vegetal-Paint Tradition, Mesa Verde Province.*
RIGHT: *Mesa Verde Black-on-white mug*, A.D. 1200–1300. *Anasazi Vegetal-Paint Tradition, Mesa Verde Province.*

Fig. 125. Mesa Verde Black-on-white dipper, A.D. 1200–1300. Anasazi Vegetal-Paint Tradition, Mesa Verde Province.

Vegetal Paint in the Chuska Province

During the middle 700s a substantial number of Kayenta Anasazi from northeastern Arizona moved eastward, over or around the northern end of the Chuska Mountains that stand astride the New Mexico–Arizona boundary. They settled in the Chuska Valley, or Chuska Province, along the western edge of the San Juan Basin, roughly midway between Gallup and Shiprock. They were the makers of the Lino Black-on-gray. The Chuska Valley already had a scattering of indigenous Basketmaker III settlements, including several major pithouse villages, not far from the modern Navajo communities of Newcomb and Two Gray Hills. The local potters of the Chuska Province also made Lino Gray utility pottery. By the middle 500s they had developed or adopted an iron-oxide pigment to decorate what came to be known as the Cibola White Ware, La Plata Black-on-white, and White Mound Black-on-white of the Anasazi Mineral-Paint Tradition (figs. 43–45).

The arrival of the Kayenta people in the Chuska Valley seems to have met no resistance from the original Chuska Anasazi, whose settlements were scattered along the tops and slopes of ridges and small mesas mainly paralleling Captain Tom Wash for about thirty-two kilometers (twenty miles) from the foot of the Chuska Mountains to the Rio Chaco. For that matter, the Kayenta people may have been invited to settle there. With much of the province sparsely inhabited, the Kayenta people were able to establish at least fifteen incipient focal communities scattered along drainages that were choice agricultural areas in the Chuska Valley. In some places the two groups may have been living almost side by side.

Kayenta potters in the Chuska Valley continued making Lino Black-on-gray, except that instead of the sand temper they had used in northeastern Arizona (which the Chuska Anasazi potters also used), they began to temper their pottery with trachyte, obtainable in volcanic outcrops in the Chuska Mountains and possibly in

Fig. 126. Gallina Black-on-white bowl, A.D. 1200–1275. Anasazi Vegetal-Paint Tradition, Gallina Province.

Fig. 127. Gallina Black-on-white bowl, A.D. 1200–1275. Anasazi Vegetal-Paint Tradition, Gallina Province.

stream gravels down in the Chuska Valley. Along with this Chuska equivalent of Lino Black-on-gray (called "Theodore Black-on-white" after Theodore Wash, a usually dry arroyo draining part of the Chuska Valley), they made trachyte-tempered Bennett Gray, a Chuska version of Lino Gray. By the late 800s, these settlers had begun to add a thick, well-polished white slip to the vessel surface to be painted with vegetal paint, producing Tunicha Black-on-white, whose fine-line designs were almost a carbon copy of the contemporary northeastern Arizona vegetal-paint type, Kana-a Black-on-white. The Chuska Valley potters may have been following the lead of Kayenta potters in northeastern Arizona, but in the succeeding two centuries, more often than not the Chuska vegetal-paint potters copied designs of iron-paint pottery types, such as Red Mesa Black-on-white and, later, Gallup Black-on-white, that were associated with the spectacular growth of Chaco Canyon and other nearby areas.

Within a short time after the arrival of the Kayenta migrants, certainly by the middle 700s, the Chuska Anasazi had also switched from sand temper to trachyte temper, though continuing their iron-paint tradition and using designs that are more commonly thought to be Chacoan. As a matter of fact, the settlements of the mineral-paint potters became concentrated into just a few communities, at least two of which were associated with abbreviated versions of specialized architecture reminiscent of the great houses at Chaco Canyon. Similar Chaco enclaves or outliers have been found at various points around the perimeter of the San Juan Basin.

From the early 1000s onward, great quantities of trachyte-tempered vegetal-paint and utility pottery from the Chuska Valley reached the great Chaco settlements, sometimes accounting for over half of the potsherds found on sites there. With limited timber resources, the Chaco people may have had to import pottery from the Chuska Valley and other provinces whose abundance of fuel for pottery firing enabled them to produce considerably beyond their own needs.

The symbiotic relationship between the Chuska Iron-Paint and Chuska Vegetal-Paint potters continued until the first few decades after A.D. 1100, when the iron-paint tradition in the area suddenly ceased. The significance of this event may be found in the apparent simultaneous collapse of the Chaco Phenomenon and the almost simultaneous cessation of the iron-paint tradition throughout all but the southern San Juan Basin. This upheaval left only the Anasazi Vegetal-Paint Tradition in the Chuska, Chaco, and Mesa Verde provinces.

During Basketmaker III and Pueblo I, in the far northeastern corner of the San Juan Basin (the Upper San Juan Province), there was a mix of mineral-paint and vegetal-paint pottery similar to that occurring in the Mesa Verde Province. Upper San Juan potters seem to have lagged behind those farther west in both utility and service pottery and by the early 1000s had only begun to copy the Red Mesa Style that had prevailed elsewhere for over one hundred years. Throughout most of the province, this was their last gasp, since by A.D. 1050 all but its northernmost localities had been abandoned, apparently due to severe down-cutting of the San Juan River and its tributaries, which left their bordering farmlands high and dry. Many victims of this event seem to have moved southeastward to the cooler areas of the Continental Divide, near Cuba, New Mexico, where they remained in geographic and cultural isolation until the late 1200s.

Arriving in the Gallina Province, the Upper San Juan emigrants were the bearers of the Anasazi Vegetal-Paint Tradition, but they were so far from mainstream pottery

Fig. 128. Gallina Black-on-white effigy horned toad, A.D. 1200–1275. Anasazi Vegetal-Paint Tradition, Gallina Province.

development that their pottery making virtually stood still for more than the next two hundred years (figs. 126, 127). Gallina utility pottery (fig. 39) didn't follow the progression of corrugated types seen in the main part of the San Juan Basin either, and some archaeologists have concluded that their cylindrical utility-jar forms were somehow ancestral to later pottery of the Navajo of northwestern New Mexico. Although the Navajo may have moved through the Gallina Province on their way to the Upper San Juan drainage, they did so 200 to 500 years after those areas had been abandoned by the Anasazi. No convincing evidence has been found that links those two cultures. Apparently, the Navajo were late arrivals in the Southwest, coming west from the Plains of northeastern New Mexico not much earlier than the sixteenth century.

The isolation of the Gallina Province seems to have been reflected in ways other than pottery. The Gallina people built massive-walled unit houses, perhaps for greater protection from severe winters, and never followed the same elaboration of dwelling and kiva architecture developed by Anasazi around the San Juan Basin. As a matter of fact, there is little in Gallina Culture to suggest the nature of their religion. An exception might be the pottery figure of a horned toad (fig. 128), a common type of lizard in the Southwest, which might have been symbolic of survival in an arid environment and, by imitative magic, characteristic of the Gallina people themselves. The piece also demonstrates a creative sensibility in an otherwise war-preoccupied people.

The Gallina people were apparently affected by the same drought that seared the San Juan Basin in the late 1300s. Current archaeological data suggest that they abandoned the Gallina Province and moved only a short distance to the nearby Jémez

Fig. 129. Jemez Black-on-white bowl, A.D. 1425–1600. Anasazi Vegetal-Paint Tradition, Jemez Province.

Mountains and the upper drainages of the Jémez River. They carried their version of the Anasazi Vegetal-Paint Tradition with them. Perhaps through their encounters with San Juan Basin Anasazi migrants and their McElmo-Mesa Verde vegetal-paint pottery, the Gallina potters adopted a highly polished, pearl gray slip and some decorative styles, ultimately producing Jémez Black-on-white (figs. 129, 130). Increasingly, Gallina potters fell in step with fourteenth- and fifteenth-century Anasazi. The potters of the Upper San Juan, Gallina, and Jémez provinces, in a roundabout way, may have been at least nominal contributors in the perpetuation of the Anasazi Vegetal-Paint Tradition as it continued into the Historic Period in the Rio Grande region.

By the 1100s and 1200s, vegetal-paint pottery was in ascendance in the Chaco, Chuska, and Mesa Verde provinces in the heart of the San Juan Basin. Painted pottery in these provinces continued to have the bold designs of the waning years of the iron-paint pottery tradition in the region (figs. 119–122), but a new treatment, the McElmo Style, emerged that stressed smaller, more carefully drawn solids and hatch-filled designs (fig. 119) that graded into the final effort of the San Juan Basin Anasazi, Mesa Verde Black-on-white (figs. 122–125).

Pueblo III vegetal-paint pottery in much of the Central Anasazi area shows an apparent Anasazi desire to achieve perfection in their skillfully shaped symmetrical, highly polished, carefully decorated service pottery that was aesthetically pleasing to the eye and had the potential of being traded to other Anasazi groups regardless of the kind of paint used. To that end, Central Anasazi potters seem to have experimented with improving their wares. Not all attempts to copy decorative styles and finishes during early Pueblo III attempts were successful, as can be seen in vessels of

Fig. 130. Jemez Black-on-white bowl, A.D. 1425–1600. Anasazi Vegetal-Paint Tradition, Jemez Province.

VEGETAL PAINT IN THE CHUSKA PROVINCE 109

Fig. 131. Pindi Black-on-white bowl, A.D. 1300–1350. Anasazi Vegetal-Paint Tradition, Tewa Basin Province.

Fig. 132. Wiyo Black-on-white bowl, A.D. 1325–1425. Anasazi Vegetal-Paint Tradition, Tewa Basin Province.

McElmo Black-on-white and Chaco-McElmo Black-on-white (figs. 118–121). Although we cannot really be sure whose work was the model that other potters attempted to match, archaeologists tend to recognize McElmo Black-on-white, characteristically not yet well polished and somewhat carelessly executed in design and paint application. By the 1200s, however, practice most frequently led to perfection in Mesa Verde Black-on-white (figs. 122–125).

Such fine work was not the exclusive domain of the inhabitants of the cliff dwellings at Mesa Verde, however. Potters in the Cibola Province were producing Wingate Black-on-red (fig. 87), whose well-polished, brilliant red slip was unique in much of the Anasazi world of pottery, where black, white, and gray were the only colors achieved. Sherds of Wingate Black-on-red are commonly found on sites dating to the twelfth and thirteenth centuries as far as the Rio Grande and throughout most parts of the Anasazi area, suggesting that to possess the pottery was prestigious.

Although local, trachyte-tempered copies of the slick-finished Mesa Verde and Chaco types may be found in the Chuska Valley, the Chuska potters seem to have been continuing the indigenous Chuska vegetal-paint tradition. Great amounts of true Mesa Verde pottery can be found in the Chuska Province, suggesting either extensive trade with the Mesa Verde Province or possibly the arrival of Mesa Verde people attempting to escape from the burgeoning populations of the Mesa Verde and Montezuma Valley areas in southwestern Colorado.

Archaeologists have long known that the Anasazi abandoned the San Juan Basin by about A.D. 1300, but initial emigration from the basin provinces probably began in the

Fig. 133. Wiyo Black-on-white bowl, A.D. 1300–1400. Anasazi Vegetal-Paint Tradition, Galisteo Province.

Fig. 134. Galisteo Black-on-white bowl, A.D. 1300–1400. Anasazi Vegetal-Paint Tradition, Galisteo Province.

early 1100s, when the calamity at Chaco Canyon occurred. Although the final abandonment of the Mesa Verde and Chuska provinces didn't occur until the late 1200s, it is likely that individual families or small communities were relocating within the region or leaving the region entirely over the course of the preceding 150 to 175 years.

The decline of mineral paint black-on-white pottery in Rio Grande provinces during the twelfth century echoed, perhaps only coincidentally, the decline of Chacoan influence following the Chaco collapse. It is possible that the shift from mineral paint was presaged by early bands of migrants from the San Juan Basin who introduced vegetal paint to the Rio Grande Anasazi. By as early as A.D. 1150 Rio Grande potters had begun changing over to vegetal paint; the transition was complete by A.D. 1200. However, the tradition of using mineral pigments persisted to the south, where well-made Socorro Black-on-white (figs. 82, 84, 86) was produced, and southeastward into the Salinas Province, where Chupadero Black-on-white (figs. 83, 85) was preferred. Mineral-paint pottery also persisted in isolation in the Taos Province in the extreme northern Rio Grande, where changes initiated in other Anasazi provinces often arrived late and were slow to be copied.

The Anasazi Vegetal-Paint Tradition persisted in the northern San Juan Basin and Mesa Verde areas until the middle to late 1200s, when the Great Drought (A.D. 1276–1299) forced the Anasazi to abandon their ancient homeland. Segments of the highly developed society of the San Juan Basin went off in various directions, many to the Middle and Northern Rio Grande provinces, others to central and west-central New Mexico, and still others to northeastern Arizona. In northeastern Arizona, the

Fig. 135. Bandelier Black-on-gray (Biscuit B) bowl, A.D. 1425–1475. Anasazi Vegetal-Paint Tradition, Tewa Basin Province.

vegetal-paint tradition, carried by Tusayan White Ware, continued until as late as A.D. 1400, when it was superceded by mineral-paint yellow ware.

Archaeological surveys have traced the general routes followed by migrants from the San Juan Basin to the Rio Grande. Beginning in the mid-1100s and throughout the 1200s, many small to medium-size pueblos were established in the middle part of the Rio Puerco, the Pajarito Plateau, the Tewa Basin, and the Galisteo Basin. The first wave of migrants found these localities occupied, but their numbers seem to have been small, and choice areas for settlement were available along well-watered valleys draining the Sangre de Cristo and Jémez Mountains. This was the time of the Rio Grande Coalition Period, and by the mid-1200s every running stream draining the western slopes of the Sangre de Cristo Mountains saw new pueblos being founded, including several along the Santa Fe River.

Fig. 136. Cuyamungue Black-on-tan (Biscuit C) olla, A.D. 1475–1600. Anasazi Vegetal-Paint Tradition, Tewa Basin Province.

Fig. 137. Cuyamungue Black-on-tan (Biscuit C) bowl, A.D. 1425–1475. Anasazi Vegetal-Paint Tradition, Tewa Basin Province.

As bearers of the Anasazi Vegetal-Paint Tradition, the new settlers throughout the Rio Grande provinces often made varieties of basically similar pottery, such as Pindi Black-on-white, Galisteo Black-on-white, and Wiyo Black-on-white. Though all reminiscent of San Juan Basin vegetal-paint types, these varieties often graded into one another and seemed to reflect a period of great unrest and resettlement.

During the 1300s, the arriving migrants who were the carriers of the Anasazi Vegetal-Paint Tradition moved into the Rio Grande provinces, filling virtually every space where water and potentially arable lands were available. They occupied much

Fig. 138. Bandelier Black-on-gray (Biscuit B) bowl, A.D. 1425–1475. Anasazi Vegetal-Paint Tradition, Tewa Basin Province.

Fig. 140. Sankawi Black-on-cream bowl, 1550–1650. Anasazi Vegetal-Paint Tradition, Tewa Basin Province.

of the Tewa Basin, including much of the Rio Grande drainage upstream from White Rock Canyon (near San Ildefonso Pueblo) northward to the vicinity of Velarde on the Rio Grande. Others occupied the Rio Chama Valley as far upstream as modern Abiquiu Reservoir and other tributaries of the Chama (El Rito Colorado and Ojo Caliente). The migrants also settled the canyon and mesas of the Pajarito Plateau west of the Rio Grande and the foothills and mesa of the Sangre de Cristo Mountains to the east. Still others settled in the Galisteo Basin and the Pecos River Valley, and a few pueblos were established both north and south of present-day Las Vegas, New Mexico.

Since earlier generations of San Juan Basin Anasazi had moved to the Rio Grande in the late 1100s and early 1200s, many of the indigenous people of the Tewa Basin were already painting their pottery with vegetal paint and may have spoken dialects

Fig. 139. Cuyamungue Black-on-tan (Biscuit C) olla, A.D. 1475–1600. Anasazi Vegetal-Paint Tradition, Tewa Basin Province.

of the language spoken by some of the newly arriving migrants. This may have facilitated their being able to cope with the thousands of migrants who needed to find suitable lands, build homes, plant crops, find raw materials for making tools and pottery, and adjust to the unfamiliar natural environment.

Aesthetically, vegetal-paint pottery of the 1300s left much to be desired (figs. 131–133). Available clays and finely divided volcanic tuff temper produced rather soft, porous, thick-walled bowls with streaky, gray-white slips and wide, carelessly drawn lines. It is no wonder that potters from the area south of a line drawn from Frijoles

VEGETAL PAINT IN THE CHUSKA PROVINCE   113

Fig. 141. *Sankawi Black-on-cream olla, 1550–1650. Anasazi Vegetal-Paint Tradition, Tewa Basin Province.*

Fig. 142. *Sankawi Black-on-cream olla, 1550–1650. Anasazi Vegetal-Paint Tradition, Tewa Basin Province.*

Canyon (Bandelier National Monument) to Pecos Pueblo (Pecos National Monument) quickly chose to abandon the gritty pottery decorated with vegetal paint and switch to harder, more durable glaze-decorated pottery made in the Middle Rio Grande and Galisteo Basin provinces.

By the late 1300s, potters of the Tewa Basin had more-or-less adjusted to the inadequacies of the local pottery-making materials and had revised their pottery-making technology. They began producing the first of the Biscuit Wares, Abiquiu Black-on-gray (or as A. V. Kidder called it, Biscuit A). Thicker and more porous than Coalition Period pottery of the early and middle 1300s, the Biscuit Wares were, in the eyes of Frank H. H. Roberts, Jr., lacking. He had studied the fine, thin-walled, mineral-paint pottery of Chaco Canyon and saw the Biscuit Wares as coarse and unsophisticated. To him, the ceramic and other developments in the Rio Grande region were inferior to those in the San Juan Basin. Consequently, he proposed re-designating the Pueblo IV period as "Regressive Pueblo." In 1955, Wendorf and Reed (1955) viewed the same developments as a relative florescence of the Rio Grande Anasazi culture and renamed the period "Rio Grande Classic."

Early Biscuit Ware bowls—no other forms were made—tended to be hemispherical in shape, with exteriors rough as sandpaper and interiors and rims coated with a moderately well-polished pearl-gray slip and decorated in vegetal paint. Paneled band designs typically encircled the interior surfaces.

By the early fifteenth century, scores of the smallish, more widely dispersed settlements of the 1300s had been abandoned, and their inhabitants appear to have moved

Fig. 143. Tewa Polychrome olla (water jar), ca. 1680. Mogollon Slipped/Anasazi Mineral Paint/Anasazi and Historic Pueblo Vegetal-Paint Traditions, Upper Pecos Valley Province.

Fig. 144. Sakona Polychrome shouldered bowl, ca. 1680. Mogollon Slipped/Anasazi Mineral-Paint/Anasazi and Historic Pueblo Vegetal-Paint Traditions, Tewa Basin Province.

Fig. 145. Ogapoge Polychrome miniature medicine jar, ca. 1720–1760. Mogollon Slipped/Anasazi Mineral Paint/Anasazi and Historic Pueblo Vegetal-Paint Traditions, Tewa Basin Province. CENTER: *Sankawi Black-on-cream miniature medicine jar, 1550–1650. Anasazi Vegetal-Paint Tradition, Tewa Basin Province.* RIGHT: *Tewa Polychrome miniature medicine jar, 1650–1730. Mogollon Slipped/Anasazi Mineral Paint/Anasazi and Historic Pueblo Vegetal-Paint Traditions, Tewa Basin Province.*

to join more strategically located villages that seemed to have advantages of land, water, and manpower. Small amounts of Biscuit A pottery have been found on many of the immense fifteenth- and sixteenth-century ruins in the Tewa Basin Province. However, architectural evidence of most of the small villages that produced this pottery has been buried by the far more extensive Late Rio Grande Classic villages on the same locations.

It is possible that, by A.D. 1425–1450, Tewa Basin people along the Rio Grande had learned about irrigation farming. This offered them the opportunity to use larger areas of valley bottomland for farming. Construction and maintenance of irrigation systems may have required more manpower than the small, widely dispersed settlements could manage. Many family-size pueblos were abandoned as the second phase of population coalescence occurred in the Tewa Basin.

Coincident with the joining of many villages came the merger of the talents of countless potters who began making Bandelier Black-on-gray (Biscuit B), whose vertical-sided, flat-bottomed bowls were more capacious containers with more extensive surfaces to be decorated. What set these later Biscuit Wares apart from Biscuit A were the bands of both broad and narrow vegetal-painted parallel lines horizontally encircling bowl exteriors and the division of these bands into panels by vertical lines, solid black triangles, and diagonal lines framing rows of dots. Interior designs were commonly in banded layouts and radiating lines. Most popular were depictions of the distinctive *awanyu* figure (figs. 135–137, 139, 141). *Awanyu*, the Tewa guardian of water, is possibly the local conception of the feathered serpent, a Mesoamerican water deity. Renderings of the *awanyu* commonly divided the interior field of bowls into halves, thirds, or quarters, while exteriors featured the figure wriggling around decorative banding. The filler of the *awanyu* body on the *olla* in figure 139 bears the alternating angled hatched technique that is characteristic of Potsuwi'i Incised of about the same period.

Slipped, polished, and painted inside and out, the popularity of the later Biscuit Wares seemed to be just one of many features of the rejuvenation of the Rio Grande Anasazi that carried into architecture, ceremonialism, craft diversification, and greater social interchange.

The Anasazi Vegetal-Paint Tradition was again on a firm foundation. By the late 1400s it was supporting pottery refinements in new vessel forms and a new pottery

Fig. 146. *Potsuwi'i Incised* olla, A.D. 1450–1500. Ancestral Tewa Black Tradition(?), Tewa Basin Province.

Fig. 147. *Kapo Black* olla, 1720–1760(?). Tewa Black Tradition, Galisteo Province.

type, Cuyamungue Black-on-tan (Biscuit C). Broad shallow bowls joined the revival of water jars (*ollas*) and began to be made with stronger, thinner walls, streaky, creamier slips applied to a brown paste, and decoration in somewhat simpler, more carelessly drawn vegetal-paint designs reminiscent of those of earlier Biscuit Ware (figs. 137, 138). Its mid-sixteenth century successor, Sankawi Black-on-cream (figs. 140, 141, 142), was an even squattier type whose jar forms became more prevalent. Its bowls were often shallow but had high, vertical, sometimes thickened rims like those in use on contemporary glaze-decorated pottery of the Middle Rio Grande and Galisteo Basin provinces. During this time the appearance of low-shouldered *ollas* with a distinctive bulge at the shoulder (fig. 142) indicates the use of the *puki*.

While the Anasazi Vegetal-Paint Tradition continues up to the present day, during the 1600s and 1700s the lineages of this tradition periodically merged with the red-slipped Anasazi Mineral-Paint Tradition in the Middle Rio Grande province and then separated, leaving behind various expressions of a new polychrome tradition. This is shown especially in the post-1680 polychrome styles of the Tewa, which were borrowed by the Keres-speaking Pueblos of Cochiti and Santo Domingo. From these events, we can, almost without question, trace one lineage of modern Rio Grande painted-pottery tradition back to Basketmaker III vegetal-paint pottery, and further back at least to a combined Mogollon-Anasazi Mineral-Paint Tradition at least as early as early Pueblo III. Beyond this, a continuity of red slipping can be traced from the earliest Mogollon red pottery, ca. A.D. 250, right up to the present-day use of red as a slip or paint in many New Mexico Pueblos. Besides being responsible for the development of the Tewa polychrome tradition, the use of the red slip ultimately led to the adoption of the plain red and polished black traditions that gained fame and fortune for many potters of the modern Tewa Pueblos.

Fig. 148. *El Paso Black-on-brown bowl,* A.D. *1200–1400. Mogollon Slipped(?)/Eastern Mogollon Vegetal-Paint Traditions, Jornada Province.*

Fig. 149. *El Paso Polychrome ceremonial bowl,* A.D. *1200–1400. Mogollon Slipped(?)/Eastern Mogollon Vegetal-Paint Traditions, Jornada Province.*

Jornada Painted Tradition

As originally defined, the Jornada Branch of the Mogollon Culture (Lehmer 1947) was a Chihuahuan desert version of the general Mogollon Culture, whose areal extent included the lower Rio Grande, Jornada del Muerto, and Tularosa Basin of south-central New Mexico, west Texas near El Paso, and adjacent parts of Chihuahua, Mexico. As in all branches of the Mogollon Culture, the Indians of the Jornada Branch made brown pottery. Archaeologists further divide the Jornada Mogollon into two sub-branches. Temper, if it was needed, was usually crushed igneous rock, moderately fine in the north and very coarse in the south. The northern group polished its plain brown pottery very much as did potters in the Mimbres Province, whereas the southern group left vessel surfaces unpolished and rough, seeming to reflect a possible third basic pottery-making tradition to enter the Southwest, perhaps from somewhere down the Rio Grande.

Most common in the southern Jornada Province was the later development of painted, thin-walled, coarse-tempered, unpolished pottery. Some early examples were painted red-on-brown; others black-on-brown; and still others in polychrome (black and red-on-brown). Collectively referred to as the "El Paso series," this pottery bears designs that are so bold and simple that, on potsherds, it is often impossible to discern overall design or whether the decoration was simply a red or black on a brown background (fig. 148) or combinations of the two to produce a polychrome (figs. 149–151).

In an area of iron-rich clays, the El Paso series was expectably done in basic brown. But is all brown pottery Mogollon in origin? Essentially, brown pottery predominates

JORNADA PAINTED TRADITION 117

Fig. 150. El Paso Polychrome jar, A.D. 1200–1400. Mogollon Slipped(?)/Eastern Mogollon Vegetal-Paint Traditions, Casas Grandes Province.

throughout northern and southern Mexico, but no archaeologist is likely to propose that all the people who made it were Mogollon. Southern Jornada potters seem to have had little desire to emulate the craft as it developed in the Mimbres or any other Mogollon province. With its coarse temper, lack of polish, extremely thin vessel walls, sometimes enormous jar forms, and flamboyant designs, the El Paso series hardly seems to fit in with the rest of the Mogollon crowd.

Some similarities exist between the architecture and crafts of the Mimbres and Jornada provinces. However, one might question whether or not ceramic traditions of the southern part of the Jornada Province really had any strong ties to the Mogollon Culture farther west. Although the association is not clear-cut, there is a possibility that at least some of the post-A.D. 1200 upland Jornada may have descended from a group of Mimbres people who, after A.D. 1150, moved eastward out of the Mimbres area and joined existing groups in the Tularosa Basin and the Sacramento Mountains.

Casas Grandes Traditions

Viewed from north of the International Boundary, the late, largely post-1300 great settlements of the Casas Grandes Province, in northern Chihuahua, bear only superficial similarities to those of the Anasazi and Mogollon in the Southwest. Seen from the south, Casas Grandes is an obvious, though perhaps smaller-scale, Mesoamerican presence within a few days' walking distance of considerably less developed Southwestern Puebloan settlements. Parochial as the viewpoint may be, it would be presumptuous to claim the late Casas Grandes communities for the Southwest simply because they made exquisite pottery and had massive multiroom pueblos. With

Fig. 151. El Paso Polychrome storage jar, A.D. 1200–1400. Mogollon Slipped(?)/Eastern Mogollon Vegetal-Paint Traditions, Jornada Province.

Fig. 152. Escondida Polychrome jar, A.D. 1275–1400. Casas Grandes Painted(?) Tradition, Casas Grandes Province.

Fig. 153. Playas Red Incised, Corralitos variant jar, A.D. 1350–1450. Casas Grandes Red(?) Tradition, Casas Grandes Province.

platform mounds, ball courts, and even ceramics (figs. 152, 153), their ties were more strongly to the Classic cultures of lower Mexico than to the Anasazi and Mogollon Pueblos, and seem to have had only selective impact on the Pueblo Southwest.

Archaeologists have long considered the prehistoric Southwest to have been the recipient, through the periodic diffusion, of technologic and probably socioeconomic cultural traits (which can also be read as traditions) from Mexico. Except for the early introductions of agriculture, pottery making, and possibly isolated elements of architecture and material culture, it is difficult to pinpoint much of what reached the developing Southwest by way of the great Casas Grandes trading center of Paquimé (DiPeso 1974). Aside from seashells for jewelry, Casas Grandes appears to have been only a link in the transmission of trade items and some aspects of ceremonialism up into the Southwest.

From the middle 1400s to the late 1500s, Tewa Province potters began making a distinctive hard, thin-walled, polished gray to gray-brown pottery with incised decoration, Potsuwi'i Incised (fig. 146). Its simple geometric designs were often accentuated with a localized application of a sparkling micaceous slip. Its origins are obscure; there is no local or nearby ancestor. A short-lived type, it had passed out of favor by the mid-1500s. Some archaeologists suggest that Tewa potters may have been responding to stimulus from Casas Grandes potters, who made a somewhat similar type, Playas Red Incised (fig. 153). In the 1930s, a few potters from San Juan Pueblo revived the incised style, including the micaceous slip. However, their incised vessels generally had thicker walls and a softer tan paste (fig. 170), which was sometimes partially red-slipped. Today, only a few San Juan potters still make the incised ware.

120 PUEBLO POTTERY POST-1600

4. PUEBLO POTTERY POST-1600

The Historic Period in the Southwest began with the establishment of a relatively permanent Spanish colony in north-central New Mexico, whose sustained impact altered many of the traditions of the Pueblos, including those of pottery making.

During the seventeenth, eighteenth, and nineteenth centuries, Pueblo potters were making pottery utensils not only for themselves but also for trade or sale to non-Indian (Hispanic and, later, Anglo) households. The potters responded to the pottery needs and preferences of the colonial inhabitants of the region by producing new vessel forms, such as soup plates, candlesticks, chalices, and large grain-storage jars, often decorated with designs more preferable to European sensibilities. By the middle to late nineteenth century, potters began to decorate their pottery with birds, flowers, and other abstract designs (figs. 101, 102) that do not follow any earlier established traditions. New forms and designs were not produced solely for the Europeans; Pueblo households made practical use of them as well. However, twentieth-century Pueblo potters continue to make some pottery exclusively for ceremonial purposes within the pueblos.

Historic Pueblo vessel construction still employed the coil-scrape technique using naturally occurring materials. Historic Period potters often adapted European tools and materials to existing Pueblo pottery-making methods. Today's Pueblo potters often use metal knives and other commercially made implements for shaping vessels and scraps of sheet metal to protect the pottery during firing. Pueblo potters also adopted the use of cattle and sheep dung as a firing fuel. Presumably, this occurred not long after they found that corrals for Spanish cattle were full of compressed masses of manure. They could quarry, dry, and stockpile the manure with much less labor than was required in woodcutting and at the same time obtain more uniform firing temperatures.

Whole vessels and potsherds from archaeological excavations at historic sites such as the Palace of the Governors in Santa Fe and seventeenth-century mission churches at Abó, Quarai, Las Humanas (Gran Quivira), Giusewa, and Hawikuh show few, if any, technological differences between prehistoric and historic pottery.

In the Middle Rio Grande, Salinas, and Jémez provinces, links to the west during the Early Historic Period are very evident. Pueblos in the Middle Rio Grande and Salinas provinces continued making glaze-decorated pottery into the 1600s, and Zuni potters revived glaze decoration after about an 150-year hiatus (A.D. 1475–1630), during which they used matte-paint decoration. However, following the Pueblo Revolt of 1680 and reconquest in 1693–1694, it appears that lead-ore sources in the

Fig. 154. Santo Domingo Polychrome jar, ca. 1920. Mogollon Slipped/Anasazi Mineral-Paint/Anasazi and Historic Pueblo (Tewa) Vegetal-Paint Traditions, Middle Rio Grande Province.

Fig. 155. Santo Domingo Polychrome dough bowl, ca. 1910–1915. Mogollon Slipped/Anasazi Mineral-Paint/Anasazi and Historic Pueblo Vegetal-Paint Traditions, Middle Rio Grande Province.

Cerrillos Hills south of Santa Fe were commandeered by the Spanish, thereby gradually ending the manufacture of glaze-decorated pottery. Whatever stocks of ore the Pueblos may have had were exhausted by the mid-1700s. Even before that time, potters in the area around modern Zia Pueblo had been forced to revert to the old traditional black-firing iron-oxide pigments to make pottery such as Puname Polychrome (fig. 114). Additionally, they continued to use red-firing pigments as solid design fillers.

Without a supply of glaze pigments, some Pueblos of the Middle Rio Grande Province ceased making painted pottery altogether, reverting solely to the manufacture of utility pottery for storing and cooking. They probably traded for painted-pottery serving vessels, a longtime practice in the Rio Grande area. The exceptions were the people of Cochiti and Santo Domingo, who by the 1700s had made their peace with the Tewa and borrowed Tewa pottery traditions, adopting vegetal paint, red and white slips, and even some designs (figs. 155, 157). This preference continues at both pueblos (figs. 155, 156 at Santo Domingo; figs. 160, 161, 162 at Cochiti). Today, Santo Domingo Pueblo is probably best known for its jewelry making and shrewd trading of arts and crafts from many other pueblos. However, following the pattern of their earlier borrowing of vegetal paint from the Tewa, some Santo Domingo potters saw a good thing in the matte-on-black pottery of the Tewa in the 1920s and 1930s and produced some of their own (fig. 158). There are still many skilled potters at Santo Domingo today who make vegetal paint black-on-cream or polychrome in traditional forms and designs.

Though some Cochiti potters may still make pottery in traditional forms using vegetal paint and decorating with orderly, well-balanced, graceful designs, many others have followed the lead of Helen Cordero, whose amusing storyteller figures have been immensely successful. Not only have other Cochiti potters taken advantage

Fig. 156. Santo Domingo Polychrome dough bowl, ca. 1870–1890. Mogollon Slipped/Anasazi Mineral-Paint/Anasazi and Historic Pueblo (Tewa) Vegetal-Paint Traditions, Middle Rio Grande Province.

of the popularity of the figures, but potters in almost every pueblo are making their versions using natural materials available in their areas. At the 1986 Indian Market in Santa Fe, an Indian craftsman from the southeastern United States exhibited a storyteller figure in welded bronze.

Given the current public demand for Southwestern pottery, some Cochiti potters, and probably those from other pueblos, are no longer trusting their wares to the vagaries of dung-fueled fires. Some potters have their own electric kilns, and others take their unfired pieces to be fired by commercial pottery-making firms. When pristine storyteller figures can fetch hundreds of dollars, potters are reluctant to subject their work to the sometimes unpredictable nature of outdoor firings.

The desire to protect the potter's investment in time and money through using modern technology is understandable, however, some potters, particularly at Acoma and Isleta, have strayed almost totally away from tradition. After firing, natural inclusions of calcium carbonate in Acoma's pottery clays gradually absorb moisture from the air, causing tiny pits to form on the vessel surfaces. This unhappy occurrence —for the makers and the buyers of their wares—has led younger potters to abandon making what was traditionally some of the finest pottery made in this century. These progressive Acoma potters have abandoned clays from traditional sources and purchase nontraditional green ware or slip-cast pottery poured as a liquid into molds. Commercially available ceramic paints are used in the execution of "traditional" designs, and the pots are fired in an electric kiln. Others may not even use ceramic pigments applied before firing, but rather choose to use acrylic paints applied after firing. The visual result may be the same, but is it traditional?

For the Tewa potters, it has largely been business as usual, since they continue to use guaco as the principal pigment. However, in the 1500s, as noted earlier, they were introduced to the use of a red-firing paint or slip brought to the area by a group of

Fig. 157. (LEFT). Powhoge Polychrome or Santo Domingo Polychrome olla, *early to mid-nineteenth century. Mogollon Slipped/Anasazi Mineral-Paint/Anasazi and Historic Pueblo Vegetal-Paint Traditions, Tewa Basin or Middle Rio Grande Province.*

Fig. 158. Santo Domingo Black-on-black seed jar, 1930s. Mogollon Slipped/Historic Pueblo (Tewa) Black Traditions, Middle Rio Grande Province.

Fig. 159. Santo Domingo Polychrome jar, ca. 1910. Mogollon Slipped/Anasazi Mineral-Paint/Anasazi and Historic Pueblo (Tewa) Vegetal-Paint Traditions, Middle Rio Grande Province.

Tewa-speaking Tano (or Southern Tewa) people. Following Spanish colonization of the Tewa Basin in 1598, the use of red on exterior parts of *ollas* and both inside and outside bowls of Cuyamungue Black-on-tan (and Sakona Black-on-tan) gradually gained favor in the form of Sakona Polychrome (fig. 144). From then on, red slips and paints worked their way onto other types as Tewa Polychrome (figs. 144, 145), Ogapoge Polychrome (fig. 145), and Powhoge Polychrome (fig. 157).

The red-firing slip contains ferric oxide, which, when fired in an oxidizing atmosphere, yields the rich red for which Tewa potters are well-known. The same slip, when fired in a reducing atmosphere, is converted to ferro-ferric oxide (Lyon 1988). It is this chemical change that produces the distinctive black ware of Santa Clara (figs. 168, 169) and San Ildefonso (fig. 163). The matte-paint designs on matte-on-black pottery are accomplished with more of the same slip material applied over the polished surface but left unpolished. Presumably, the earlier eighteenth-century Tewa type, Kapo Black (fig. 147), is a result of this chemical change.

The same red was used as the background color of the especially handsome San Ildefonso Black-on-red pottery made by two members of one family (Dominguita Martinez and her daughter Tonita Roybal) of the late nineteenth and early twentieth centuries (Chapman 1970). The striking red-firing slip appears from the rim to just below the shoulder on many red-on-tan vessels made at San Juan Pueblo and formerly at Santa Clara. It is also used effectively both within polychrome designs and to frame the upper and lower parts of decorative bands on pottery from other Tewa pueblos (figs. 164, 165, 166, 167). Thus, the use of a red slip by the Tewa may be traced south to the Middle Rio Grande glaze-producing area, westward through the Acoma and Zuni areas, and, depending on its earlier antecedents, to either the Four Corners Anasazi or the Mogollon Culture and the earliest years of pottery in the Southwest.

PUEBLO POTTERY POST-1600 125

Fig. 160. Cochiti Polychrome bowl, early 1900s. Mogollon Slipped/Anasazi and Historic Pueblo (Tewa) Vegetal-Paint Traditions, Middle Rio Grande Province.

Fig. 161. Cochiti Polychrome storage jar, 1930–1935. Mogollon Slipped/Anasazi Mineral-Paint/Anasazi and Historic Pueblo Vegetal-Paint Traditions, Middle Rio Grande Province.

Fig. 162. Cochiti Polychrome jar, 1946. Mogollon Slipped/Anasazi Mineral-Paint/Anasazi and Historic Pueblo Vegetal-Paint Traditions, Middle Rio Grande Province.

Fig. 163. San Ildefonso Black-on-black jar, 1919. Mogollon Slipped/Anasazi Mineral-Paint/Anasazi and Historic Pueblo Vegetal-Paint/Tewa Red and Tewa Black Traditions, Tewa Basin Province.

Fig. 164. San Ildefonso Polychrome jar, 1925–1935. Mogollon Slipped/Anasazi Mineral-Paint/Anasazi and Historic Pueblo Vegetal-Paint Traditions, Tewa Basin Province.

PUEBLO POTTERY POST-1600 129

Fig. 165. San Ildefonso Polychrome prayer meal bowl, 1922. Mogollon Slipped/Anasazi Mineral-Paint/Anasazi and Historic Pueblo Vegetal-Paint Traditions, Tewa Basin Province.

Fig. 166. San Ildefonso Polychrome seed jar, 1976. Mogollon Slipped/Anasazi Mineral-Paint/Anasazi and Historic Pueblo Vegetal-Paint Traditions, Tewa Basin Province.

Fig. 167. Santa Clara Red-on-tan, Appliqué/Sculpted jar, 1975. Mogollon Slipped/Anasazi Mineral-Paint/ Anasazi and Historic Pueblo Vegetal-Paint/Tewa Red and Tewa Black Traditions, Tewa Basin Province.

Perhaps influenced by sixteenth-century Potsuwi'i Incised, potters at Santa Clara have further experimented with carving, impressing, sculpting (fig. 167), and, perhaps most recently, sgraffito (fig. 171), wherein strikingly intricate designs are engraved or embossed with sharply pointed metal tools that cut through a slipped, but unfired, vessel surface. The results are pure art, since the pottery pieces engraved are almost totally closed forms, with only a tiny hole to allow gases to escape during firing. Potters sometimes selectively fire parts of the pieces in a reducing atmosphere to obtain dense blacks while oxidizing other parts to achieve the traditional reds. There are no shortages of creative people producing this pottery, and potters of many Pueblos have applied their skills to similar work. Although the germ of continuity is there, one might ask if this kind of treatment harks back to Potsuwi'i Incised. The full impact of such new pottery traditions cannot be predicted.

Fig. 168. Santa Clara Black closed bowl, pre-1942. Mogollon Slipped/Tewa Red and Tewa Black Traditions, Tewa Basin Province.

Fig. 169. Santa Clara Black melon bowl, 1978. Mogollon Slipped/Anasazi Mineral-Paint/Anasazi and Historic Pueblo Vegetal-Paint/Tewa Red and Tewa Black Traditions, province unknown.

Fig. 170. San Juan Incised jar, 1958. Mogollon Slipped/ Anasazi Mineral-Paint/Anasazi and Historic Pueblo Vegetal-Paint/Tewa Red Traditions, Tewa Basin Province.

Fig. 171. Santa Clara Red Sgraffito "jewel"; miniature "medicine jar," 1981. Mogollon Slipped/Anasazi Mineral-Paint/Anasazi and Historic Pueblo Vegetal-Paint/Tewa Red Traditions, Tewa Basin Province.

Fig. 172. San Juan Carved Polychrome jar, 1940. Mogollon Slipped/Anasazi Mineral-Paint/Anasazi and Historic Pueblo Vegetal-Paint/Tewa Red Traditions, Tewa Basin Province.

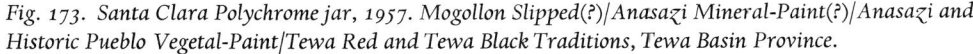

Fig. 173. Santa Clara Polychrome jar, 1957. Mogollon Slipped(?)/Anasazi Mineral-Paint(?)/Anasazi and Historic Pueblo Vegetal-Paint/Tewa Red and Tewa Black Traditions, Tewa Basin Province.

Fig. 174. Pecos Glaze Polychrome (Revival) "medicine" bowl, 1977. Mogollon Slipped/Anasazi Mineral-Paint Traditions, province unknown.

CONCLUSION

There never has been any real doubt that the Pueblo pottery tradition could be traced back to its introduction into the Southwest. While the prehistoric Pueblo people were creative in their own right, no archaeological information suggests that pottery was independently invented here in the Southwest.

The Mogollon disappeared from the scene, and their descendants, if they could once be discerned by their distinctive pottery styles, became so absorbed into the culture of the Anasazi, and possibly others as well, that their culture can be recognized no longer. Although it might be considered to be partly by default, the modern Pueblo Indians are the inheritors of the combined traditions of the Anasazi and Mogollon.

The apparent distinction between pottery made for cooking and storage versus that used for serving seems to have been established, even before the advent of painted pottery, with the making of either slipped, well-smoothed, or polished serving vessels. Because these vessels involved extra care in their making, early potters seem to have chosen not to immerse such vessels into cooking fires where they would have been quickly coated with soot, thus obscuring their handiwork. In other words, prehistoric potters first decided what the function of the vessel was to be and then made one of the appropriate clay, temper, finish, and decoration for that function. Pottery served a function for which the Anasazi, even if they had tried, could find no suitable substitute until the late nineteenth century, when their descendants were introduced to mass-produced containers of metal, glass, chinaware, and, ultimately, plastic.

Traditional pottery classification still serves important roles in observing technological and aesthetic trends and showing the effects of such externals as nearby cultural groups, environmental change, and adaptation. But occasionally it is worthwhile to stray from the straight and narrow and examine continuities rather than dividing them into smaller and smaller units. Many of the traditions discussed here can provide new perspectives on an already intensively studied subject.

In developing this discourse on traditions, I have drawn on my general familiarity with the spatial and chronological distributions of pottery types in New Mexico and the contiguity of the provinces in which they were dominant. Simplistic as it may seem, the basic theory is that contiguous provinces not separated by major geographic barriers are likely to be in frequent contact with one another and would be most likely to share ceramic traditions. The geographic barriers need not be major mountain chains but simply waterless expanses such as grasslands, areas with no population, or ones with few pottery-making resources and practices. Also worth consideration is the possibility that the prehistoric Indians might have exhibited the normal human trait of being reluctant to trade with groups with whom they had little in common.

Just as all possible pottery types have not yet been recognized and described, all possible traditions and sub-traditions have yet to be cited. Spatial and chronological gaps are gradually being filled as archaeological research goes into new areas. As can be seen, the traditions here discussed do not necessarily follow the same lines and distributions as pottery wares and types. The latter are far more specific because the archaeologists have designed them to be. They may tend to reflect local geology and how the potters used it and may show that traditions could extend from one major culture area into another in the same way that they cross province lines. The tendency to equate pottery type or ware boundaries with cultural boundaries may be specious. Traditions and cultural provinces are often more closely tied to differences in natural environment—geological exposures, topography, elevation, prevailing vegetation, and local climate—to which people have adapted over long periods. Some, but not all, disruptions of pottery traditions appear to have been related to brief but severe climatic fluctuations that led populations to relocate to areas with different environments. In such cases, adapting to clays of different geologic origins and firing qualities may have posed problems for potters of relocated settlements.

Also not to be discounted is the possibility that potters of migrant groups might, for diplomacy's sake, adopt the pottery-making techniques of the people into whose midst they moved, not wanting to set themselves apart from the host group. When migrants from the San Juan Basin moved to the Rio Grande in the late 1200s, one of the most conspicuous attributes they seem to have left behind was the circular kiva with its encircling bench, pilasters, and recess above the ventilator. Fourteenth-century Anasazi of the Middle Rio Grande and Galisteo Basin provinces, though for over one hundred years accustomed to decorating their pottery with vegetal paint, readily switched to glaze paint in the early 1300s as a result of stimulus from the Zuni and Acoma provinces. However, ancestral Tewa people chose to retain vegetal-paint decoration, favoring designs markedly different from those of the Middle Rio Grande. On the other hand, potters in the Jémez Province, though continuing to use vegetal paint, adopted at least some of the design motifs of the glaze-paint area.

All changes in pottery traditions may never be fully explainable. Some may reflect the influence of outside groups, or of host groups, or of differences in pottery-making resources and experimentation with them, but others may only be attributed to human nature. The pottery traditions discussed here are traditions of materials that constitute only a small, perhaps minor, aspect of the overall culture, as is the case with all human cultures. The culture of the modern Pueblo Indians is a reflection of countless simultaneous traditions that were developed, merged with others, perpetuated, separated, forgotten, remembered, revived, or lost irretrievably.

Perpetuation of the traditions herein described must have been, and continues to be, a largely unconscious act. Continuing to do what has always been done involves diligence among all concerned, but in doing so there is the satisfaction that equilibrium has not been affected. To work contrary to tradition, on the other hand, is very likely to involve conscious, though not necessarily malicious, intent and probably an equal amount of diligence. However, between these two extremes there is probably a degree of latitude in performance wherein chance, ignorance, or apathy come into play. Today's Pueblo potters must be aware of these factors, as should be the many buyers of their craft. The values of the makers, traders, and buyers have a bearing on where the Pueblo pottery traditions will go from here.

APPENDIX OF POTTERY VESSEL DATA

Vessels are listed in numerical order according to figure number. All dimensions are in millimeters. All sites and provinces are in New Mexico unless otherwise indicated.

FIG. 1.
Catalog No. 49971/11
Collection Museum of New Mexico
Culture Mogollon
Province Mimbres (northern), Quemado area
Site LA 5407, Feature 39
Tradition Unknown
Type Unnamed, semifired, fiber-tempered
Form Basket-liner bowl
Dimensions Height 88 to 102; maximum diameter 381
Period/Date Mogollon 2 (Pine Lawn Phase); A.D. 400–600

FIG. 2.
Catalog No. 51071/11
Collection Museum of New Mexico
Culture Mogollon
Province Mimbres (northern), Quemado area
Site LA 5407, Feature 39
Tradition Brown/Plain
Type Alma Plain
Form Small jar
Dimensions Height 215; maximum diameter 162
Period/Date Mogollon 2 (Pine Lawn Phase); A.D. 400–600

FIG. 3.
Catalog No. 51073/11
Collection Museum of New Mexico
Culture Mogollon
Province Mimbres (northern), Quemado area
Site LA 5407, Feature 39
Tradition Brown/Plain
Type Alma Plain
Form Seed jar
Dimensions Height 206; maximum diameter 235
Period/Date Mogollon 2 (Pine Lawn Phase); A.D. 400–600

FIG. 4.
Catalog No. 51069/11
Collection Museum of New Mexico
Culture Mogollon
Province Mimbres (northern), Quemado area
Site LA 5407, Feature 39
Tradition Mogollon Brown
Type Brown/Plain
Form Seed jar
Dimensions Height 254; maximum diameter 286
Period/Date Mogollon 2 (Pine Lawn Phase); A.D. 400–600

FIG. 5.
Catalog No. 46632/11
Collection Museum of New Mexico
Culture Mogollon
Province Mimbres (northern), near Reserve
Site LA 5936, Feature 2
Tradition Brown/Plain
Type Alma Plain
Form Olla
Dimensions Height 427; maximum diameter 330
Period/Date Mogollon 2 (Pine Lawn Phase); A.D. 400–600
Also illustrated in: Whiteford et al. 1989, fig. 6

FIG. 6.
Catalog No. 49565/11
Collection Museum of New Mexico
Culture Mogollon
Province Mimbres (southern), Silver City area
Site Unknown
Tradition Brown/Slipped (?)/Reduced
Type Three Circle Neck Corrugated, Smudged Interior
Form Jar
Dimensions Height 305; maximum diameter 318
Period/Date Mogollon 4 (Three-circle Phase); A.D. 900–1000
Also illustrated in: Whiteford et al. 1989, fig. 12

FIG. 7.
Catalog No. 8763/11
Collection School of American Research Collections in the Museum of New Mexico
Culture Mogollon
Province Mimbres (northern)
Site Unknown
Tradition Brown/Slipped/Reduced
Type Tularosa Patterned Corrugated, Smudged Variety
Form Bowl
Dimensions Height 231; maximum diameter 290
Period/Date Mogollon 4–5 (Reserve or Tularosa Phase); A.D. 1050–1250

FIG. 8.
- Catalog No.: 21989/11
- Collection: Museum of New Mexico
- Culture: Mogollon
- Province: Mimbres (southern), Arenas Valley
- Site: Cameron Creek Village (LA 190)
- Tradition: Brown/Slipped/Reduced
- Type: Unnamed, fine coil with punctate decoration and smudged interior
- Form: Bowl
- Dimensions: Height 117; maximum diameter 241
- Period/Date: Mogollon 4 (Mimbres Phase); A.D. 1100–1150
- Comment: Similar to the roughly contemporary pottery type, Los Lunas Smudged, that occurs in the Acoma-Laguna and Middle Rio Grande provinces.

FIG. 9.
- Catalog No.: 21046/11
- Collection: Museum of New Mexico
- Culture: Mogollon
- Province: Mimbres (northern)
- Site: Unknown
- Tradition: Brown/Slipped/Reduced
- Type: Tularosa Fillet Rim
- Form: Bowl
- Dimensions: Height 89; maximum diameter 191
- Period/Date: Mogollon 5 (Apache Creek or Tularosa Phase); A.D. 1100–1250

FIG. 10.
- Catalog No.: 8392/11
- Collection: School of American Research Collections in the Museum of New Mexico
- Culture: Mogollon
- Province: Mimbres (southern), near Silver City
- Site: Unknown
- Tradition: Brown/Slipped/Red Paint
- Type: Mogollon Red-on-brown
- Form: Bowl
- Dimensions: Height 94; maximum diameter 281
- Period/Date: Mogollon 3 (San Francisco Phase); A.D. 700–900
- Comment: Exterior coils apparently not completely bonded by scraping, leaving dimpled appearance; then slipped red and polished.

FIG. 11.
- Catalog No.: 8393/11
- Collection: School of American Research Collections in the Museum of New Mexico
- Culture: Mogollon
- Province: Mimbres (southern), near Silver City
- Site: Unknown
- Tradition: Brown/Slipped/Red Paint
- Type: Mogollon Red-on-brown
- Form: Bowl
- Dimensions: Height 109; maximum diameter 241
- Period/Date: Mogollon 3 (San Francisco Phase); A.D. 700–900
- Comment: Exterior treatment the same as that in fig. 10.
- Also illustrated in: Brody 1977, fig. 30

FIG. 12.
- Catalog No.: 20419/11
- Collection: Museum of New Mexico
- Culture: Mogollon
- Province: Mimbres (northern); possibly Reserve area
- Site: Unknown
- Tradition: Gray-Brown/Slipped/Mineral Paint
- Type: Mangas Black-on-white (also known as Mimbres Bold Face Black-on-white)
- Form: Bowl
- Dimensions: Height 125; maximum diameter 201
- Period/Date: Mogollon 4 (Three-Circle Phase); A.D. 900–1000
- Comment: Compare decorative style with the Anasazi-type Kiatuthlanna Black-on-white bowl, fig. 50, from the Allantown site.

FIG. 13.
- Catalog No.: 8521/11
- Collection: School of American Research Collections in the Museum of New Mexico
- Culture: Mogollon
- Province: Mimbres (southern), Mimbres Valley
- Site: Mattocks Ruin (LA 676)
- Tradition: Gray-Brown/Slipped/Mineral Paint
- Type: Mimbres Black-on-white
- Form: Bowl
- Decoration: Geometric
- Dimensions: Height 121; maximum diameter 273
- Period/Date: Mogollon 4 (Mimbres Phase); A.D. 1000–1150
- Also illustrated in: Whiteford et al. 1989, fig. 30

FIG. 14.
- Catalog No.: 19923/11
- Collection: School of American Research Collections in the Museum of New Mexico
- Culture: Mogollon
- Province: Mimbres (southern), Mimbres Valley area
- Site: Eby Site (LA 15016)
- Tradition: Gray-Brown/Slipped/Mineral Paint
- Type: Mimbres Black-on-white
- Form: Bowl
- Decoration: Geometric
- Dimensions: Height 98; maximum diameter 251
- Period/Date: Mogollon 4 (Mimbres Phase); A.D. 1000–1150
- Also illustrated in: Whiteford et al. 1989, fig. 26

FIG. 15.
- Catalog No.: 19911/11
- Collection: School of American Research Collections in the Museum of New Mexico
- Culture: Mogollon
- Province: Mimbres (southern), Mimbres Valley
- Site: Old Town Ruin (LA 1113)
- Tradition: Gray-Brown/Slipped/Mineral Paint
- Type: Mimbres Black-on-white
- Form: Jar
- Decoration: Geometric
- Dimensions: Height 279; maximum diameter 308
- Period/Date: Mogollon 4 (Mimbres Phase); A.D. 1000–1150

FIG. 16.
- Catalog No.: 8617/11
- Collection: School of American Research Collections in the Museum of New Mexico
- Culture: Mogollon
- Province: Mimbres (southern), Lake Valley area
- Site: Unknown
- Tradition: Gray-Brown/Slipped/Mineral Paint
- Type: Mimbres Black-on-white
- Form: Ring-shaped canteen
- Decoration: Geometric
- Dimensions: Height 102; maximum diameter 279
- Period/Date: Mogollon 4 (Mimbres Phase); A.D. 1100–1200
- Also illustrated in: Brody 1977, plate 6; Whiteford et al. 1989, fig. 28

FIG. 17.
Catalog No.   17953/11
Collection   Museum of New Mexico
Culture   Mogollon
Province   Mimbres (southern), Mimbres Valley
Site   Rock House Ruin (LA 1118), Feature 7
Tradition   Gray-Brown/Slipped/Mineral Paint
Type   Mimbres Black-on-white
Form   Bowl
Decoration   Pictorial—Stylized serpent heads
Dimensions   Height 89; maximum diameter 241
Period/Date   Mogollon 4 (Mimbres Phase);
               A.D. 1000–1150

FIG. 18 (left).
Catalog No.   21526/11
Collection   Museum of New Mexico
Culture   Rio Grande Anasazi
Province   Tewa Basin (Pajarito Plateau)
Site   Puyé (LA 47), probably South House
Tradition   Tan/Vegetal Paint
Type   Cuyamungue Black-on-tan (Biscuit C)
Form   Miniature medicine jar
Dimensions   Height 73; maximum diameter 102
Period/Date   Late Rio Grande Classic Period (Pueblo IV); A.D. 1475–1600

FIG. 18 (center).
Catalog No.   20165/11
Collection   Museum of New Mexico
Culture   Anasazi
Province   Cibola or Chaco
Site   Unknown
Tradition   Gray/Slipped/Mineral Paint
Type   Gallup Black-on-white
Form   Miniature medicine jar
Dimensions   Height 89; maximum diameter 83
Period/Date   Pueblo II–III; A.D. 1000–1100

FIG. 18 (right).
Catalog No.   19905/11
Collection   School of American Research Collections in the Museum of New Mexico
Culture   Mogollon
Province   Mimbres (southern)
Site   Warm Springs Site (LA 19071)
Tradition   Gray-Brown/Slipped/Mineral Paint
Type   Mimbres Black-on-white
Form   Miniature medicine jar
Decoration   Geometric
Dimensions   Height 81; maximum diameter 92
Period/Date   Mogollon 4 (Mimbres Phase);
               A.D. 1000–1150

FIG. 19.
Catalog No.   20407/11
Collection   Museum of New Mexico
Culture   Mogollon
Province   Mimbres (southern)
Site   Cameron Creek Village (LA 190)
Tradition   Gray-Brown/Slipped/Mineral Paint
Type   Mimbres Black-on-white
Form   Bowl
Decoration   Pictorial—Two fish
Dimensions   Height 134; maximum diameter 302
Period/Date   Mogollon 4 (Mimbres Phase);
               A.D. 1000–1150

FIG. 20.
Catalog No.   8539/11
Collection   School of American Research Collections in the Museum of New Mexico
Culture   Mogollon
Province   Mimbres (southern), Mimbres Valley
Site   Mattocks Ruin (LA 676)
Tradition   Gray-Brown/Slipped/Mineral Paint
Type   Mimbres Black-on-white
Form   Bowl
Decoration   Pictorial—Whiptail scorpion
Dimensions   Height 102; maximum diameter 286
Period/Date   Mogollon 4 (Mimbres Phase);
               A.D. 1000–1150
Also illustrated in: Whiteford et al. 1989, fig. 29

FIG. 21.
Catalog No.   19928/11
Collection   School of American Research Collections in the Museum of New Mexico
Culture   Mogollon
Province   Mimbres (southern), Mimbres Valley area
Site   Eby Site (LA 15016)
Tradition   Gray-Brown/Slipped/Mineral Paint
Type   Mimbres Black-on-white
Form   Bowl
Decoration   Pictorial—Fish
Dimensions   Height 102; maximum diameter 286
Period/Date   Mogollon 4 (Mimbres Phase);
               A.D. 1000–1150
Also illustrated in: Whiteford et al. 1989, fig. 20

FIG. 22.
Catalog No.   37942/11
Collection   Museum of New Mexico
Culture   Mogollon
Province   Mimbres (southern), Mimbres Valley
Site   Rock House Ruin (LA 1118), Feature 5
Tradition   Gray-Brown/Slipped/Mineral Paint
Type   Mimbres Black-on-white
Form   Bowl
Decoration   Pictorial—Horned toad
Dimensions   Height 79; maximum diameter 183
Period/Date   Mogollon 4 (Mimbres Phase);
               A.D. 1000–1150
Also illustrated in: Brody 1977, fig. 126

FIG. 23.
Catalog No.   1630/11
Collection   Museum of New Mexico
Culture   Mogollon
Province   Mimbres (southern), Mimbres Valley
Site   Rock House Ruin (LA 1118), Feature 5
Tradition   Gray-Brown/Slipped/Mineral Paint
Type   Mimbres Black-on-white
Form   Small bowl
Decoration   Pictorial—Possible mask or representation of Mexican deity Xipe-teca
Dimensions   Height 58; maximum diameter 125
Period/Date   Mogollon 4 (Mimbres Phase);
               A.D. 1000–1150

FIG. 24.
Catalog No.   8249/11
Collection   School of American Research Collections in the Museum of New Mexico
Culture   Anasazi
Province   Cibola (Puerco River, Arizona, area)
Site   Allantown (LA 664), Puerco River area
Tradition   Gray/Slipped/Plain
Type   Lino Gray, Fugitive Red
Form   Pitcher
Dimensions   Height 184; maximum diameter 152
Period/Date   Basketmaker III; A.D. 600–800
Also illustrated in: Whiteford et al. 1989, fig. 8

FIG. 25.
Catalog No.   47372/11
Collection   Museum of New Mexico
Culture   Anasazi
Province   Cibola (Manuelito area)
Site   LA 4487, Feature 46
Tradition   Gray/Slipped/Plain
Type   Lino Gray, Fugitive Red
Form   Pitcher
Dimensions   Height 173; maximum diameter 127
Period/Date   Basketmaker III; A.D. 700–800

FIG. 26 (left).
Catalog No. 20485/11
Collection Museum of New Mexico
Culture Anasazi
Province Chaco (Chaco Canyon?)
Site Unknown
Tradition Gray/Unslipped/Plain
Type Lino Gray
Form Ring-shaped canteen
Dimensions Height 73; maximum body diameter 130
Period/Date Basketmaker III; A.D. 600–800

FIG. 26 (right).
Catalog No. 8243/11
Collection School of American Research Collections in the Museum of New Mexico
Culture Anasazi
Province Cibola (Puerco River, Arizona, area)
Site Allantown (LA 664)
Tradition Gray/Unslipped/Plain
Type Lino Gray
Form Trilobed pitcher
Dimensions Height 121; maximum lateral diameter 105
Period/Date Basketmaker III; A.D. 600–800

FIG. 27.
Catalog No. 8284/11
Collection School of American Research Collections in the Museum of New Mexico
Culture Anasazi
Province Cibola (Puerco River, Arizona, area)
Site Allantown (LA 664)
Tradition Gray/Unslipped/Textured
Type Kana-a Gray
Form Pitcher
Dimensions Height 485; maximum diameter 419
Period/Date Pueblo I; A.D. 800–875
Also illustrated in: Roberts 1940, plate 5c
Whiteford et al. 1989, fig. 9

FIG. 28 (left).
Catalog No. 21207/11
Collection Museum of New Mexico
Culture Rio Grande Anasazi
Province Tewa Basin (Pajarito Plateau)
Site Puyé (LA 47)
Tradition Gray/Slipped/Textured
Type Sapawe Micaceous
Form "Duck pot"
Dimensions Height 127; length 152; width 137
Period/Date Rio Grande Classic Period (Pueblo IV); A.D. 1350–1700
Comment A widespread form occurring at least as far south as central Mexico. A cooking vessel that allows the orifice to be close to the edge of the fire instead of at its center.

FIG. 28 (right).
Catalog No. 46382/11
Collection Museum of New Mexico
Culture Rio Grande Anasazi
Province Probably Tewa Basin
Site Unknown
Tradition Gray/Slipped/Textured
Type Sapawe Micaceous
Form "Duck pot"
Dimensions Height 89; length 163; width 130
Period/Date Rio Grande Classic Period (Pueblo IV); A.D. 1350–1700
Comment See Comment for fig. 28 (left).

FIG. 29.
Catalog No. 37956/11
Collection Museum of New Mexico
Culture Anasazi
Province Mesa Verde (middle San Juan Valley)
Site Smithy Site (LA 3317)
Tradition Gray/Unslipped/Textured
Type Mesa Verde Corrugated
Form Jar
Dimensions Height 290; maximum diameter 280
Period/Date Pueblo III (Mesa Verde Phase); A.D. 1200–1300
Comment Found buried in the floor of a dwelling room with its rim flush with the floor level; shaped sandstone disk used as a cover. It has no bottom and may have been used as a urinal.

FIG. 30.
Catalog No. 20514/11
Collection Museum of New Mexico
Culture Anasazi
Province Chaco or Cibola
Site Unknown
Tradition Gray/Unslipped/Textured
Type Coolidge Corrugated
Form Jar
Dimensions Height 173; maximum diameter 151
Period/Date Pueblo II; A.D. 1000–1075

FIG. 31.
Catalog No. 47722/11
Collection Museum of New Mexico
Culture Anasazi
Province Chaco (Chaco Canyon?)
Site Unknown
Tradition Gray/Unslipped/Textured
Type Chaco Corrugated
Form Jar
Dimensions Height 184; maximum diameter 179
Period/Date Pueblo II; A.D. 1000–1075
Also illustrated in: Whiteford et al. 1989, fig. 19

FIG. 32.
Catalog No. 20555/11
Collection Museum of New Mexico
Culture Anasazi
Province Chaco or Cibola
Site Unknown
Tradition Gray/Unslipped/Textured
Type Coolidge Corrugated
Form Jar
Dimensions Height 216; maximum diameter 222
Period/Date Pueblo II; A.D. 1000–1075

FIG. 33.
Catalog No. 51738/11
Collection Museum of New Mexico
Culture Anasazi
Province Chaco
Site Unknown
Tradition Gray/Unslipped/Textured
Type Chaco Corrugated
Form Storage jar
Dimensions Height 396; maximum diameter 420
Period/Date Pueblo II–III; A.D. 1075–1125

FIG. 34.
Catalog No. 43869/11
Collection Museum of New Mexico
Culture Anasazi
Province Chaco
Site Unknown
Tradition Gray/Unslipped/Textured
Type Chaco Corrugated
Form Jar
Dimensions Height 312; maximum diameter 360
Period/Date Pueblo II–III; A.D. 1075–1125

FIG. 35.
Catalog No. 43649/11
Collection Museum of New Mexico
Culture Anasazi
Province Upper San Juan
Site Unknown
Tradition Gray/Unslipped/Plain
Type Rosa Gray
Form Seed jar
Dimensions Height 213; maximum diameter 273
Period/Date Basketmaker III (Rosa Phase); A.D. 700–850
Comment Base exterior has impressions of a coiled basket.
Also illustrated in: Whiteford et al. 1989, fig. 7

FIG. 36.
Catalog No. 43101/11
Collection Museum of New Mexico
Culture Anasazi
Province Upper San Juan (Arboles, Colorado, area)
Site Sambrito Village (LA 4195), Feature 9
Tradition Gray/Unslipped/Plain
Type Piedra Gray
Form Large bowl
Dimensions Height 254; maximum diameter 427
Period/Date Pueblo I (Piedra Phase); A.D. 850–950

FIG. 37.
Catalog No. 44330/11
Collection Museum of New Mexico
Culture Anasazi
Province Upper San Juan (Arboles, Colorado, area)
Site Sanchez Site (LA 4086), Feature 28
Tradition Gray/Unslipped/Plain
Type Piedra Gray
Form Jar
Dimensions Height 390; maximum diameter 306
Period/Date Pueblo I (Piedra Phase); A.D. 850–950

FIG. 38.
Catalog No. 42973/11
Collection Museum of New Mexico
Culture Anasazi
Province Upper San Juan (Arboles, Colorado, area)
Site Sambrito Village (LA 4195), Feature 38, Pit A, fill
Tradition Gray/Unslipped/Plain
Type Piedra Gray
Form Pitcher (ovoid body)
Dimensions Height 211; greatest body diameter 155; smallest body diameter 127
Period/Date Pueblo I (Piedra Phase); A.D. 850–950
Comment Difference in body diameters to produce an oval shape was intentional.

FIG. 39.
Catalog No. 47735/11
Collection Museum of New Mexico
Culture Rio Grande Anasazi
Province Gallina (Lindrith area)
Site LA 11850, Feature 4
Tradition Gray/Unslipped/Textured
Type Gallina Banded Utility
Form Beaker
Dimensions Height 284; maximum diameter 183
Period/Date Pueblo III (Largo-Gallina Phase); A.D. 1200–1275

FIG. 40.
Catalog No. 47321/11
Collection Museum of New Mexico
Culture Rio Grande Anasazi
Province Tewa Basin (Tesuque Valley)
Site Pojoaque Grant Site (LA 835)
Tradition Gray/Unslipped/Textured
Type "Pojoaque Neckbanded"
Form Jar
Dimensions Height 361; maximum diameter 284
Period/Date Rio Grande Developmental Period (Pueblo I–II); A.D. 850–950
Comment Found buried in the floor of a pit house.

FIG. 41.
Catalog No. 44312/11
Collection Museum of New Mexico
Culture Anasazi
Province Upper San Juan (Arboles, Colorado, area)
Site Sanchez Site (LA 4086), Feature 14
Tradition Gray/Unslipped/Textured
Type Piedra Neckbanded
Form Tripod pitcher
Dimensions Height 182; maximum diameter 185
Period/Date Pueblo I (Piedra Phase); A.D. 850–950

FIG. 42.
Catalog No. 47322/11
Collection Museum of New Mexico
Culture Rio Grande Anasazi
Province Tewa Basin (Tesuque Valley)
Site Pojoaque Grant Site (LA 835), Kiva A
Tradition Gray/Unslipped/Textured
Type "Pojoaque Corrugated"
Form Jar
Dimensions Height 401; maximum diameter 356
Period/Date Late Rio Grande Developmental Period (Pueblo I–II); A.D. 900–1000
Comment Found buried in the floor of a pit house.

FIG. 43.
Catalog No. 47371/11
Collection Museum of New Mexico
Culture Anasazi
Province Cibola (Manuelito area)
Site LA 4487, Feature 43
Tradition Gray/Unslipped/Mineral Paint
Type La Plata/White Mound Black-on-white
Form Bowl
Dimensions Height 72; maximum diameter 150
Period/Date Basketmaker III; A.D. 600–700

FIG. 44.
Catalog No. 8494/11a
Collection School of American Research Collections in the Museum of New Mexico
Culture Anasazi
Province Cibola (Manuelito area)
Site Unknown
Tradition Gray/Unslipped/Mineral Paint
Type La Plata/White Mound Black-on-white
Form Seed jar
Dimensions Height 81; maximum diameter 95
Period/Date Basketmaker III; A.D. 600–700

FIG. 45.
Catalog No. 8441/11
Collection School of American Research Collections in the Museum of New Mexico
Culture Anasazi
Province Cibola (Manuelito area)
Site Unknown
Tradition Gray/Unslipped/Mineral Paint
Type White Mound Black-on-white
Form Double bowl
Dimensions Height 70; length 184
Period/Date Late Basketmaker III; A.D. 700–800

FIG. 46.
Catalog No. 9007/11
Collection Museum of New Mexico
Culture Rio Grande Anasazi
Province Middle Rio Grande (north Albuquerque)
Site LA 3290
Tradition Gray/Unslipped/Mineral Paint
Type San Marcial Black-on-white
Form Bowl
Dimensions Height 84; maximum diameter 181
Period/Date Rio Grande Development Period (Late Basketmaker III–Early Pueblo I); A.D. 750–875

FIG. 47.
Catalog No. 47373/11
Collection Museum of New Mexico
Culture Anasazi
Province Cibola (Manuelito area)
Site LA 4487, Feature 46
Tradition Gray/Unslipped/Mineral Paint
Type La Plata/White Mound Black-on-white
Form Bowl
Dimensions Height 77; maximum diameter 145
Period/Date Basketmaker III–Pueblo I; A.D. 600–750
Comment Water-soluble red-iron oxide (hematite) pigment applied to bowl exterior after firing.

FIG. 48.
Catalog No. 18625/11
Collection School of American Research Collections in the Museum of New Mexico
Culture Anasazi
Province Unknown
Site Unknown
Tradition Gray/Unslipped/Mineral Paint
Type White Mound Black-on-white
Form Bowl
Dimensions Height 89; maximum diameter 216
Period/Date Late Basketmaker III–Early Pueblo I; A.D. 700–800

FIG. 49.
Catalog No. 8143/11
Collection School of American Research Collections in the Museum of New Mexico
Culture Anasazi
Province Chuska
Site Unknown
Tradition Gray/Slipped/Mineral Paint
Type Crozier Black-on-white
Form Bowl
Dimensions Height 81; maximum diameter 175
Period/Date Pueblo I; A.D. 800–875

FIG. 50.
Catalog No. 8224/11
Collection School of American Research Collections in the Museum of New Mexico
Culture Anasazi
Province Cibola (Puerco River, Arizona, area)
Site Allantown (LA 664)
Tradition Gray/Slipped/Mineral Paint
Type Kiatuthlanna Black-on-white
Form Bowl
Dimensions Height 82; maximum diameter 197
Period/Date Pueblo I; A.D. 800–875
Comment Compare decorative style with the Mangas Black-on-white, fig. 12.
Also illustrated in: Roberts 1940, plate 25d
Brody 1977, fig. 42

FIG. 51.
Catalog No. 47375/11
Collection Museum of New Mexico
Culture Anasazi
Province Cibola
Site LA 4487, Feature 55
Tradition Gray/Slipped/Mineral Paint
Type Kiatuthlanna Black-on-white
Form Bowl
Dimensions Height 74; maximum diameter 121
Period/Date Pueblo I; A.D. 800–875

FIG. 52.
Catalog No. 8191/11
Collection School of American Research Collections in the Museum of New Mexico
Culture Anasazi
Province Cibola (Puerco River, Arizona, area)
Site Unknown
Tradition Gray/Slipped/Mineral Paint
Type Kiatuthlanna Black-on-white
Form Bowl
Dimensions Height 84; maximum diameter 147
Period/Date Pueblo I; A.D. 800–875

FIG. 53.
Catalog No. 20094/11
Collection School of American Research Collections in the Museum of New Mexico
Culture Anasazi
Province Mesa Verde or Upper San Juan
Site Unknown
Tradition Gray/Unslipped/Mineral Paint
Type Piedra Black-on-white
Form Effigy pitcher
Dimensions Height 192; maximum diameter 178
Period/Date Pueblo I; A.D. 850–950
Comment Found near Gallup, New Mexico.

FIG. 54.
Catalog No. 42905/11
Collection Museum of New Mexico
Culture Anasazi
Province Upper San Juan (Arboles, Colorado, area)
Site Sambrito Village (LA 4195), Feature 7
Tradition Gray/Unslipped/Mineral Paint
Type Piedra Black-on-white
Form Bowl
Dimensions Height 81; maximum diameter 206
Period/Date Pueblo I (Piedra Phase); A.D. 850–950
Comment Pictorial design implies birds were hunted by catching them in a net.

FIG. 55.
Catalog No. 8277/11
Collection School of American Research Collections in the Museum of New Mexico
Culture Anasazi
Province Cibola (Puerco River, Arizona, area)
Site Allantown (LA 664)
Tradition Gray/Slipped/Mineral Paint
Type Red Mesa Black-on-white
Form Pitcher
Dimensions Height 166; maximum diameter 153
Period/Date Pueblo I–II; A.D. 875–1000
Also illustrated in: Roberts 1940, plate 13b

FIG. 56.
Catalog No. 19850/11
Collection Museum of New Mexico
Culture Anasazi
Province Chaco
Site Unknown
Tradition Gray/Slipped/Mineral Paint
Type Red Mesa Black-on-white
Form Bowl
Dimensions Height 92; maximum diameter 224
Period/Date Pueblo I–II; A.D. 875–1000

FIG. 57.
Catalog No. 8222/11
Collection School of American Research Collections in the Museum of New Mexico
Culture Anasazi
Province Cibola (Puerco River, Arizona, area)
Site Allantown (LA 664)
Tradition Gray/Slipped/Mineral Paint
Type Red Mesa Black-on-white
Form Bowl
Dimensions Height 74; maximum diameter 144
Period/Date Pueblo I–II; A.D. 875–1000
Also illustrated in: Roberts 1940, plate 25b

FIG. 58.
Catalog No. 45837/11
Collection Museum of New Mexico
Culture Rio Grande Anasazi
Province Middle Rio Grande (Zia Pueblo area)
Site Toribio Site (LA 9193), Feature 13
Tradition Gray/Slipped/Mineral Paint
Type Red Mesa Black-on-white
Form Pitcher
Dimensions Height 237; maximum diameter 220
Period/Date Rio Grande Developmental Period (Pueblo I–II); A.D. 875–1050

FIG. 59.
Catalog No. 19646/11
Collection Museum of New Mexico
Culture Anasazi
Province Chaco or Cibola
Site Unknown
Tradition Gray/Slipped/Mineral Paint
Type Red Mesa (or early Gallup) Black-on-white
Form Bowl
Dimensions Height 82; maximum diameter 185
Period/Date Pueblo II; A.D. 950–1000
Comment Interlocking spiral figures apparently are serpents.

FIG. 60.
Catalog No. 45839/11
Collection Museum of New Mexico
Culture Rio Grande Anasazi
Province Middle Rio Grande (Zia Pueblo area)
Site Toribio Site (LA 9193), Feature 14
Tradition Gray/Slipped/Mineral Paint
Type Red Mesa Black-on-white
Form Bowl
Dimensions Height 87; maximum diameter 197
Period/Date Rio Grande Developmental Period (Pueblo I–II); A.D. 875?–1050

FIG. 61.
Catalog No. 45838/11
Collection Museum of New Mexico
Culture Rio Grande Anasazi
Province Middle Rio Grande (Zia Pueblo area)
Site Toribio Site (LA 9193), Feature 13
Tradition Gray/Slipped/Mineral Paint
Type Red Mesa Black-on-white
Form Seed jar with pierced lug handles
Dimensions Height 164; maximum diameter 217
Period/Date Rio Grande Developmental Period (Pueblo I–II); A.D. 875–1050

FIG. 62.
Catalog No. 43334/11
Collection Museum of New Mexico
Culture Anasazi
Province Chaco(?)
Site Unknown
Tradition Gray/Slipped/Mineral Paint
Type Red Mesa Black-on-white
Form Beaker
Dimensions Height 227; maximum diameter 180
Period/Date Pueblo II; A.D. 950–1050
Also illustrated in: Whiteford et al. 1989, fig. 14

FIG. 63.
Catalog No. 51742/11
Collection Museum of New Mexico
Culture Anasazi
Province Chaco
Site LA 4986, Feature 52
Tradition Gray/Slipped/Mineral Paint
Type Red Mesa Black-on-white
Form Bowl
Dimensions Height 82; maximum diameter 186
Period/Date Pueblo II; A.D. 900–1025

FIG. 64.
Catalog No. 43323/11
Collection Museum of New Mexico
Culture Anasazi
Province Chaco (Chaco Canyon area)
Site Chetro Ketl (LA 838)
Tradition Gray/Slipped/Mineral Paint
Type Gallup Black-on-white
Form Bowl
Dimensions Height 64; maximum diameter 154
Period/Date Pueblo II; A.D. 1000–1100

FIG. 65.
Catalog No. 49912/11
Collection Museum of New Mexico
Culture Anasazi
Province Chaco or Cibola (Gallup area)
Site Unknown
Tradition Gray/Slipped/Mineral Paint
Type Gallup Black-on-white
Form Seed jar
Dimensions Height 136; maximum diameter 190
Period/Date Pueblo II; A.D. 1000–1100

FIG. 66.
Catalog No. 8842/11
Collection Museum of New Mexico
Culture Anasazi
Province Chaco or Cibola
Site Unknown
Tradition Gray/Slipped/Mineral Paint
Type Gallup/Puerco Black-on-white
Form Seed jar
Dimensions Height 127; maximum diameter 241
Period/Date Pueblo II; A.D. 1000–1100
Also illustrated in: Whiteford et al. 1989, fig. 18

FIG. 67.
Catalog No. 18530/11
Collection Museum of New Mexico
Culture Anasazi
Province Acoma (Rio San Jose Valley)
Site McCarty Site (LA 6401), Feature 9
Tradition Gray/Slipped/Mineral Paint
Type Gallup Black-on-white
Form Bowl
Dimensions Height 86; maximum diameter 218
Period/Date Pueblo II; A.D. 1000–1100

FIG. 68.
Catalog No. 8552/11
Collection School of American Research Collections in the Museum of New Mexico
Culture Anasazi
Province Chaco (Escavada Wash area)
Site Unknown
Tradition Gray/Slipped/Mineral Paint
Type Gallup/Chaco Black-on-white
Form Olla
Dimensions Height 365; maximum diameter 366
Period/Date Pueblo II; A.D. 1000–1100

FIG. 69.
Catalog No. 18534/11
Collection Museum of New Mexico
Culture Anasazi
Province Chaco (southern San Juan Basin)
Site LA 2985, Feature 31
Tradition Gray/Slipped/Mineral Paint
Type Chaco Black-on-white
Form Pitcher
Dimensions Height 172; maximum diameter 148
Period/Date Late Pueblo II; A.D. 1075–1130

FIG. 70.
Catalog No.   20175/11
Collection   Museum of New Mexico
Culture   Anasazi
Province   Cibola (Puerco River Valley)
Site   Unknown
Tradition   Gray/Slipped/Mineral Paint
Type   Puerco Black-on-white, Escavada Variety
Form   Jar
Dimensions   Height 298; maximum diameter 310
Period/Date   Pueblo II; A.D. 1000–1100
Comment   Jar has a "kickup" on the bottom to facilitate carrying jar on the head or for stability on a flat surface.

FIG. 71.
Catalog No.   25251/11
Collection   Museum of New Mexico
Culture   Anasazi
Province   Chaco
Site   Unknown
Tradition   Gray/Slipped/Mineral Paint
Type   Escavada Black-on-white
Form   Bowl
Dimensions   Height 103; maximum diameter 229
Period/Date   Pueblo II; A.D. 1000–1100

FIG. 72.
Catalog No.   18628/11
Collection   School of American Research Collections in the Museum of New Mexico
Culture   Anasazi
Province   Cibola (Puerco River Valley)
Site   Unknown
Tradition   Gray/Slipped/Mineral Paint
Type   Gallup/Escavada Black-on-white
Form   Bird effigy pitcher
Dimensions   Height 130; maximum length 138
Period/Date   Pueblo II; A.D. 1000–1100

FIG. 73.
Catalog No.   8815/11
Collection   Museum of New Mexico
Culture   Anasazi
Province   Unknown
Site   Unknown
Tradition   Gray/Slipped/Mineral Paint
Type   Escavada Black-on-white
Form   Bowl
Dimensions   Height 199; maximum diameter 82
Period/Date   Pueblo II; A.D. 1000–1100

FIG. 74.
Catalog No.   19680/11
Collection   Museum of New Mexico
Culture   Anasazi
Province   Chaco (Chaco Canyon)
Site   Chetro Ketl Talus Unit I (LA 2470)
Tradition   Gray/Slipped/Mineral Paint
Type   Mancos Black-on-white
Form   Bowl
Dimensions   Height 89; maximum diameter 194
Period/Date   Pueblo II; A.D. 1000–1075

FIG. 75.
Catalog No.   20022/11
Collection   Museum of New Mexico
Culture   Anasazi
Province   Cibola
Site   Unknown
Tradition   Gray/Slipped/Mineral Paint
Type   Reserve Black-on-white
Form   Pitcher
Dimensions   Height 219; maximum diameter 197
Period/Date   Pueblo II–III; A.D. 1000–1125
Comment   Pitcher handle bears picture of a masked figure resembling later kachinas.

FIG. 76.
Catalog No.   19720/11
Collection   Museum of New Mexico
Culture   Anasazi
Province   Cibola
Site   Unknown
Tradition   Gray/Slipped/Mineral Paint
Type   Tularosa Black-on-white
Form   Pitcher
Dimensions   Height 170; maximum diameter 177
Period/Date   Pueblo III (Tularosa Phase); A.D. 1125–1250

FIG. 77.
Catalog No.   46533/11
Collection   Museum of New Mexico
Culture   Anasazi
Province   Cibola (east-central Arizona)
Site   LA 11374
Tradition   Gray/Slipped/Mineral Paint
Type   Tularosa Black-on-white
Form   Dipper
Dimensions   Height of bowl 69; diameter of bowl 145; length 293
Period/Date   Pueblo III (Tularosa Phase); A.D. 1125–1250

FIG. 78.
Catalog No.   19806/11
Collection   Museum of New Mexico
Culture   Anasazi
Province   Cibola
Site   Unknown
Tradition   Gray/Slipped/Mineral Paint
Type   Tularosa Black-on-white
Form   Pitcher
Dimensions   Height 168; maximum diameter 168
Period/Date   Pueblo III (Tularosa Phase); A.D. 1125–1250

FIG. 79.
Catalog No.   43341/11
Collection   School of American Research Collections in the Museum of New Mexico
Culture   Anasazi
Province   Cibola
Site   Unknown
Tradition   Gray/Slipped/Mineral Paint
Type   Klagetoh Black-on-white
Form   Stirrup-shaped canteen
Dimensions   Height 178; maximum diameter 127
Period/Date   Pueblo III (Tularosa Phase); A.D. 1125–1250 or 1300
Comment   A relatively rare form; some specimens known as early as Basketmaker III; fairly common in later Rio Grande glaze types; may be ancestral to nineteenth-century "wedding vase" form in the Rio Grande. Prehistoric stirrup-shaped vessels are known as far south as Peru.
Also illustrated in: Whiteford et al. 1989, fig. 37

FIG. 80.
Catalog No.   43080/11
Collection   Museum of New Mexico
Culture   Anasazi
Province   Cibola
Site   Unknown
Tradition   Gray/Slipped/Mineral Paint
Type   Tularosa Black-on-white
Form   Pitcher with parrot effigy handle
Dimensions   Height 151; maximum diameter 134
Period/Date   Pueblo III (Tularosa Phase); A.D. 1125–1300

FIG. 81.
Catalog No. 49842/11
Collection Museum of New Mexico
Culture Anasazi
Province Acoma(?)
Site Unknown
Tradition Gray/Slipped/Mineral Paint
Type Cebolleta / Tularosa Black-on-white
Form Bird effigy jar
Dimensions Height 191; length 260
Period/Date Pueblo III; A.D. 1150–1250 (est.)
Also illus-
trated in: Whiteford et al. 1989, fig. 24

FIG. 82.
Catalog No. 8182/11
Collection School of American Research Collections in the Museum of New Mexico
Culture Anasazi
Province Acoma (Grants area)
Site Unknown
Tradition Gray/Slipped(?)/Mineral Paint
Type Socorro Black-on-white
Form Olla
Dimensions Height 309; maximum diameter 302
Period/Date Pueblo III (Cebolleta Phase); A.D. 1050–1275
Also illus-
trated in: Dittert and Plog 1980, fig. 114

FIG. 83.
Catalog No. 46345/11
Collection Museum of New Mexico
Culture Anasazi
Province Northern Jornada (Sacramento Mountains)
Site LA 5380
Tradition Gray/Slipped/Mineral Paint
Type Chupadero Black-on-white
Form Bowl
Dimensions Height 91; maximum diameter 279
Period/Date Pueblo III (Lincoln Phase); A.D. 1200–1375)

FIG. 84.
Catalog No. 8179/11
Collection School of American Research Collections in the Museum of New Mexico
Culture Anasazi
Province Acoma (Grants area)
Site Unknown
Tradition Gray/Slipped(?)/Mineral Paint
Type Socorro Black-on-white
Form Bowl
Dimensions Height 229; maximum diameter 330
Period/Date Pueblo III (Cebolleta Phase); A.D. 1050–1275

FIG. 85.
Catalog No. 51011/11
Collection Museum of New Mexico
Culture Anasazi
Province Northern Jornada (Sacramento Mountains)
Site Filingin Site (LA 16297)
Tradition Gray/Slipped/Mineral Paint
Type Chupadero Black-on-white
Form Olla
Dimensions Height 321; maximum diameter 349
Period/Date Pueblo III (Corona Phase?); A.D. 1100–1200
Comment Vessel interior shows characteristic striation.

FIG. 86.
Catalog No. 8440/11
Collection School of American Research Collections in the Museum of New Mexico
Culture Anasazi
Province Acoma (Grants area)
Site Unknown
Tradition Gray/Slipped(?)/Mineral Paint
Type Socorro Black-on-white
Form Olla
Dimensions Height 413; maximum diameter 387
Period/Date Pueblo III (Cebolleta Phase); A.D. 1050–1275

FIG. 87.
Catalog No. 43321/11
Collection Museum of New Mexico
Culture Anasazi
Province Cibola (Puerco River area)
Site Unknown
Tradition Yellow-Gray/Slipped/Mineral Paint
Type Wingate Black-on-red
Form Bowl
Dimensions Height 105; maximum diameter 235
Period/Date Pueblo II–III; A.D. 1050–1200

FIG. 88.
Catalog No. 42938/11
Collection Museum of New Mexico
Culture Rio Grande Anasazi
Province Middle Rio Grande
Site Unknown
Tradition Gray-Tan/Slipped/Mineral Glaze Paint
Type Agua Fria Glaze-on-red (Glaze A)
Form Bowl
Dimensions Height 111; maximum diameter 301
Period/Date Rio Grande Classic Period (Early Pueblo IV); A.D. 1315–1425

FIG. 89.
Catalog No. 42939/11
Collection Museum of New Mexico
Culture Rio Grande Anasazi
Province Galisteo (Upper Pecos Valley area)
Site Pecos Pueblo (LA 625)
Tradition Gray-Tan/Slipped/Mineral Glaze Paint Paint/Mogollon Slipped(?)
Type Cieneguilla Glaze-on-yellow (Glaze A)
Form Bowl
Dimensions Height 130; maximum diameter 327
Period/Date Rio Grande Classic Period (Pueblo IV); A.D. 1325–1425
Comment Compare decorative style with Wiyo Black-on-white bowl, fig. 133, of the Anasazi Vegetal Paint Tradition.

FIG. 90.
Catalog No. 11456/11
Collection Museum of New Mexico
Culture Rio Grande Anasazi
Province Middle Rio Grande (Bernalillo area)
Site Kuaua (LA 187)
Tradition Gray-Tan/Slipped/Mineral Glaze Paint
Type Espinoso Glaze-polychrome (Glaze C)
Form Bowl
Dimensions Height 57; maximum diameter 133
Period/Date Rio Grande Classic Period (Pueblo IV); A.D. 1425–1490

FIG. 91.
Catalog No. 42952/11
Collection Museum of New Mexico
Culture Rio Grande Anasazi
Province Salinas (Mountainair area)
Site Quarai (LA 95)
Tradition Gray-Tan/Slipped/Mineral Glaze Paint
Type Puaray Glaze-polychrome
Form Shouldered bowl
Dimensions Height 89; maximum diameter 243
Period/Date Rio Grande Classic Period (Pueblo IV); A.D. 1515–1650
Comment Sometimes called Tiguex Glaze-polychrome.

FIG. 92.
Catalog No. 8587/11
Collection School of American Research Collections in the Museum of New Mexico
Culture Rio Grande Anasazi
Province Galisteo
Site Vicinity of San Marcos Pueblo (LA 98)
Tradition Gray-Tan/Slipped/Mineral Glaze Paint
Type Puaray Glaze-polychrome (Glaze E)
Form Olla
Dimensions Height 229; maximum diameter 330
Period/Date Rio Grande Classic Period (Pueblo IV); A.D. 1515–1600

FIG. 93.
Catalog No. 43875/11
Collection Museum of New Mexico
Culture Rio Grande Anasazi
Province Middle Rio Grande
Site Unknown
Tradition Gray-Tan/Slipped/Mineral Glaze Paint
Type Kotyiti Glaze-on-yellow (Glaze F)
Form Shouldered bowl
Dimensions Height 99; maximum diameter 321
Period/Date Rio Grande Classic Period (Pueblo IV); 1650–1700

FIG. 94.
Catalog No. 50382/11
Collection Museum of New Mexico
Culture Rio Grande Anasazi
Province Middle Rio Grande
Site Frijolito (LA 78)
Tradition Gray-Tan/Slipped/Mineral Glaze Paint
Type Puaray Glaze-polychrome (Glaze E)
Form Olla
Dimensions Height 255; maximum diameter 395
Period/Date Rio Grande Classic Period (Pueblo IV); A.D. 1515–1600

FIG. 95.
Catalog No. 8551/11
Collection School of American Research Collections in the Museum of New Mexico
Culture Rio Grande Anasazi
Province Middle Rio Grande
Site Old San Felipe (LA 2047)
Tradition Gray-Tan/Slipped/Mineral Glaze Paint
Type Kotyiti Glaze-polychrome (Glaze F)
Form Olla
Dimensions Height 216; maximum diameter 254
Period/Date Rio Grande Classic Period (Late Pueblo IV); 1650–1700
Comment A late glaze decoration on an early Tewa form.
Also illustrated in: Batkin 1987, p. 92

FIG. 96.
Catalog No. 7878/12
Collection School of American Research Collections in the Museum of New Mexico
Culture Historic Pueblo
Province Acoma(?)
Pueblo Zuni
Tradition Gray/Slipped/Mineral Paint
Type Ashiwi Polychrome
Form Olla
Dimensions Height 318; maximum diameter 235
Maker Unknown
Period/Date Pueblo V; 1710–1750
Comment Found near Cubero, New Mexico.
Also illustrated in: Mera 1939, p. 144, plate LVII
Harlow 1973, pp. 260, 263
Harlow 1974, p. 141

FIG. 97.
Catalog No. 8032/12
Collection School of American Research Collections in the Museum of New Mexico
Culture Historic Pueblo
Province Cibola
Pueblo Zuni
Tradition Gray/Slipped/Mineral Paint
Type Zuni Polychrome
Form Stew bowl
Dimensions Height 134; maximum diameter 360
Maker Unknown
Period/Date Pueblo V; 1850–1890
Also illustrated in: Harlow 1973, plate 34a

FIG. 98.
Catalog No 36593/12
Collection Museum of New Mexico
Culture Historic Pueblo
Province Cibola
Pueblo Zuni
Tradition Gray/Slipped/Mineral Paint
Type Zuni Polychrome
Form Olla
Dimensions Height 276; maximum diameter 359
Period/Date Pueblo V; 1860–1875
Also illustrated in: Harlow 1973, pp. 268–269

FIG. 99.
Catalog No. 7834/12
Collection School of American Research Collections in the Museum of New Mexico
Culture Historic Pueblo
Province Acoma
Pueblo Acoma
Tradition Gray/Slipped/Mineral Paint
Type Late Ako Polychrome or Early Acomita Polychrome
Form Olla
Dimensions Height 305; maximum diameter 343
Maker Unknown
Period/Date Pueblo V; 1750–1800
Also illustrated in: Mera 1939, p. 152, plate LXI
Harlow 1973, p. 240, plate 27d
Whiteford et al. 1989, fig. 45

FIG. 100.
Catalog No. 7753/12
Collection School of American Research Collections in the Museum of New Mexico
Culture Historic Pueblo
Province Acoma
Pueblo Laguna
Tradition Gray/Slipped/Mineral Paint
Type Acomita Polychrome, Laguna Variant
Form Olla
Dimensions Height 279; maximum diameter 305
Maker Unknown
Period/Date Pueblo V; 1780–1820
Comment Although named for an Acoma village, Harlow says this olla was made at Laguna.
Also illustrated in: Harlow 1973, plate 28b

FIG. 101.
Catalog No. 35748/12
Collection Museum of New Mexico
Culture Historic Pueblo
Province Acoma
Pueblo Acoma
Tradition Gray/Slipped/Mineral Paint
Type Acoma Polychrome
Form Olla
Dimensions Height 292; maximum diameter 349
Maker Unknown
Date 1900–1920
Comment The perching bird and meandering rainbow band are typical of Acoma pottery of this period.

Also illustrated in: Toulouse 1977, plate 8

FIG. 102.
Catalog No. 35758/12
Collection Museum of New Mexico
Culture Historic Pueblo
Province Acoma
Pueblo Acoma
Tradition Gray/Slipped/Mineral Paint
Type Acoma Polychrome
Form Canteen or water jar with double spout
Dimensions Height 349; maximum diameter 279
Maker Unknown
Date 1920–1940

FIG. 103.
Catalog No. 12035/12
Collection Museum of New Mexico
Culture Historic Pueblo
Province Acoma
Pueblo Acoma
Tradition Gray/Slipped/Mineral Paint
Type Acoma Polychrome
Form Olla
Dimensions Height 341; maximum diameter 341
Maker Unknown
Date c. 1900
Comment The wavy "piecrust" rim appears to have been adopted before 1900 and continues to the present. Surface pitting, a chronic problem for Acoma potters—and even prehistoric ones—is visible at several points around the exterior and is largely due to incomplete washing of the clay and removal of impurities.

FIG. 104.
Catalog No. 45135/12
Collection Museum of New Mexico
Culture Historic Pueblo
Province Acoma
Pueblo Acoma
Tradition Gray/Slipped/Mineral Paint
Type Acoma Polychrome
Form Olla
Dimensions Height 229; maximum diameter 292
Maker Mary Histia
Date 1951

FIG. 105.
Catalog No. 25830/12
Collection Museum of New Mexico
Culture Historic Pueblo
Province Acoma
Pueblo Acoma
Tradition Gray/Slipped/Mineral Paint
Type Acoma Black-on-white
Form Seed jar
Dimensions Height 114; maximum diameter 165
Maker Marie Chino
Date 1961
Comment Use of fine-line brushwork bears some similarity to Mimbres decoration and was only one of several prehistoric decorative techniques adopted by Acoma potters in the 1950s and later.

Also illustrated in: Peterson 1984, fig. 301

FIGS. 106 and 107.
Catalog No. 50427/12
Collection Museum of New Mexico
Culture Historic Pueblo
Province Acoma
Pueblo Acoma
Tradition Gray/Slipped/Mineral Paint
Type Acoma Polychrome
Form Seed jar
Dimensions Height 171; maximum diameter 248
Maker Rose Chino Garcia
Date 1984

FIG. 108.
Catalog No. 25831/12
Collection Museum of New Mexico
Culture Historic Pueblo
Province Acoma
Pueblo Acoma
Tradition Gray/Slipped/Mineral Paint
Type Acoma Black-on-white
Form Seed jar
Dimensions Height 121; maximum diameter 165
Maker Marie Chino
Date 1961
Comment An apparent revival and adaptation of the hatch-filled and solid motif reminiscent of those found on Socorro Black-on-white, figs. 82–86.

Also illustrated in: Garcia-Mason 1979, fig. 14d

FIG. 109.
Catalog No. 49555/12
Collection Museum of New Mexico
Culture Historic Pueblo
Province Acoma
Pueblo Acoma
Tradition Gray/Slipped/Mineral Paint
Type Acoma Black-on-white
Form Seed jar or closed bowl
Dimensions Height 140; maximum diameter 197
Maker Lucy Lewis
Date 1960s
Also illustrated in: Toulouse 1977, p. 65

FIG. 110.
Catalog No. 25834/12
Collection Museum of New Mexico
Culture Historic Pueblo
Province Acoma
Pueblo Acoma
Tradition Gray/Slipped
Type Acoma White, Tooled Corrugated
Form Jar
Dimensions Height 140; maximum diameter 165
Maker Marie Chino
Date 1961

FIG. 111.
Catalog No. 50433/12
Collection Museum of New Mexico
Culture Historic Pueblo
Province Cibola
Pueblo Zuni
Tradition Gray/Slipped/Mineral Paint
Type Zuni Polychrome
Form Jar
Dimensions Height 160; maximum diameter 216
Maker Anderson Peynetsa
Date 1984

FIG. 112.
Catalog No.   12295/12
Collection   Museum of New Mexico
Culture   Historic Pueblo
Province   Middle Rio Grande
Pueblo   Zia
Tradition   Tan/Slipped/Mineral Paint
Type   Zia Polychrome
Form   Olla
Dimensions   Height 254; maximum diameter 278
Maker   Harviana Toribio
Date   1940
Also illus-
trated in: Toulouse 1977, p. 79

FIG. 113.
Catalog No.   50428/12
Collection   Museum of New Mexico
Culture   Historic Pueblo
Province   Acoma
Pueblo   Laguna
Tradition   Gray/Slipped/Mineral Paint
Type   Laguna Polychrome
Form   Olla
Dimensions   Height 264; maximum diameter 305
Maker   Gladys Paquin
Date   1984

FIG. 114.
Catalog No.   7887/12
Collection   School of American Research Collec-
              tions in the Museum of New Mexico
Culture   Historic Pueblo
Province   Middle Rio Grande
Pueblo   Zia, but obtained at Jemez
Tradition   Tan/Slipped/Mineral Paint
Type   Puname Polychrome
Form   Olla
Dimensions   Height 254; maximum diameter 298
Maker   Unknown
Period/Date   Rio Grande Historic Period (Pueblo
              V); 1710–1750
Also illus-
trated in: Mera 1939, p. 112, plate XLI
              Harlow 1973, plate 23d

FIG. 115.
Catalog No.   35754/12
Collection   School of American Research Collec-
              tions in the Museum of New Mexico
Culture   Historic Pueblo
Province   Middle Rio Grande
Pueblo   Zia
Tradition   Tan/Slipped/Mineral Paint
Type   Zia Polychrome
Form   Dough bowl
Dimensions   Height 232; maximum diameter 495
Maker   Vicentita Pino
Date   Acquired in 1951

FIG. 116.
Catalog No.   8244/11
Collection   School of American Research Collec-
              tions in the Museum of New Mexico
Culture   Kayenta Anasazi
Province   Cibola (Puerco River, Arizona, area)
Site   Allantown (LA 664)
Tradition   Gray/Unslipped/Vegetal Paint
Type   Lino Black-on-gray
Form   Pitcher
Dimensions   Height 216; maximum diameter 121
Period/Date   Basketmaker III; A.D. 600–700
Also illus-
trated in: Roberts 1940, plate 10c

FIG. 117.
Catalog No.   43098/11
Collection   Museum of New Mexico
Culture   Anasazi
Province   Upper San Juan (Arboles, Colorado,
              area)
Site   Sambrito Village (LA 4195), Feature
              15
Tradition   Gray/Unslipped/Vegetal Paint
Type   Bancos Black-on-white
Form   Fish effigy
Dimensions   Length 218; maximum diameter 102
Period/Date   Pueblo I (Piedra Phase); A.D. 900–950
Comment   Possibly a ceremonial vessel,
              probably in the form of a local fish
              (humpback sucker).

FIG. 118.
Catalog No.   19640/11
Collection   Museum of New Mexico
Culture   Anasazi
Province   San Juan Basin (locality unknown)
Site   Unknown
Tradition   Gray/Slipped/Vegetal Paint
Type   McElmo Black-on-white
Form   Bowl
Dimensions   Height 133; maximum diameter 289
Period/Date   Pueblo III; A.D. 1100–1200

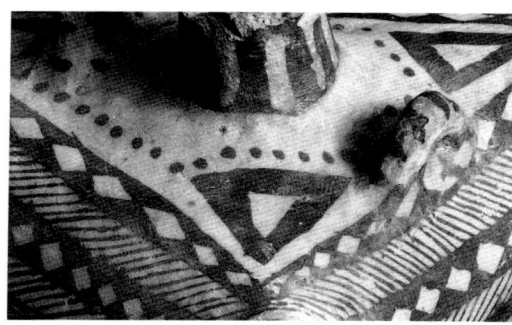

FIG. 119.
Catalog No.   25124/11
Collection   Museum of New Mexico
Culture   Anasazi
Province   Southern San Juan Basin (Tohatchi
              locality)
Site   LA 2497
Tradition   Gray/Slipped/Vegetal Paint
Type   Chaco-McElmo Black-on-white
Form   Dipper
Dimensions   Height of bowl 58; diameters of bowl
              127 by 102; length 284
Period/Date   Early Pueblo III; A.D. 1100–1200
Comment   Hollow handle contains small
              pebbles to make a rattle.
Also illus-
trated in: Whiteford et al. 1989, fig. 23

FIG. 120.
Catalog No.   43335/11
Collection   Museum of New Mexico
Culture   Anasazi
Province   Chaco (Chaco Canyon)
Site   Chetro Ketl, Talus Unit 1 (LA 2470)
Tradition   Gray/Slipped/Vegetal Paint
Type   Chaco-McElmo Black-on-white
Form   Canteen; triangular body
Dimensions   Height 126; maximum side length
              255
Period/Date   Early Pueblo III; A.D. 1100–1200

FIG. 121 (left).
Catalog No.   8822/11
Collection   Museum of New Mexico
Culture   Anasazi
Province   Mesa Verde (locality unknown)
Site   Unknown
Tradition   Gray/Slipped/Vegetal Paint
Type   McElmo or Mesa Verde Black-on-
              white
Form   Pitcher
Dimensions   Height 178; maximum diameter 121
Period/Date   Pueblo III (McElmo/Mesa Verde
              Phase); A.D. 1100–1300

FIG. 121 (right).
Catalog No.   43336/11
Collection   Museum of New Mexico
Culture   Anasazi
Province   Middle San Juan (Animas Valley)
Site   Unknown
Tradition   Gray/Slipped/Vegetal Paint
Type   McElmo Black-on-white
Form   Pitcher
Dimensions   Height 146; maximum diameter 116
Period/Date   Pueblo III (McElmo Phase);
              A.D. 1100–1200

FIG. 122 (left).
Catalog No. 35744/11
Collection Museum of New Mexico
Culture Anasazi
Province Mesa Verde (locality unknown)
Site Unknown
Tradition Gray/Slipped/Vegetal Paint
Type Mesa Verde Black-on-white
Form Bowl
Dimensions Height 76; maximum diameter 165
Period/Date Pueblo III (Mesa Verde Phase); A.D. 1200–1300

FIG. 122 (right).
Catalog No. 19686/11
Collection Museum of New Mexico
Culture Anasazi
Province Mesa Verde (Animas Valley)
Site Unknown
Tradition Gray/Slipped/Vegetal Paint
Type Mesa Verde Black-on-white
Form Bowl
Dimensions Height 67; maximum diameter 171
Period/Date Pueblo III (Mesa Verde Phase); A.D. 1200–1300

FIG. 123 (left).
Catalog No. 8823/11
Collection Museum of New Mexico
Culture Anasazi
Province Mesa Verde (locality unknown)
Site Unknown
Tradition Gray/Slipped/Vegetal Paint
Type Mesa Verde Black-on-white
Form Mug
Dimensions Height 81; maximum diameter 91
Period/Date Pueblo III (Mesa Verde Phase); A.D. 1200–1300

FIG. 123 (right).
Catalog No. 19616/11
Collection Museum of New Mexico
Culture Anasazi
Province Mesa Verde (Animas Valley)
Site Unknown
Tradition Gray/Slipped/Vegetal Paint
Type Mesa Verde Black-on-white
Form Mug
Dimensions Height 90; maximum diameter 96
Period/Date Pueblo III (Mesa Verde Phase); A.D. 1200–1300

FIG. 124 (left).
Catalog No. 19622/11
Collection Museum of New Mexico
Culture Anasazi
Province Mesa Verde (Animas Valley)
Site Unknown
Tradition Gray/Slipped/Vegetal Paint
Type Mesa Verde Black-on-white
Form Mug
Dimensions Height 109; maximum diameter 108
Period/Date Pueblo III (Mesa Verde Phase); A.D. 1200–1300

FIG. 124 (right).
Catalog No. 19621/11
Collection Museum of New Mexico
Culture Anasazi
Province Mesa Verde (Animas Valley)
Site Unknown
Tradition Gray/Slipped/Vegetal Paint
Type Mesa Verde Black-on-white
Form Mug
Dimensions Height 95; maximum diameter 108
Period/Date Pueblo III (Mesa Verde Phase); A.D. 1200–1300

FIG. 125.
Catalog No. 43347/11
Collection Museum of New Mexico
Culture Anasazi
Province Mesa Verde (locality unknown)
Site Unknown
Tradition Gray/Slipped/Vegetal Paint
Type Mesa Verde Black-on-white
Form Dipper
Dimensions Bowl height 62; maximum bowl diameter 144; overall length 304
Period/Date Pueblo III (Mesa Verde Phase); A.D. 1200–1300

FIG. 126.
Catalog No. 8457/11
Collection School of American Research Collections in the Museum of New Mexico
Culture Anasazi
Province Gallina (Gallina River Valley)
Site Unknown
Tradition Gray/Slipped/Vegetal Paint
Type Gallina Black-on-white
Form Bowl
Dimensions Height 176; maximum diameter 203
Period/Date Pueblo III (Largo-Gallina Phase); A.D. 1200–1275

FIG. 127.
Catalog No. 8461/11
Collection School of American Research Collections in the Museum of New Mexico
Culture Anasazi
Province Gallina (Gallina River Valley)
Site Unknown
Tradition Gray/Slipped/Vegetal Paint
Type Gallina Black-on-white
Form Bowl
Dimensions Height 101; maximum diameter 181
Period/Date Pueblo III (Largo-Gallina Phase); A.D. 1200–1275

FIG. 128.
Catalog No. 47420/11
Collection Museum of New Mexico
Culture Anasazi
Province Gallina (Llaves area)
Site LA 12063, South Unit house, floor
Tradition Gray/Slipped/Vegetal Paint
Type Gallina Black-on-white
Form Effigy horned toad
Dimensions Height 76; length 133; width 102
Period/Date Pueblo III (Largo-Gallina Phase); A.D. 1200–1275
Also illustrated in: Whiteford et al. 1989, p. 43

FIG. 129.
Catalog No. 790/11
Collection Museum of New Mexico
Culture Rio Grande Anasazi
Province Jemez
Site Unshagi (LA 123)
Tradition Gray/Slipped/Vegetal Paint
Type Jemez Black-on-white
Form Bowl
Dimensions Height 120; maximum diameter 306
Period/Date Rio Grande Classic Period (Pueblo IV); A.D. 1425–1600
Also illustrated in: Reiter 1938, plate XVb, item H; Dittert and Plog 1980, fig. 154

FIG. 130.
Catalog No. 8576/11
Collection School of American Research Collections in the Museum of New Mexico
Culture Rio Grande Anasazi
Province Jemez
Site Unshagi (LA 123)
Tradition Gray/Slipped/Vegetal Paint
Type Jemez Black-on-white
Form Bowl
Dimensions Height 133; maximum diameter 318
Period/Date Rio Grande Classic Period (Pueblo IV); A.D. 1425–1600

FIG. 131.
Catalog No. 1914/11
Collection Museum of New Mexico
Culture Rio Grande Anasazi
Province Tewa Basin (Santa Fe River Valley)
Site Pindi Pueblo (LA 1)
Tradition Gray/Slipped/Vegetal Paint
Type Pindi Black-on-white
Form Bowl
Dimensions Height 129; maximum diameter 305
Period/Date Rio Grande Coalition Period (Late Pueblo III–Early Pueblo IV); A.D. 1300–1350
Also illustrated in: Stubbs and Stallings 1953, fig. 58F

FIG. 132.
Catalog No. 35750/11
Collection Museum of New Mexico
Culture Rio Grande Anasazi
Province Tewa Basin (Santa Fe River Valley)
Site Pindi Pueblo (LA 1)
Tradition Gray/Slipped/Vegetal Paint
Type Wiyo Black-on-white
Form Bowl
Dimensions Height 142; maximum diameter 340
Period/Date Rio Grande Coalition Period (Late Pueblo III–Early Pueblo IV); A.D. 1325–1425
Comment Pairs of repair holes along a prehistoric crack in the bowl would have been laced with sinew that, as it dried, would shrink, drawing the crack together tightly.
Also illustrated in: Stubbs and Stallings 1953, fig. 46b; Dittert and Plog 1980, fig. 155

FIG. 133.
Catalog No. 50373/11
Collection Museum of New Mexico
Culture Rio Grande Anasazi
Province Galisteo (Upper Pecos Valley)
Site Pecos Pueblo (LA 625)
Tradition Gray/Slipped/Vegetal Paint
Type Wiyo Black-on-white
Form Bowl
Dimensions Height 128; maximum diameter 311
Period/Date Rio Grande Coalition (Late Pueblo III–Early Pueblo IV); A.D. 1300–1400
Comment Compare decorative style with that of the Cieneguilla Glaze-on-yellow, fig. 89.

FIG. 134.
Catalog No. 43677/11
Collection Museum of New Mexico
Culture Rio Grande Anasazi
Province Galisteo (Upper Pecos Valley)
Site Pecos Pueblo (LA 625), North House
Tradition Gray/Slipped/Vegetal Paint
Type Galisteo Black-on-white
Form Bowl
Dimensions Height 127; maximum diameter 279
Period/Date Rio Grande Coalition Period (Late Pueblo III–Early Pueblo IV); A.D. 1300–1400

FIG. 135.
Catalog No. 1437/11
Collection Museum of New Mexico
Culture Rio Grande Anasazi
Province Tewa Basin
Site Unknown
Tradition Gray/Slipped/Vegetal Paint
Type Bandelier Black-on-gray (Biscuit B)
Form Bowl
Dimensions Height 89; maximum diameter 235
Period/Date Rio Grande Classic Period (Middle Pueblo IV); A.D. 1425–1475

FIG. 136.
Catalog No. 21214/11
Collection Museum of New Mexico
Culture Rio Grande Anasazi
Province Tewa Basin (Pajarito Plateau)
Site Puyé (LA 47), probably South House
Tradition Tan/Slipped/Vegetal Paint
Type Cuyamungue Black-on-tan (Biscuit C)
Form Olla
Dimensions Height 222; maximum diameter 363
Period/Date Rio Grande Classic Period (Middle to Late Pueblo IV); A.D. 1475–1600

FIG. 137.
Catalog No. 21852/11
Collection Museum of New Mexico
Culture Rio Grande Anasazi
Province Tewa Basin (Pajarito Plateau)
Site Otowi (LA 169)
Tradition Tan/Slipped/Vegetal Paint
Type Cuyamungue Black-on-tan (Biscuit C)
Form Bowl
Dimensions Height 127; maximum diameter 308
Period/Date Rio Grande Classic Period (Pueblo IV); A.D. 1425–1475
Also illustrated in: Harlow 1973, plate 1c

FIG. 138.
Catalog No. 21445/11
Collection Museum of New Mexico
Culture Rio Grande Anasazi
Province Tewa Basin (Pajarito Plateau)
Site Unknown
Tradition Gray/Slipped/Vegetal Paint
Type Cuyamungue Black-on-tan (Biscuit C)
Form Bowl
Dimensions Height 133; maximum diameter 322
Period/Date Rio Grande Classic (Middle Pueblo IV); A.D. 1425–1475
Comment Although not uncommon, the "salt dish" projecting from the rim is of unknown function. A small hole at one end of this feature is perhaps to hold a feather.

FIG. 139.
Catalog No. 47026/11
Collection Museum of New Mexico
Culture Rio Grande Anasazi
Province Tewa Basin (Tesuque Valley)
Site Cuyamungue Pueblo (LA 38), Room 30
Tradition Tan/Slipped/Vegetal Paint
Type Cuyamungue Black-on-tan (Biscuit C)
Form Olla
Dimensions Height 216; maximum diameter 330
Period/Date Rio Grande Classic (middle-to-late Pueblo IV); A.D. 1475–1600

FIG. 140.
Catalog No. 21447/11
Collection Museum of New Mexico
Culture Rio Grande Anasazi
Province Tewa Basin (Pajarito Plateau)
Site Otowi (LA 169)
Tradition Tan/Slipped/Vegetal Paint
Type Sankawi Black-on-cream
Form Bowl
Dimensions Height 80; maximum diameter 241
Period/Date Rio Grande Classic Period (Late Pueblo IV); 1550–1650

POTTERY VESSEL DATA 151

FIG. 141.
Catalog No.   21919/11
Collection   Museum of New Mexico
Culture   Rio Grande Anasazi
Province   Tewa Basin (Pajarito Plateau)
Site   Tyuonyi (LA 82)
Tradition   Tan/Slipped/Vegetal Paint
Type   Sankawi Black-on-cream
Form   Olla
Dimensions   Height 268; maximum diameter 359
Period/Date   Rio Grande Classic Period (Late Pueblo IV); 1550–1650
Comment   From 1910 excavations by Hewett.
Also illustrated in: Harlow 1973, plate 4a

FIG. 142.
Catalog No.   8167/11
Collection   School of American Research Collections in the Museum of New Mexico
Culture   Rio Grande Anasazi
Province   Tewa Basin (Pajarito Plateau)
Site   Tsirege (LA 170)
Tradition   Tan/Gray/Slipped/Vegetal Paint
Type   Sankawi Black-on-cream
Form   Olla
Dimensions   Height 304; maximum diameter 385
Period/Date   Rio Grande Classic Period (Late Pueblo IV); 1550–1650
Comment   Has a "kickup" (concavity) in bottom to facilitate carrying olla on head and for stability on a flat surface.

FIG. 143.
Catalog No.   21864/11
Collection   Museum of New Mexico
Culture   Historic Pueblo
Province   Tano (Upper Pecos Valley)
Pueblo   Pecos (LA 625)
Tradition   Tan/Slipped/Vegetal Paint
Type   Tewa Polychrome
Form   Olla (water jar)
Dimensions   Height 270; maximum diameter 305
Date   c. 1680
Also illustrated in: Harlow 1973, plate 6d

FIG. 144.
Catalog No.   44862/11
Collection   Museum of New Mexico
Culture   Historic Pueblo
Province   Tewa Basin (Santa Fe River Valley)
Site   Palace of the Governors (LA 4451)
Tradition   Tan/Slipped/Vegetal Paint
Type   Sakona Polychrome
Form   Shouldered bowl
Dimensions   Height 115; maximum diameter 332
Maker   Unknown
Period/Date   Late Rio Grande Classic Period or Early Historic Period (Pueblo IV–V); probably c. 1680
Comment   Found on a floor level of a long-demolished west part of the Palace of the Governors, more than five feet below Lincoln Avenue in downtown Santa Fe. Named by Harlow (Chapman 1970, fig. 3) as Black-on-tan but has a possible uneven faint pink slip on base, thereby making it a polychrome. This may be early evidence of the influence of Tano bearers on red-slipped, glaze-decorated pottery in the Puyé area west of Santa Clara Pueblo. Associated with a sherd of Fig Springs Polychrome (Mexican? Majolica).
Also illustrated in: Harlow 1973, plate 5b
                       Whiteford et al. 1989, fig. 47

FIG. 145 (left).
Catalog No.   11310/12
Collection   School of American Research Collections in the Museum of New Mexico
Culture   Historic Pueblo
Province   Tewa Basin (Pojoaque Valley)
Pueblo   San Ildefonso(?)
Tradition   Tan/Slipped/Mineral Paint and Vegetal Paint
Type   Ogapoge Polychrome
Form   Miniature medicine jar
Dimensions   Height 76; maximum diameter 89
Period/Date   Rio Grande Historic Period (Pueblo V); c. 1720–1760
Comment   An early informant states that such vessels were used in a kiva altar where they were suspended from a bowstring. Compare with similar vessel forms from other sites, periods, and areas.

FIG. 145 (center).
Catalog No.   21277/11
Collection   Museum of New Mexico
Culture   Rio Grande Anasazi
Province   Tewa Basin (Pajarito Plateau)
Site   Unknown
Tradition   Tan/Slipped/Vegetal Paint
Type   Sankawi Black-on-cream
Form   Miniature medicine jar
Dimensions   Height 60; maximum diameter 60
Period/Date   Rio Grande Classic Period (Late Pueblo IV); 1550–1650

FIG. 145 (right).
Catalog No.   11308/12
Collection   School of American Research Collections in the Museum of New Mexico
Culture   Historic Pueblo
Province   Tewa Basin (Pojoaque Valley)
Pueblo   San Ildefonso
Tradition   Tan/Slipped/Vegetal Paint
Type   Tewa Polychrome
Form   Miniature medicine jar
Dimensions   Height 79; maximum diameter 92
Period/Date   Rio Grande Period (Pueblo V); 1650–1730

FIG. 146.
Catalog No.   22023/11
Collection   Museum of New Mexico
Culture   Rio Grande Anasazi
Province   Tewa Basin (Chama Valley near Abiquiu)
Site   Unknown
Tradition   Gray/Slipped/Reduced
Type   Potsuwi'i Incised
Form   Olla
Dimensions   Height 237; maximum diameter 353
Period/Date   Rio Grande Classic Period (Pueblo IV); A.D. 1450–1500
Comment   The origin of this type is obscure; it had no known local predecessor. H. P. Mera (1932) saw possible links to the lower Mississippi, though others suggest the Casas Grandes region of northern Mexico. Bottom of vessel has a "kickup" or concavity to facilitate balancing vessel on head and to provide stability when setting on a flat surface.

FIG. 147.
Catalog No. 8439/11
Collection School of American Research Collections in the Museum of New Mexico
Culture Historic Pueblo
Province Galisteo
Pueblo Pecos (LA 625)
Tradition Gray/Slipped/Reduced
Type Kapo Black
Form Olla
Dimensions Height 307; maximum diameter 334
Period/Date Rio Grande Historic Period (Pueblo V); 1720–1760(?)
Comment Probably traded to Pecos from the Tewa Basin.
Also illustrated in: Harlow 1973, plate 16e
Batkin 1987, p. 40

FIG. 148.
Catalog No. 8389/11
Collection School of American Research Collections in the Museum of New Mexico
Culture Mogollon
Province Jornada (southern)
Site Unknown
Tradition Brown/Slipped/Mineral Paint
Type El Paso Polychrome
Form Bowl
Dimensions Height 117; maximum diameter 247
Period/Date El Paso Phase; A.D. 1200–1400

FIG. 149.
Catalog No. 8784/11
Collection School of American Research Collections in the Museum of New Mexico
Culture Mogollon
Province Jornada (southern)
Site LA 2335
Tradition Brown/Slipped/Mineral Paint
Type El Paso Polychrome
Form Ceremonial bowl
Dimensions Height 116; maximum diameter 137
Period/Date El Paso Phase; A.D. 1200–1400

FIG. 150.
Catalog No. 21417/11
Collection Museum of New Mexico
Culture Mogollon (Chihuahua)
Province Casas Grandes
Site Unknown
Tradition Brown/Slipped/Mineral Paint
Type El Paso Polychrome
Form Jar
Dimensions Height 140; diameter of orifice 115; maximum diameter 201
Period/Date El Paso Phase; A.D. 1200–1400

FIG. 151.
Catalog No. 8619/11
Collection School of American Research Collections in the Museum of New Mexico
Culture Mogollon
Province Jornada (Lake Valley vicinity)
Tradition Brown/Slipped/Mineral Paint
Type El Paso Polychrome
Form Storage jar
Dimensions Height 505; maximum diameter 531
Period/Date El Paso Phase; A.D. 1200–1400

FIG. 152.
Catalog No. 8332/11
Collection School of American Research Collections in the Museum of New Mexico
Culture Chihuahua Mogollon
Province Casas Grandes (near Colonia Juarez)
Site Unknown
Tradition Yellow-Tan/Slipped/Mineral Paint
Type Escondida Polychrome
Form Jar
Dimensions Height 160; maximum diameter 218
Period/Date Medio Period; A.D. 1275–1400
Comment A Casas Grandes equivalent of the Middle Gila type, Tonto Polychrome.

FIG. 153.
Catalog No. 8378/11
Collection School of American Research Collections in the Museum of New Mexico
Culture Chihuahua Mogollon
Province Casas Grandes
Site Unknown
Tradition Brown/Slipped/Mineral Paint
Type Playas Red Incised, Corralitos Variant
Form Jar
Dimensions Height 178; maximum diameter 208
Period/Date Medio and Tardio Periods; A.D. 1350–1450
Comment The Casas Grandes incised treatment has been suggested as the stimulus for the prehistoric Tewa type, Potsuwi'i Incised.

FIG. 154.
Catalog No. 18901/12
Collection School of American Research Collections in the Museum of New Mexico
Culture Historic Pueblo
Province Middle Rio Grande
Pueblo Santo Domingo
Tradition Tan/Slipped/Vegetal Paint
Type Santo Domingo Polychrome
Form Jar
Decoration Decorated in the "Aguilar Style"; see Comment for fig. 159.
Dimensions Height 305; maximum diameter 343
Date c. 1920

FIG. 155.
Catalog No. 12258/12
Collection Museum of New Mexico
Culture Historic Pueblo
Province Middle Rio Grande
Pueblo Santo Domingo
Tradition Tan/Slipped/Vegetal Paint
Type Santo Domingo Polychrome
Form Dough bowl
Dimensions Height 242; maximum diameter 547
Maker Unknown
Date c. 1910–1915
Also illustrated in: Toulouse 1977, p. 66

FIG. 156.
Catalog No. 35755/12
Collection School of American Research Collections in the Museum of New Mexico
Culture Historic Pueblo
Province Middle Rio Grande
Pueblo Santo Domingo
Tradition Tan/Slipped/Vegetal Paint
Type Santo Domingo Polychrome
Form Dough bowl
Dimensions Height 305; maximum diameter 559
Maker Unknown
Date c. 1870–1890

FIG. 157.
Catalog No. 12220/12
Collection Museum of New Mexico
Culture Historic Pueblo
Province Tewa Basin or Middle Rio Grande
Pueblo San Ildefonso or Santo Domingo
Tradition Tan/Slipped/Vegetal Paint
Type Powhoge Polychrome or Santo Domingo Polychrome
Form Olla
Dimensions Height 565; maximum diameter 568
Maker Unknown
Period/Date Rio Grande Historic Period (Pueblo IV); early- to mid-nineteenth century

FIG. 158.
Catalog No. 7727/12
Collection School of American Research Collections in the Museum of New Mexico
Culture Historic Pueblo
Province Middle Rio Grande
Pueblo Santo Domingo
Tradition Tan/Slipped/Reduced
Type Santo Domingo Black-on-black
Form Seed jar
Dimensions Height 114; maximum diameter 203
Maker Maria Calabaza
Date 1930s
Comment A clear attempt to copy the black-on-black of San Ildefonso Pueblo.

FIG. 159.
Catalog No. 47660/12
Collection Museum of New Mexico
Culture Historic Pueblo
Province Middle Rio Grande
Pueblo Santo Domingo
Tradition Tan/Slipped/Vegetal Paint
Type Santo Domingo Polychrome
Form Jar
Dimensions Height 284; maximum diameter 283
Maker Uncertain (see Comment)
Date c. 1910
Comment Batkin (1987, p. 99) refers to this as being in the "Aguilar Style," named after Felipita Aguilar Garcia, Asunción Aguilar Cate, and Mrs. Ramos Aguilar.

FIG. 160.
Catalog No. 7808/12
Collection School of American Research Collections in the Museum of New Mexico
Culture Historic Pueblo
Province Middle Rio Grande
Pueblo Cochiti
Tradition Tan/Slipped/Vegetal Paint
Type Cochiti Polychrome
Form Bowl
Dimensions Height 152; maximum diameter 343
Date Early 1900s

FIG. 161.
Catalog No. 36380/12
Collection Museum of New Mexico
Culture Historic Pueblo
Province Middle Rio Grande
Pueblo Cochiti
Tradition Tan/Slipped/Vegetal Paint
Type Cochiti Polychrome
Form Storage jar
Dimensions Height 400; maximum diameter 491
Maker Stephanita Herrera
Date 1930–1935

FIG. 162.
Catalog No. 12269/12
Collection Museum of New Mexico
Culture Historic Pueblo
Province Middle Rio Grande
Pueblo Cochiti
Tradition Tan/Slipped/Vegetal Paint
Type Cochiti Polychrome
Form Jar
Dimensions Height 546; maximum diameter 401
Maker Trinidad Montoya
Date Acquired in 1946
Comment Decorations are based on recollections of stories of Cochiti buffalo hunts told to the potter when she was a child.

FIG. 163.
Catalog No. 19494/12
Collection Museum of New Mexico
Culture Historic Pueblo
Province Tewa Basin (Pojoaque Valley)
Pueblo San Ildefonso
Tradition Tan/Slipped/Reduced
Type San Ildefonso Black-on-black
Form Jar
Dimensions Height 232; maximum diameter 330
Makers Maria and Julian Martinez
Date 1919
Comment Reportedly one of the first two of this type made by Maria and Julian Martinez.
Also illustrated in: Marriott 1948, pp. 218–19
Peterson 1977, fig. 259

FIG. 164.
Catalog No. 18783/12
Collection Museum of New Mexico
Culture Historic Pueblo
Province Tewa Basin (Pojoaque Valley)
Pueblo San Ildefonso
Tradition Tan/Slipped/Vegetal Paint
Type San Ildefonso Polychrome
Form Jar
Dimensions Height 359; maximum diameter 451
Maker Maria Martinez
Date 1925–1935
Comment Not signed, though Maria said she made it.

FIG. 165.
Catalog No. 18922/12
Collection Museum of New Mexico
Culture Historic Pueblo
Province Tewa Basin (Pojoaque Valley)
Pueblo San Ildefonso
Tradition Tan/Slipped/Vegetal Paint
Type San Ildefonso Polychrome
Form Prayer meal bowl
Dimensions Height 135; length 201; width 127
Maker Maria Martinez
Date 1922
Comment Won second prize in its class at the first Southwest Indian Fair at Santa Fe, 1922. Design apparently copied from a Tesuque Polychrome dough bowl in the Museum of New Mexico Collections. Compare hatch-filled figure with that in Harlow 1973, plate 12f, and Whiteford et al. 1989, fig. 80.

FIG. 166.
Catalog No. 48033/12
Collection Museum of New Mexico
Culture Historic Pueblo
Province Tewa Basin (Pojoaque Valley)
Pueblo San Ildefonso
Tradition Tan/Slipped/Vegetal Paint
Type San Ildefonso Polychrome
Form Seed jar
Dimensions Height 191; maximum diameter 241
Maker Blue Corn (Crucita Calabaza)
Date 1976
Also illustrated in: Toulouse 1977, p. 76
Edelman 1979, fig. 8c

FIG. 167.
Catalog No. 47651/12
Collection Museum of New Mexico
Culture Historic Pueblo
Province Tewa Basin (Espanola Valley)
Pueblo Santa Clara
Tradition Tan/Slipped
Type Santa Clara Red-on-tan, Appliqué/Sculpted
Form Jar
Dimensions Height 217; maximum diameter 197
Maker Jody Folwell
Date 1975
Comment Won first prize in its category at 1975 Southwestern Association on Indian Affairs (SWAIA) Indian Market, Santa Fe.

FIG. 168.
Catalog No. 18911/12
Collection School of American Research Collections in the Museum of New Mexico
Culture Historic Pueblo
Province Tewa Basin (Espanola Valley)
Pueblo Santa Clara
Tradition Tan/Slipped/Reduced
Type Santa Clara Black
Form Closed bowl
Dimensions Height 130; maximum diameter 271
Maker Unknown
Date Pre–1942

FIG. 169.
Catalog No. 49543/12
Collection Museum of New Mexico
Culture Historic Pueblo
Province Tewa Basin (Espanola Valley)
Pueblo Santa Clara
Tradition Tan/Slipped/Reduced
Type Santa Clara Black
Form Melon bowl
Dimensions Height 122; greatest diameter 163
Maker Mela Youngblood
Date 1978
Comment Won first prize in its category at 1978 Southwestern Association on Indian Affairs (SWAIA) Indian Market, Santa Fe.

FIG. 170.
Catalog No. 19349/12
Collection Museum of New Mexico
Culture Historic Pueblo
Province Tewa Basin (Espanola Valley)
Pueblo San Juan
Tradition Tan/Slipped/Textured
Type San Juan Incised
Form Jar
Dimensions Height 234; maximum diameter 283
Maker Tomasita Montoya
Date 1958
Comment Incising revived at San Juan in early 1930s copying the prehistoric type, Potsuwi'i Incised, fig. 147.

FIG. 171.
Catalog No. 49747/12b
Collection Museum of New Mexico
Culture Historic Pueblo
Province Tewa Basin (Espanola Valley)
Pueblo Santa Clara Pueblo
Tradition Tan/Slipped
Type Santa Clara Red Sgraffito
Form "Jewel"; miniature "medicine jar"
Dimensions Height 57; maximum diameter 108
Maker Joseph Lonewolf
Date 1981

FIG. 172.
Catalog No. 18880/12
Collection Museum of New Mexico
Culture Historic Pueblo
Province Tewa Basin (Espanola Valley)
Pueblo San Juan
Tradition Tan/Slipped/Mineral Paint
Type San Juan Carved Polychrome
Form Jar
Dimensions Height 300; maximum diameter 324
Maker Reyecita Trujillo
Date 1940
Also illustrated in: Toulouse 1977, p. 74
Harlow 1973, plate 18c
Dittert and Plog 1980, fig. 87

FIG. 173.
Catalog No. 19337/12   19377
Collection Museum of New Mexico
Culture Historic Pueblo
Province Tewa Basin (Espanola Valley)
Pueblo Santa Clara
Tradition Tan/Slipped/Mineral Paint
Type Santa Clara Polychrome
Form Jar
Dimensions Height 156; maximum diameter 155
Makers Lela and Luther Gutierrez
Date 1957
Also illustrated in: Toulouse 1977, p. 75

FIG. 174.
Catalog No. 48663/11
Collection Museum of New Mexico
Culture Historic Pueblo
Province Jemez
Pueblo Jemez
Tradition Tan/Slipped/Mineral Glaze Paint
Type Pecos Glaze Polychrome (Revival)
Form "Medicine" bowl
Dimensions Height 70; maximum diameter 213
Maker Evelyn M. Vigil
Date 1977

GLOSSARY

A

Acoma Province. Anasazi province in New Mexico bounded by Mount Taylor (north), Rio Puerco (east), San Agustin Plains (south), and the Grants lava flow (west); utility pottery of this region periodically shows Mogollon influence or presence.

Anasazi Culture. Prehistoric, sedentary, agricultural, pottery-making culture of the northern Southwest; considered to be largely the ancestral culture to the modern Pueblo Indians of New Mexico and the Hopi of Arizona. *See also* Mogollon Culture.

Anthropomorphic. Of human shape, generally in reference to representational painted pottery decoration and to some forms of effigies.

Aplastic. See Temper.

Appliqué. Generally an uncommon prehistoric treatment wherein short, linear, or spiral ropes (sometimes animal figures, as in Tularosa Black-on-white) of clay are attached as handles or as decoration to the exteriors of pottery vessels.

Awanyu. Representation of the mythical keeper of the water of springs and streams in the Tewa Basin Province. Commonly depicted on prehistoric (Pueblo IV) Biscuitware and rarely in this manner on historic Tewa pottery. Modern San Ildefonso and Santa Clara potters depict Awanyu as the horned or plumed serpent, a religious figure derived from Mexico and occasionally appearing on prehistoric Pueblo pottery and rock art.

B

Band Design. Painted decoration occurring on bowl interiors and exteriors and jar exteriors wherein the design is restricted to the area between two generally widely separated horizontal framing lines, leaving areas above and below the band undecorated or with different decoration.

Basketmaker (sometimes *Basker Maker*). The stages of Anasazi development when only basketry or hide containers were made (Basketmaker I and Basketmaker II); that is, before the introduction of pottery making, or when the idea of pottery making was first introduced, experimented with, and disseminated (Basketmaker III).

Basketmaker–Pueblo Culture. A general name given to the prehistoric, sedentary (largely), agricultural, pottery-making (largely) culture of the northern Southwest. Replaced by the name "Anasazi" in the 1930s.

Beaker. Tall, generally cylindrical container with parallel or slightly tapering sides.

Bichrome. Pottery with a single-color painted decoration applied to a natural or slipped background color. Sometimes called "duochrome."

Biscuit Ware. Principal Tewa Basin Anasazi painted ware during Pueblo IV; thick and porous, it was so named because of its similarity to the bisque or biscuit stage (before the second firing) of modern glazed pottery. Three Biscuitware types are recognized: Biscuit A, or Abiquiu Black-on-gray; Biscuit B, or Bandelier Black-on-gray; and Biscuit C, or Cuyamungue Black-on-tan, the latter the immediate ancestor of Sankawi Black-on-cream.

Black-on-Black. Painted decoration technique developed c. 1919 by Maria and Julian Martinez of San Ildefonso Pueblo, wherein slipped pottery vessels are highly polished, then decorated with designs painted with the same slip material that is left unpolished, and finally fired in a reducing atmosphere to produce two shades of black—one highly polished, the other matte or dull. The same vessel fired in an oxidizing atmosphere would produce two shades of red.

Bowl. A neckless, hemispherical, or subhemispherical vessel whose orifice diameter is usually its greatest dimension, though some vessels with slightly incurving rims may be considered to be bowls.

Brown-Firing Clay. A residual clay produced by the breakdown of iron-rich volcanic deposits. In an oxidizing atmosphere, the iron minerals may be converted to iron oxide, producing a brown or rust-colored surface and paste color.

Brown Ware. Pottery whose basic fired color is brown, even though this color may be masked with a usually red slip.

Brushing. See Scoring.

Burnish. See Polish.

C

Canteen. Usually a small flask for carrying water, though large canteens with capacities of a gallon or more were made during Pueblo IV and Pueblo V.

"Capitan" Figure. A design often found on Pueblo IV glaze-decorated pottery of the Middle Rio Grande Province. It may represent the very sacred pole still carried in modern Corn Dances of the Rio Grande pueblos. It may also be a Middle Rio Grande conception of the "awanyu" figure occurring during the same period in the Tewa Basin Province.

Carbon Paint. Black-firing pigment that is the boiled-down residue of the leaves and stems of commonly occurring native plants in the northern Southwest. In New Mexico and the Mesa Verde

Province in Colorado, the plant was probably Rocky Mountain bee plant, or beeweed (*Cleome serrulata*); in northeastern Arizona, tansy mustard (*Descurainia richardsonii*) was preferred. In the Rio Grande area today, the paint is called guaco. Characteristics of carbon paint include a slight blurring at the edges of painted lines (especially when compared to iron paint); blacks that tend to be watery and not dense; and an appearance that the painted surface was polished after painting (polish carries over the painted decoration in contrast to iron-paint pottery). Recent investigations suggest that the black results not from charring of the plant material during firing but from the presence of organic iron compounds.

Carved. A technique developed at Santa Clara Pueblo requiring relatively thick vessel walls decorated through the careful carving of selected parts of the vessel wall to produce sculpted designs.

Ceramic. A prepared clay product that, when fired to optimum temperature, results in an irreversible physical and chemical alteration—sometimes fused—of its constituents (clay and temper) to the extent that the product becomes relatively durable and retains its desired shape as a pottery bowl or jar.

Chaco Province. Province of the Anasazi Culture in northwestern New Mexico, including the middle drainages of the Chaco River and the southern and southwestern parts of the San Juan Basin.

Chuska Province. Province of the Anasazi Culture in the western San Juan Basin primarily between the Chuska Mountains (on the New Mexico–Arizona boundary) and the northward flowing segment of the Chaco River.

Cibola Province (Anasazi Culture). The area between the Continental Divide on the east, U.S. Highway 666 on the west, and from the Puerco River south of the San Juan Basin to near Reserve, New Mexico.

Clapboard Corrugated. See Plain Corrugated.

Clay. A soil comprised largely of anhydrous aluminum silicates having a high plasticity index in relation to its liquid limit, with grains of less than 0.005 millimeter (mm).

Clay Paint. Clays occurring in or purposefully ground to a sufficiently fine texture so that it can be applied and controlled with a brush for line-work decoration.

Coiling. The construction of vessel walls through the welding or pinching together of successive ropes or coils of clay. (Compare with "wheel-thrown pottery").

Coil-Paddle-and-Anvil-Technique. Pottery-making technique of the prehistoric Hohokam Culture of southern Arizona in which following the construction of the vessel by coiling, the coil junctures are compressed and concealed through hammering the exterior vessel wall with a wooden paddle at the point where, on the interior, the curved surface of a stone anvil is placed; sometimes simply called the paddle-and-anvil technique. See also Coil-scrape Technique.

Coil-Scrape Technique. The pottery-finishing technique used by the Anasazi and Mogollon cultures whereby coil junctures are compressed and obliterated by scraping them with a curved edge tool, such as a worked potsherd or a gourd rind. See also Coil-paddle-and-anvil Technique.

Cord-Marked. An uncommon decorative treatment in the Southwest wherein cordage is pressed into the leather-hard surface of a vessel. Occurs almost exclusively in the extreme southwestern parts of New Mexico and adjacent Mexico. Non-Anasazi (Woodland Cultural Tradition) Indians of the Panhandle Aspect in northeastern New Mexico and adjacent states characteristically made cord-marked pottery between A.D. 1000 and 1500.

Corrugated (or *Corrugation*). Intentionally leaving unobliterated the narrow (usually 3 to 8 mm wide) coils on the exterior surface of primarily utility vessels, which may function in enhancing heat absorption in cooking, aid evaporation as water containers, provide a more secure grip when carrying, or for decoration.

Crazing, Crackling. Extremely fine cracks found on surfaces of some vessels often resulting from shrinkage of thick slips, especially on Pueblo III types, such as Mesa Verde Black-on-white, St. Johns Polychrome, and Tularosa Black-on-white, as well as modern Cochiti and Santo Domingo black-on-cream types.

D

Design. The arrangements of details, particularly form and decoration, that are integral to a pottery work.

Design Symmetry. Tendency for the structure of pottery decoration (elements, motifs, and color) to be symmetrical and appearing in motion in relation to a single axis (a line), point, or intersecting axes. It assumes that all members of a given group, through living together and communicating, will use the same symmetrical structure in decorating their pottery.

Dipper. Scooplike vessel for serving water or food; early versions appear to replicate the shape and function of gourds cut in half lengthwise. Later dippers were essentially small bowls with a long solid or hollow handle, the latter sometimes having small pebbles inside to produce a rattling sound. Painted and unpainted dippers were more common in provinces in the San Juan and Little Colorado drainages (Basketmaker III to Pueblo III) and generally uncommon in Rio Grande provinces.

Double Vessel. Pottery vessels comprised of two bowls linked together at the rim and with a reinforcing strap at the base or sharing a common vessel wall; jar or canteen forms whose necks are joined at a single orifice.

Dough Bowl. Very large bowls in which to mix bread dough (and probably other functions), generally made from the late eighteenth century to the early twentieth century by various Rio Grande pueblos, especially Santo Domingo, Cochiti, and Zia.

Duck Pot. Elongated vessel with its neck and orifice placed asymmetrically toward one end, thereby making the vessel resemble a duck's body or a shoe.

Duochrome. See Bichrome.

E

Eccentric Form. Atypical or uncommon vessel shapes, such as ring, tripod, double, stirrup, lobed, and (except in Pueblo IV) rectangular forms; often thought to have had ceremonial functions.

Effigy. An anthropomorphic or zoomorphic vessel sufficiently large to have a hollow rather than solid interior. Though exceedingly rare, some prehistoric San Juan Basin specimens copy anthropomorphic effigies of northern Mexico.

F

Figurine. A small anthropomorphic or (more commonly) zoomorphic figure usually having a solid interior; possibly made for test-firing of pottery clays. Some appear to have been toys and others possibly fetishes.

Fire Cloud. A roundish or irregular discoloration on a vessel exterior; usually the result of burning fuel coming in direct contact with the vessel during firing and causing localized reduction. In prehistoric times, the potter would protect the pots to be fired by covering them with large sherds from broken pots. This may also be done today, though pieces of sheet metal may also be used.

Framing Lines. Painted lines that enclose a design element that may be solid-filled or filled with hatching. Single or multiple framing lines may enclose band or panel designs, as in Mimbres Black-on-white and Mesa Verde Black-on-white.

Fugitive Slip or Paint. An unfired water-soluble pigment applied to the surface of a vessel *after* firing, as in Lino gray, Fugitive red variant, and including modern watercolor paints formerly used by Tesuque, Jemez, and some other pueblos. Also, an imperfectly fired slip or pigment that does not adhere well to the vessel surface.

G

Galisteo Basin Province (Anasazi Culture). Principally, the extensive drainage area between the southern end of the Sangre de Cristo Mountains and the northern end of the Sandia Mountains, but with extensions eastward to the upper Pecos Valley, south to near Leyba, and west to the vicinity of Cochiti Pueblo on the Rio Grande.

Gallina Province (also Largo-Gallina Province). A divergent Anasazi group in north-central New Mexico that separated from groups in the Upper San Juan Province and moved southeast to occupy lands on both sides of the Continental Divide in the Largo (west) and Gallina (east) drainages.

Glaze Paint. A mineral pigment containing iron, manganese, and/or copper minerals, together with a lead mineral, such as cerussite, which acts as a flux, causing other minerals to melt at a lower temperature and fuse as a glaze. Colors achieved include black, brown, apple green, and purple, the latter two primarily in the Puerco-Zuni Province.

Glaze Wares. Pottery decorated with glaze-producing pigments; glazes were not used to waterproof vessels. Glazes were used as solid-design elements or as framing lines for solid-red elements. Accidental lead glazes occurred early (Basketmaker III) in the Upper San Juan Province, intentionally later in the Puerco-Zuni and Upper Little Colorado provinces (Late Pueblo III), and still later in the Acoma, Middle Rio Grande, Salinas, and Rio Abajo provinces (Pueblo IV).

Gray-Firing Clay. Generally clay of sedimentary origin often high in carbon content and low in red-firing iron minerals; associated most frequently with Anasazi Culture sites on the Colorado Plateau.

Gray Ware. Unslipped and unpainted utility pottery made from gray-firing clay; such grayware is diagnostic of Anasazi provinces. Early Anasazi painted pottery was unslipped and thus could be considered gray ware, though even such a color designation may be imprecise. Compare with Brown ware.

H

Hakataya Culture. Fourth and most recently defined of the prehistoric pottery-making cultures of the Southwest, occupying west-central Arizona and adjacent parts of California and northwest Mexico. Considered to be ancestral to modern Yuman-speaking tribes of the same area. Their pottery was made using the coil-paddle-and-anvil technique.

Hatching. Painted (also incised in the Tewa Basin in Pueblo IV) decoration consisting of straight or occasionally wavy closely spaced lines used diagonally or at right angles as fillers between framing lines. Sometimes called "hachure."

Historic. In New Mexico, generally the period since sustained Spanish influence on the Pueblo Indians began; that is, beginning in 1598 with the establishment of permanent Spanish settlements (excluding earlier brief contact by explorers such as Coronado).

Hohokam Culture. One of the four basic prehistoric pottery-making cultures of the Southwest whose greatest extent included central and south-central Arizona, from near Flagstaff south to the International Boundary. Their pottery was made using the coil-paddle-and-anvil technique.

I

Incising. A decorative technique using a pointed instrument to draw simple designs on the plain exterior surface of pottery vessels; periodically popular in some Anasazi, Mogollon, and Hohokam provinces. Sometimes used in combination with corrugation.

Indented Corrugated. Generally utility pottery whose individual coils have been purposefully left deeply to moderately finger-indented on the exterior during the coiling construction of the vessel wall. "Exuberant" corrugated, with wide coils with vertically or diagonally aligned broad, deep indentations on vessel necks, was common in the Chaco and Chuska provinces (Late Pueblo I to Early Pueblo II). Later Pueblo II and contemporary Mogollon versions had narrower coils and smaller but generally carefully aligned indentations; in Pueblo III, coils appear increasingly irregular in width and indentation and begin a trend toward coil obliteration.

Iron-Manganese Paint. Mineral pigment, usually mostly an iron oxide but containing some manganese mineral. Often the pigment type used on White Mountain redware types.

Iron Paint. Mineral pigment made from various iron minerals (hematite, limonite, and magnetite), probably mixed with a vegetal medium as a binder. Used commonly by most Anasazi provinces in New Mexico and Colorado (Basketmaker III through Late Pueblo II) and later in Salinas, Cibola, and Mimbres provinces. Distinguished from vegetal or "carbon" paint in the sharpness of edges of lines, general denseness of color (black or oxidized to brown and even red), matte surface (not appearing to have been polished over the paint, as does vegetal paint), and greater tendency to flake off or be fugitive.

J

Jar. Any vessel with a definable (constricted) orifice, with or without a neck. *See* Olla.

Jemez Province. Anasazi province largely confined to the upper drainages of the Jemez River northwest of Albuquerque, New Mexico, and whose populations were the prehistoric ancestors of the modern pueblo of Jemez. Apparently largely vacant by Late Pueblo III.

Jornada Province. Easternmost province of the Mogollon Culture, largely in south-central New Mexico and adjacent parts of Texas and Chihuahua, Mexico, and generally east and southeast of the Mimbres Province.

K

Kickup. A concavity in the bottoms of ollas (water jars) common during Late Pueblo IV and into the modern period. Presumably to permit balancing the vessel on one's head but also providing greater stability when the vessel is placed on a flat surface.

Kiva Jar. Distinctive seed jar form of Mesa Verde Black-on-white having a recess around its rim to hold a lid.

L

Ladle. See *Dipper*.

Line-Break. A common feature of Anasazi pottery decoration where an encircling band design or painted rim has been intentionally left incomplete, supposedly to allow the spirit of the vessel to escape.

Lobed Vessel. Usually a canteenlike vessel comprised of two or more segments joined at a single orifice.

Lug. A simple handle (often more than one) projecting from the side of a vessel to facilitate lifting or perhaps functioning as cleats for suspending the vessel over a fire or above the ground.

M

Matte-on-Black. See *Black-on-black*.

Matte Paint. An unpolished, often dull-surfaced paint, as with many nonglazing mineral paints or slip clays used as paint.

Mesa Verde Province. One of the northernmost Anasazi provinces located in the extreme southwestern Colorado, the middle San Juan River Valley in New Mexico, and extending slightly into the adjoining corners of Arizona and Utah.

Micaceous. Having a paste containing conspicuous amounts of pulverized mica or mica schist as temper. Also, having a slip of micaceous clay (not necessarily with a micaceous paste). Especially common in the Tewa Basin and Middle Rio Grande provinces during Pueblo IV.

Middle Rio Grande Province (Anasazi Culture). Generally the Rio Grande drainages south of a line drawn between Frijoles Canyon (near Los Alamos) and Pecos Pueblo to the vicinity of Belen, New Mexico, not including the Galisteo Basin Province and the Jemez Province.

Middle Rio Puerco Province (Anasazi Culture). Northwest of Albuquerque along the drainages of the Rio Puerco (sometimes with the qualifier "of the east" to distinguish it from the Puerco River that flows through Gallup, New Mexico), generally north of Interstate 40.

Mimbres Province (Mogollon Culture). One of the principal provinces of the Mogollon Culture, located largely in southwestern New Mexico but extending somewhat into southeastern Arizona and the northern parts of the states of Chihuahua and Sonora, Mexico.

Mineral Paint. Naturally occurring pigment that, when mixed with a binder or compacted by polishing, when fired will sinter and adhere to a pottery vessel. Though defined separately, glaze-producing pigments of the late Pueblo III and Pueblo IV periods are mineral paints.

Miniature. Very small (generally less than 10 centimeters [cm] in diameter) pottery vessels; interpreted as not being used as household utensils. Possibly for ceremonial use, as children's toys, or to test pottery materials for firing. Sometimes made by coiling; other times by modeling. See *Pinch Pot*.

Modeled. Shaping small vessels or figurines with the fingers only and without use of the coiling technique.

Mogollon Culture. One of the four basic Southwestern cultures occupying an area comprising southeastern and east-central Arizona, the southwestern and south-central parts of New Mexico, and adjacent parts of the states of Chihuahua and Sonora, Mexico.

Mug. A small cylindrical vessel with a vertical handle on one side, such as a cup.

N

Neckbanded (or Neck Banded). Jar or pitcher forms of utility pottery whose broad neck coils have not been obliterated.

Neck Corrugated. Jar forms of utility pottery where narrow plain and/or indented corrugated coils are allowed to remain only around the neck or upper one-third to one-half of vessel exteriors; coils around the vessel bottom have been completely obliterated to produce a smooth surface. This treatment succeeds neckbanding at about the same time in both the Anasazi (Late Pueblo I and Early Pueblo II [A.D. 850–875 to A.D. 950–1000]) and Mogollon (Mimbres and Cibola provinces) culture areas and somewhat later in the Jornada Province.

O

Obliterated Corrugated. Indented or plain corrugations that have been intentionally or inadvertently partially smoothed, leaving only faint undulations on the exteriors of utility pottery. Sometimes called "blind corrugated."

Olla (pronounced "oy-yah"). The Spanish term usually applied to a medium-size to large water storage jar. Large Pueblo III examples may have deeply indented finger grips near the base to facilitate pouring.

Oxidizing Atmosphere. A stage in pottery firing when the pottery is exposed to oxygen (air), bringing about oxidation of iron minerals and carbon in the clay.

P

Painted Ware. Pottery with usually permanently painted decoration using mineral or vegetal pigments. Except in its earliest types, most painted pottery is slipped before painting. Characteristically, painted pottery is used for serving foods and liquids (bowls, ollas, pitchers, dippers, cups) as well as for ceremonial purposes.

Pajarito Plateau. The mesa and canyon localities around the flanks of the Jemez Mountains which were settlement areas of three Anasazi provinces: southwestern (Jemez), southern and southeastern (Middle Rio Grande), and northeastern and northern (Tewa Basin).

Panel Design. Painted decoration on vessel interiors and/or exteriors in which the designs may be as isolated elements or as part of a horizontal band that has been divided into segments by vertical lines.

Paste. The combination of clay and tempering material needed for the manufacture of most prehistoric pottery.

Patterned Corrugated. Usually utility pottery whose corrugated coils have been selectively indented or left plain to produce simple geometric designs or as alternating plain and indented coils.

Pecos Classification. A numbered sequence of periods or stages (Basketmaker I–III and Pueblo I–V) of the Anasazi Culture that describes the introduction or evolution of its principal attributes, such as subsistence, village plan, dwelling plan, or pottery style.

Pictorial Design. A representational (such as human, animal, or ritual figures) rather than geometric painted design. Occurring only rarely on Anasazi pottery until Pueblo IV (Hopi, Zuni, and Middle Rio Grande provinces); common and best known on bowl interiors of Mimbres Black-on-white (A.D. 1000 to 1150) and some Hohokam Culture types.

Pinch Pot. A small modeled rather than coiled vessel formed by pressing the thumb into a ball of clay, with accompanying thinning and shaping of the vessel wall.

Pitcher. Jar form usually taller than wide, with a

constricted orifice and a single vertical handle attached near the rim and usually to a lower part of the body. A prepared pouring spout is usually absent in prehistoric pitchers.

Plain Corrugated. Coiling treatment of utility ware exterior where narrow (3 to 8.5 mm) coils have not been embellished with pinching or indenting; may be called clapboard corrugated, especially when the lower edge of the coil is considerably everted, as with clapboards on a house. The treatment generally developed out of neckbanding in Late Pueblo I, initially occurring as a neck-corrugated but eventually covering most of the vessel exterior. Once developed, it was often used interchangeably with indented corrugated or in combination with the latter as patterned corrugated. Occasionally further decorated with simple incised lines.

Plainware. General designation for unslipped, unpainted utility, regardless of firing color of the clay.

Polish. To polish an unslipped or slipped vessel, usually through compaction of the leather-hard surface by rubbing with a dense, very smooth stream pebble. The syllable "burn" in burnish is sometimes thought to refer to a lustrous black surface, as with modern San Ildefonso black-on-black. Without the controlled-reduction firing of that type, it would fire red but would still be burnished. Most Anasazi-painted pottery is polished but not always to a high degree; until late Pueblo III in some provinces, its utility pottery was not. *See also* Stone-stroked.

Polychrome. Having two or more painted or slipped colors on the same vessel (not necessarily all on the same surface of the vessel).

Potsherd. A fragment of a pottery vessel; sometimes simply called a sherd or shard. Edges of potsherds were sometimes ground smooth to be used as pottery-making tools (scrapers or pukis), gaming pieces, spindle whorls, and shallow dishes. Beginning in Late Pueblo I, Anasazi potters in some provinces ground up potsherds for temper or grog—usually for painted pottery but sometimes for utility, as well.

Pottery Assemblage. All the locally made and non-locally made pottery types found associated with one another on a given archaeological site.

Pottery Series. A group of pottery types within a pottery ware having a specific attribute in common and generally assumed to have been made in a sequence through time.

Pottery Type. A class of pottery that shares all the basic ceramic descriptors (firing color, temper, surface treatment, design, and general form) and is shown to have a definable areal distribution and time range.

Prayer Meal Bowl. Various small round or rectangular bowls, sometimes with stepped sides or ends, for containing specially prepared cornmeal for ritual blessings. May have painted or appliqué symbolic decoration.

Pre-Columbian. The period before the discovery of America by Christopher Columbus in 1492. The term is generally not used in reference to Southwestern Indian materials.

Prehistoric. In the Southwest, the period before the establishment of permanent Spanish colonies, whose presence would influence the cultural development of the native Indian cultures. In New Mexico, the first colony was established in 1598 near present-day San Juan Pueblo.

Province. Primarily a geographic subdivision of the area occupied by one of the four basic Southwestern prehistoric cultures and whose associated cultural traits are sufficiently different from those of other provinces.

Pueblo. The Spanish term for town or village. Variously applied to villages of the modern Tanoan, Keres, and Zuni Indians of New Mexico and the Hopi of Arizona; the culture of these Indian groups; and ruined dwellings, regardless of size, formerly inhabited by prehistoric or historic Indians having Pueblo or Pueblo-like culture.

Puerco-Zuni Province. Anasazi province located largely west of the Continental Divide, south of the San Juan Basin, north of U.S. Highway 60, and east of U.S. Highway 666.

Puki. A basin-shaped pottery or basketry container which provided some prehistoric or historic Southwestern Indians with a work platform in which they could start their coiled pottery vessels. Although the puki can be slowly rotated as the coiling progresses, it is not an incipient potter's wheel.

R

Reducing Atmosphere. The pottery-firing condition in which air is excluded, thereby preventing oxidation—and often a change in color—of the mineral constituents of the clays and paints.

Redware. Usually pottery having one or both surfaces slipped with a red-firing clay; some early Mogollon brownware tends to fire reddish and may be called a redware.

Refractory Clay. In the prehistoric Southwest, unfluxed (untempered) clay whose maturing or sintering temperature cannot be achieved using normal aboriginal firing methods; for example, pure kaolin.

Rim Form. The shape and attitude of a vessel rim achieved through modeling or sculpturing.

Ring Vessel. A specialized tubular or doughnut-shaped canteen form with a projecting orifice.

Rio Abajo Province. A province sometimes sharing both Mogollon and Anasazi attributes straddling the Rio Grande from just south of Belen, New Mexico, southward to the northern end of Elephant Butte Reservoir; also includes settlements along some drainages west of the Rio Grande. The province primarily includes the defined range of the Piro (a Pueblo group) of the early historic period.

Rod (or Rope) Handle. A vessel handle formed with a solid coil or rope of clay; attached to one exterior side of a bowl, as in a dipper or ladle, or placed either vertically or horizontally on bowl, jar, pitcher, or mug exteriors. Compare with strap handle.

S

Salinas Province. Province mainly east, southeast, and south of the southern end of the Manzano Mountains in the vicinity of Mountainair, New Mexico. This Pueblo group often shares attributes of both the Anasazi and Mogollon cultures.

Scoring. Intentional roughening of a vessel surface, apparently with a corncob or a bunch of stiff grass, as in the Mogollon Brown Ware type, Alma Scored (scored around the neck only) and Chupadero Black-on-white (on the unpainted surface of bowls and jars) from the Salinas and Jornada provinces.

Seed Jar. A usually wide, neckless jar with a narrow orifice; a low center of gravity presumably prevented it from tipping and spilling its contents.

Series. Pottery types within a pottery ware in a small geographical area that appear to follow one another in a time sequence.

Sgraffito. A modern Pueblo technique of pottery decoration whereby a slipped vessel is intricately incised before firing, exposing a contrasting paste color.

Sherd Temper. Temper made from pulverized potsherds. Its first use in New Mexico occurred in such Pueblo I painted types as Red Mesa Black-on-white (Cibola White Ware) and Tunicha Black-on white (Chuska White Ware). Other later types, such as Mancos Black-on-white (Mesa Verde White Ware) and Wingate Black-on-red (White Mountain Red Ware), also used sherd temper, as did gray-firing utility types in the Chaco and Puerco-Zuni provinces. Sherd temper is in traditional Acoma and Zuni painted pottery.

Slip. An application of very fine-grained clay to one or both surfaces of a vessel to cover color or texture imperfections in the paste, provide a surface of uniform texture for polishing, and provide contrast for painted or sgraffito decoration. A slip may cover only part of a vessel surface.

Slip Casting. Pottery made by pouring fluid slip of clay and temper into a dry plaster mold. The latter absorbs excess water until the vessel wall is of desired thickness, then the excess slip is poured off and the vessel allowed to dry. Such greenware vessels may be decorated and fired (usually in an electric kiln) or sold unfired or decoration and firing by others. Some Acoma potters have adopted this method due to problems of pitting of pottery made from native clay and with the explanation that the painted designs are traditional, and examples of slip cast pottery are known for Zuni, Zia, and Isleta (see Blair and Blair 1986: 172–173).

Smoothed. A vessel surface that has been scraped or sanded to the desired contour but has not been polished.

Smudged. The intentional blackening of one or both vessel surfaces through controlled-reduction firing.

Stirrup Jar. A specialized canteen form with two necks projecting from the top of the vessel that are joined to form a single orifice.

Stone-Stroked. A polishing technique on large vessels of the historic period, whereby the potter restricts the direction of movement of the polishing stone to produce generally parallel polishing marks.

Strap Handle. A broad, flat, usually vertical handle attached to one side of a vessel, usually a pitcher, mug, or dipper. Attachment of the handle ends may be simple welding—firmly compressed against the vessel exterior—or riveted—inserted in holes through the vessel wall, flared, and compressed against the interior.

Striated. See Scoring.

T

Taos Province. Northernmost Anasazi province in the Rio Grande drainage; includes the areas of Taos and Picuris pueblos.

Temper. Coarse to fine sand, crushed sandstone, igneous or metamorphic rock, or crushed potsherds added to clay to counteract shrinkage during drying and firing. Sometimes called "aplastic."

Tewa Basin Province (Anasazi Culture). The eastern and western drainages of the Rio Grande from near Velarde downstream to White Rock Canyon (near Los Alamos) and the Rio Chama drainage below Abiquiu Reservoir; generally the ancestral area of the modern Tewa Pueblos.

Textured. Any form of modifying the surface (usually the exterior) of a vessel through incising, scoring, punching, corrugating, or sculpting.

Tooled. Texturing using a sharp implement, such as a bone awl, the end of a stick, or the end of a hollow reed.

Tradition. A term referring to the conscious adherence to or long-term continuous use of a basic manufacturing technique or decorative theme.

U

Upper San Juan Province. Anasazi province occupying the drainages of the San Juan River in New Mexico and Colorado, roughly between Blanco, New Mexico, and Pagosa Springs, Colorado.

Utility Ware. Pottery whose primary function is for cooking or storing of foods. Usually womewhat porous with a rough or textured (such as corrugated or incised) exterior surface and a smoothed (Anasazi) or polished (Mogollon) interior surface. In archaeological contexts, vessel exteriors may be encrusted with soot from cooking fires.

V

Vegetal Paint. See "Carbon" Paint.

Vegetal Temper. Shredded plant material (or bast), such as juniper bark, used to bind together the clay for largely unfired pottery of the very early ceramic period.

W

Ware. A group of pottery types, usually from a specific province or group of provinces, that consistently shares the same descriptive attributes; for example, Chuska White Ware (with the term "Ware" capitalized) has coiled construction, gray-firing clay, crushed trachyte or sherd temper containing trachyte, and a white slip. *See* Series. Also, a generic, nonspecific term (not capitalized—brown ware) for generally similar pottery.

Wedding Jar. Specialized Tewa vessel form recognized in the mid-nineteenth century, usually having a globular body and two long pouring spouts linked near the top by a handle. Subsequently copied by some non-Tewa potters.

Whiteware. Usually pottery having a gray paste and an applied white slip; usually the basic ware for black-on-white painted pottery.

Z

Zoomorphic. In the form of an animal or bird; referring to either two-dimensional painted decoration or three-dimensional modeled effigies or figurines.

SELECTED BIBLIOGRAPHY

NOTE: Entries marked with an asterisk are largely nontechnical or semitechnical publications.

Anonymous
1975* *The Pottery Jewels of Joseph Lonewolf*. Scottsdale, Ariz.: Dandick Publications.

Anyon, Roger, and Steven A. LeBlanc
1984 *The Galaz Ruin: A Prehistoric Mimbres Village in Southwestern New Mexico*. Albuquerque: Maxwell Museum of Anthropology and University of New Mexico Press.

Arnold, Dean E.
1985 *Ceramic Theory and Cultural Process*. Cambridge: Cambridge University Press.

Bandelier, Adolph F.
1966–1984 *The Southwestern Journals of Adolph F. Bandelier (1880–1892)*, vols. I–IV. Eds. Charles H. Lange, Carroll L. Riley, and Elizabeth M. Lange. Albuquerque: University of New Mexico Press.

Batkin, Jonathan
1987* *Pottery of the Pueblos of New Mexico, 1700–1940*. Colorado Springs: Taylor Museum of the Colorado Springs Fine Arts Center.

Blair, Mary Ellen, and Lawrence R. Blair
1986* *Margaret Tafoya: A Tewa Potter's Heritage and Legacy*. West Chester, Penn.: Schiffer Publishing.

Bower, Nathan W., et al.
1986 "A Preliminary Analysis of Rio Grande Glazes of the Classic Period Using Scanning Electron Microscopy with X-ray Fluorescence." *Journal of Field Archaeology* 13:307–315.

Bradfield, Wesley
1929 *Cameron Creek Village: A Site in the Mimbres Area, Grant County, New Mexico*. Monographs of the School of American Research 1. Santa Fe.

Breternitz, David A.
1966 *An Appraisal of Tree-ring Dated Pottery in the Southwest*. Anthropological Papers of the University of Arizona 10. Tucson: University of Arizona Press.

Breternitz, David A., Arthur H. Rohn, Jr., and Elizabeth A. Morris
1974 *Prehistoric Ceramics of the Mesa Verde Region*. Museum of Northern Arizona Ceramic Series 5. Flagstaff.

Brew, J. O.
1946 *Archaeology of Alkali Ridge, Southeastern Utah*. Papers of the Peabody Museum of American Archaeology and Ethnology 21. Cambridge.

Brody, J. J.
1977* *Mimbres Painted Pottery*. Santa Fe and Albuquerque: School of American Research and University of New Mexico Press.

Brody, J. J., and Steven A. LeBlanc, eds.
1983* *Mimbres Pottery: Ancient Art of the American Southwest*. New York: Hudson Hills Press.

Bunzel, Ruth L.
1929* *The Pueblo Potter: A Study of Creative Imagination in Primitive Art*. Columbia University Contributions to Anthropology 8. New York. Reprint. New York: Dover Publications, 1972.

Carlson, Roy L.
1963 *Basket Maker III Sites Near Durango, Colorado*. University of Colorado Studies, Series in Anthropology 8. Boulder.

1970 *White Mountain Redware: A Pottery Tradition of East-central Arizona and Western New Mexico*. Anthropological Papers of the University of Arizona 19. Tucson.

Cattanach, George S., Jr.
1980 *Long House, Mesa Verde National Park, Colorado: Wetherill Mesa Excavations*. Publication in Archaeology 7-H. Washington, D.C.: National Park Service.

Chapman, Kenneth M.
1936 *The Pottery of Santo Domingo Pueblo*. Laboratory of Anthropology Monograph 1. Santa Fe.

1938 *Pueblo Indian Pottery of the Post Spanish Period*. Laboratory of Anthropology Series. Bulletin 4. Santa Fe.

1970 *The Pottery of San Ildefonso Pueblo*. School of American Research Monograph 28. Albuquerque: University of New Mexico Press.

Chapman, Kenneth M., and Bruce T. Ellis
1951 "The Line-break, Problem Child of Pueblo Pottery." *El Palacio* 58, 1:251–289.

Coe, Ralph T.
1986 *Lost and Found Traditions: Native American Art 1965–1985*. New York: University of Washington Press and American Federation Arts.

Colton, Harold S.
1953* *Potsherds: An Introduction to the Study of Prehistoric Southwestern Ceramics and Their Use in Historic Reconstruction*. Museum of Northern Arizona Bulletin 25. Flagstaff.

Colton, Harold S., and Lyndon L. Hargrave
1937 *Handbook of Northern Arizona Pottery Wares*. Museum of Northern Arizona Bulletin 11. Flagstaff.

Dittert, Alfred E., Jr., and Fred Plog
1980* *Generations in Clay: Pueblo Pottery of the American Southwest*. Flagstaff: Northland Press.

Edelman, Sandra A.
1979 "San Ildefonso Pueblo." In *Handbook of North American Indians*, vol. 9, *Southwest*. Ed. Alfonso Ortiz, pp. 308–316. Washington, D.C.: Smithsonian Institution.

Eggan, Fred
1979 "Pueblos: Introduction." In *Handbook of North American Indians*, vol. 9, *Southwest*. Ed. Alfonso Ortiz, pp. 224–235. Washington, D.C.: Smithsonian Institution.

Frank, Larry, and Francis H. Harlow
1974 *Historic Pottery of the Pueblo Indians, 1600–1880*. Boston: New York Graphic Society.

Fuller, Steve
1984 *Late Anasazi Pottery Kilns in the Yellowjacket District, Southwestern Colorado*. CASA Papers 4. Cortez, Colo.: Complete Archeological Services.

Garcia-Mason, Velma
1979 "Acoma Pueblo." In *Handbook of North American Indians*, vol. 9, *Southwest*. Ed. Alfonso Ortiz. Washington, D.C.: Smithsonian Institution.

Guthe, Carl E.
1925 *Pueblo Pottery Making: A Study at the Village of San Ildefonso*. Papers of the Southwest Expedition, Phillips Academy 2. New Haven: Yale University Press.

Hardin, Margaret Ann
1983* *Gifts of Mother Earth: Ceramics in the Zuni Tradition*. Phoenix: Heard Museum.

Harlow, Francis H.
1970 "History of Painted Tewa Pottery." In *The Pottery of San Ildefonso Pueblo* by Kenneth M. Chapman, pp. 37–51. Santa Fe: School of American Research.

1973 *Matte-paint Pottery of the Tewa, Keres and Zuni Pueblos*. Santa Fe: Museum of New Mexico Press.

1977 *Modern Pueblo Pottery, 1880–1960*. Flagstaff: Northland Press.

Haury, Emil W.
1936 *The Mogollon Culture of Southwestern New Mexico*. Medallion Papers 20. Globe, Ariz.: Gila Pueblo.

1976 *The Hohokam: Desert Farmers and Craftsmen, Excavations at Snaketown, 1964–1965*. Tucson: University of Arizona Press.

Haury, Emil W., et al.
1956 *An Archaeological Approach to the Study of Cultural Stability*. Memoirs of the Society for American Archaeology 11, pp. 31–57. Salt Lake City.

Hawley, Florence M.
1950 *Field Manuel of Prehistoric Southwestern Pottery Types*. University of New Mexico Bulletin, Anthropological Series 1/4. Albuquerque.

Hayes, Alden C., and James A. Lancaster
1975 *Badger House Community, Mesa Verde National Park, Colorado: Wetherill Mesa Excavations*. Publication in Archeology 7-E. Washington, D.C.: National Park Service.

Hayes, Alden C., Jon Nathan Young, and A. H. Warren
1981 *Excavation of Mound 7, Gran Quivira National Monument, New Mexico*. Publication in Archeology 16. Washington, D.C.: National Park Service.

Hedges, Ken, and Alfred E. Dittert, Jr.
1984* *Heritage in Clay: The 1912 Pueblo Pottery Collections of Wesley Bradfield and Thomas S. Dozier*. San Diego Museum Papers 17.

Hill, W. W.
1982 *An Ethnography of Santa Clara Pueblo, New Mexico*. Ed. and anno. Charles H. Lange. Albuquerque: University of New Mexico Press.

Holmes, William H.
1878 "Report on the Ancient Ruins of Southwestern Colorado, Examined During the Summers of 1875 and 1876." In *10th Annual Report of the U.S. Geological and Geographical Survey of the Territories for 1876*, pp. 383–408. Washington, D.C.

Jackson, William H.
1876 "Ancient Ruins in Southwestern Colorado." In *8th Annual Report of the U.S. Geological and Geographical Survey of the Territories for 1874*, pp. 367–381. Washington, D.C.

1878 "Report on Ruins Examined in 1875 and 1877." In *10th Annual Report of the U.S. Geological and Geographical Survey of the Territories for 1876*, pp. 411–450. Washington, D.C.

Judd, Neil M.
1954 *The Material Culture of Pueblo Bonito*. Smithsonian Miscellaneous Collections 124. Washington, D.C.: Smithsonian Institution.

Kidder, Alfred V.
1915 *Pottery of the Pajarito Plateau and of Some Adjacent Regions in New Mexico*. Memoir 2/6. Lancaster, Penn.: American Anthropological Association.

Kidder, Alfred V., and Anna O. Shepard
1936 "The Technology of Pecos Pottery." In *The Pottery of Pecos*, Vol. 2, Part 2. New Haven: Yale University Press.

Lambert, Marjorie F.
1966* *Pueblo Indian Pottery: Materials, Tools, and Techniques*. Santa Fe: Museum of New Mexico Press.

Lange, Charles H.
1959 *Cochiti, a New Mexico Pueblo Past and Present*. Austin: University of Texas Press. Reprint. Carbondale: Southern Illinois University Press, 1968.

LeBlanc, Steven A.
1982 "The Advent of Pottery in the Southwest." In *Southwestern Ceramics: A Comparative Review*. *The Arizona Archaeologist* 15:27–51. Arizona Archaeological Society, Phoenix.

1982 "Temporary Change in Mogollon Ceramics." In *Southwestern Ceramics: A Comparative Review*, *The Arizona Archaeologist* 15:106–127. Arizona Archaeological Society, Phoenix.

1983* *The Mimbres People: Ancient Pueblo Painters of the American Southwest*. London: Thames and Hudson.

LeFree, Betty
1975* *Santa Clara Pottery Today*. School of American Research Monograph 29. Albuquerque: University of New Mexico Press.

Lister, Robert H.
1958 *Archaeological Excavations in the Northern Sierra Madre Occidental, Chihuahua and Sonora, Mexico*. University of Colorado Studies, Series in Anthropology 7. Boulder.

Lister, Robert H., and Florence C. Lister
1978 *Anasazi Pottery: Ten Centuries of Prehistoric Ceramic Art in the Four Corners Country of the Southwestern United States*. Albuquerque: Maxwell Museum of Anthropology and University of New Mexico Press.

Lyon, Luke
1988 "Tewa Red and Tewa Black Pottery." *Pottery Southwest* 15, 1:4–5.

McGimsey, Charles R., III
1980 *Mariana Mesa: Seven Prehistoric Settlements in West-central New Mexico*. Peabody Museum of Archaeology and Ethnology 72. Cambridge: Harvard University.

Marriott, Alice
1948 *Maria: The Potter of San Ildefonso*. Norman: University of Oklahoma Press.

Martin, Paul S., and Elizabeth Willis
1940 *Anasazi Painted Pottery in Field Museum of Natural History*. Anthropology Memoirs 5. Chicago: Field Museum of Natural History.

Mera, Harry P.
1934 *A Survey of the Biscuit Ware Area in Northern New Mexico.* Laboratory of Anthropology, Technical Series Bulletin 6. Santa Fe.

1935 *Ceramic Clues to the Prehistory of North Central New Mexico.* Laboratory of Anthropology, Technical Series Bulletin 8. Santa Fe.

1937 *The Rainbird: A Study in Pueblo Design.* Laboratory of Anthropology Memoir 2. Santa Fe. Reprint. New York: Dover Publications, 1970.

1939 *Style Trends of Pueblo Pottery in the Rio Grande and Little Colorado Cultural Areas from the Sixteenth to the Nineteenth Century.* Laboratory of Anthropology Memoir 3. Santa Fe.

1940 *Population Changes in the Rio Grande Glaze-paint area.* Laboratory of Anthropology, Technical Series Bulletin 9. Santa Fe.

Morris, Earl H.
1919 *The Aztec Ruin.* American Museum of Natural History, Anthropological Paper 26. New York.

Nelson, N. C.
1914 *Pueblo Ruins of the Galisteo Basin, New Mexico.* American Museum of Natural History, Anthropological Paper, 15/1. New York.

Nesbitt, Paul H.
1931 *The Ancient Mimbreños, Based on Investigations at the Mattocks Ruin, Mimbres Valley, New Mexico.* Logan Museum, Bulletin 4. Beloit, Wis.

Olinger, Bart
1987 "Pottery Studies Using X-ray Fluorescence, Part 1, an Introduction, Nambe Pueblo as an Example." *Pottery Southwest* 14, 1:1–3.

Oppelt, Norman T.
1976* *Southwestern Pottery: An Annotated Bibliography and List of Types and Wares.* 2 vols. Occasional Publications in Anthropology, Archaeology Series 7. Greeley: Museum of Anthropology, University of Northern Colorado.

Ortiz, Alfonso, ed.
1979* *Handbook of North American Indians,* vol. 9, *Southwest.* Washington, D.C.: Smithsonian Institution.

Pepper, George H.
1920 *Pueblo Bonito.* American Museum of Natural History, Paper 27. New York.

Peterson, Susan
1977* *The Living Tradition of Maria Martinez.* Tokyo: Kodansha International.

1984* *Lucy M. Lewis: American Indian Potter.* Tokyo: Kodansha International.

Reiter, Paul
1938 *The Jemez Pueblo of Unshagi, New Mexico, with Notes on the Earlier Excavations at "Amoxiumqua" and Giusewa* (in two parts). Monographs of the School of American Research 5–6. Santa Fe.

Roberts, Frank H. H., Jr.
1929 *Shabikesh'chee Village: A Late Basket Maker Site in the Chaco Canyon, New Mexico.* Bureau of American Ethnology Bulletin 92. Washington, D.C.

1930 *Early Pueblo Ruins in the Piedra District, Southwestern Colorado.* Bureau of American Ethnology Bulletin 96. Washington, D.C.

1931 *The Ruins at Kiatuthlanna, Eastern Arizona.* Bureau of American Ethnology, Bulletin 100. Washington, D.C.

1932 *The Village of the Great Kivas on the Zuni Reservation.* Bureau of American Ethnology, Bulletin 111. Washington, D.C.

1940 *Archaeological Remains in the Whitewater District, Eastern Arizona. Part 2: Artifacts and Burials.* Bureau of American Ethnology, Bulletin 126. Washington, D.C.

Rodee, Marion, and James Ostler
1986* *Zuni Pottery.* West Chester, Penn.: Schiffer Publishing.

Rohn, Arthur H.
1971 *Mug House, Mesa Verde National Park, Colorado: Wetherill Mesa Excavations.* Archeological Research Series 7–D. Washington, D.C.: National Park Service.

Schroeder, Albert H., ed.
1982 *Southwestern Ceramics: A Comparative Review.* Arizona Archaeologist 15. Phoenix.

Schroeder, Gail D.
1964 "San Juan Pottery: Methods and Incentives." *El Palacio* 71, 1.

Shepard, Anna O.
1980* *Ceramics for the Archaeologist.* Washington, D.C.: Carnegie Institution of Washington, Publication 609.

Smith, Watson
1962 "Schools, Pots, and Potters." *American Anthropologist,* 64, 6:1165–1178.

Smith, Watson, Richard B. Woodbury, and Nathalie F. S. Woodbury
1966 *The Excavation of Hawikuh by Frederick Webb Hodge: Report of the Hendricks-Hodge Expedition 1917–1923.* Contributions from the Museum of the American Indian, Heye Foundation 20. New York.

Spivey, Richard L.
1979* *Maria.* Flagstaff: Northland Press.

Stanislawski, Michael B.
1978* *Pots, Potters, and Potsherds: Ethnoarchaeology of Hopi and Hopi-Tewa Pottery Making and Settlement.* Discovery. Santa Fe: School of American Research.

Stevenson, James
1883 *Illustrated Catalogue of Collections Obtained from Indians of New Mexico and Arizona in 1879.* Bureau of American Ethnology Annual Report 2. Washington, D.C.

1884 *Illustrated Catalog of Collections Obtained from the Pueblos of Zuni, New Mexico, and Wolpi, Arizona, in 1881.* Bureau of American Ethnology Annual Report 3. Washington, D.C.

Stirling, Matthew W.
1942 *Origin Myth of Acoma and Other Records.* Bureau of American Ethnology Bulletin 135. Washington, D.C.

Stubbs, Stanley A., and William S. Stallings, Jr.
1953 *The Excavation of Pindi Pueblo, New Mexico.* Monographs of the School of American Research 18. Santa Fe.

Swannack, Jervis D., Jr.
1969 *Big Juniper House, Mesa Verde National Park, Colorado: Wetherill Mesa Excavations.* Archeological Research Series 7–C. Washington, D.C.: National Park Service.

Swarthout, Jeanne, and Alan Dulaney
1982 *A Description of Ceramic Collections from the Railroad and Transmission Line Corridors: The Coronado Project Archaeological Investigations.* Museum of Northern Arizona Research Paper 26, Coronado Series 5. Flagstaff.

Tanner, Clara Lee
1969* *Southwest Indian Crafts.* Tucson: University of Arizona Press.

1976* *Prehistoric Southwestern Craft Arts.* Tucson: University of Arizona Press.

Taylor, Walter W.
1948 *A Study of Archaeology.* Memoir 69. Menasha: American Anthropological Association.

Toulouse, Betty
1977* *Pueblo Pottery of New Mexico Indians: Ever Constant, Ever Changing.* Santa Fe: Museum of New Mexico Press.

Trimble, Stephen
1987* *Talking with the Clay: The Art of Pueblo Pottery.* Santa Fe: School of American Research Press.

Warren, A. H.
1980 *Production and Distribution of Pottery in Chaco Canyon and Northwestern New Mexico.* Manuscript in the library of the Museum of Indian Arts and Culture, Museum of New Mexico. Santa Fe.

Washburn, Dorothy Koster
1977 *A Symmetry Analysis of Upper Gila Area Ceramic Design.* Papers of the Peabody Museum of Archaeology and Ethnology 68. Cambridge: Harvard University.

Washburn, Dorothy K., ed.
1984* *The Elkus Collection: Southwest Indian Art.* San Francisco: California Academy of Sciences.

Wheat, Joe Ben
1955 *Mogollon Culture Prior to A.D. 1000.* Memoirs of the Society for American Archaeology 10. Salt Lake City.

Whiteford, Andrew Hunter, et al.
1989 *I am Here: Two Thousand Years of Southwest Indian Arts and Culture.* Santa Fe: Laboratory of Anthropology, Museum of Indian Arts and Culture, and Museum of New Mexico Press.

Willey, Gordon R., and Philip Phillips
1958 *Method and Theory in American Archaeology.* Chicago: University of Chicago Press.

Withers, Arnold M.
1985 *Three Circle Red-on-white — An Alternative to Oblivion.* Papers of the Archaeological Society of New Mexico 10:15–25. Santa Fe.

INDEX

Boldface indicates pages with plates.

Abajo Black-on-orange, 49
Abiquiu Black-on-gray, 114
Abó, 121
Acoma Black-on-white, 97, 99
Acoma Polychrome, 94–99
Acoma Province, 9(map), 61, 69, 76, 87, 136
Acoma Pueblo, 123, 125
Acoma White, Tooled, Corrugated, 99
Acomita Polychrome (Laguna variant), 93
Agua Fria Glaze-on-red, 86
Ako Polychrome, 93
Alma Incised, 28
Alma Neckbanded, 31
Alma Plain, **26**, 27, **28**, 29, 32, 39
Alma Punched, 28
Alma Rough, 28
Alma Scored, 28
American Museum of Natural History, 6, 8
Anasazi, 44
 Central, 58, 61, 65, 69, 76, 102, 103, 109
 Eastern, 61, 76, 102
 Mineral-Paint Tradition, 17(map), 49, 57–59, 61–77, 78, 88, 106, 116. See also Pigments (mineral)
 origins, 24
 term, 10, 12
 Utility Tradition, 45–56, 59, 67, 102, 107, 108
 Vegetal-Paint Tradition, 18–19(maps), 59, 76, 87, 88, 89, 90, 102–105, 107, 109, 111–113, 115, 116. See also Pigments (vegetal)
 Western, 57, 58, 102, 103
Antiquities legislation, 7
Archaeological Institute of America, 6, 7
Archaic culture, 23
Ashiwi Polychrome, **90**
Awanyu figure, 115

Bancos Black-on-white, **102**
Bandelier, Adolph F., 6
Bandelier Black-on-gray, **112**, 113, 115
Basketmaker-Pueblo sequence, 8, 10, 11, 12
Basketmaker III, 45, 47, 50, 61, 106

designs, 65
 glaze-paint, 64, 81
 pigments, 61, 64, 75, 103, 107
Basketry, 23, 27, 29
 clay liners for, 24, **25**
 designs from, 58, 59, 65
 impressions, 24, 50, **53**
Beakers, **55**, **71**
Bennett Gray, 107
Biscuit Ware, 8, 39, 89, **112**, **113**, 114–116
Brew, J.O., 10
Brody, J.J., 36
Brown-firing pottery, 17(map), 27–28, 43. See also Mogollon Brown Tradition
Brushes (for paint), 102
Burial goods, 38

Camino Real, 6
Canteens, **38**, **48**, **79**, **95**, **104**
Captain Tom Wash, 106
Carbon-14 dating. See Radiocarbon dating
Carbon paint, 102. See also Pigments (vegetal)
Casa Grande, 6
Casas Grandes Province, 9(map), 43, 50, 86, 119–120
Cebolleta-Tularosa Black-on-white, 81
Ceremonial vessels, 117, 121
Cerrillos (New Mexico), 86, 122
Chaco Black-on-white, 72, **74**, **75**, **103**, **104**
Chaco Canyon Province, 6, 8, 9(map), 15
 painted pottery, 67, 68, 73, 76
 pigments, 61, 81, 107, 109
 Pueblo Bonito, 6
 temper, 47
 trade, 49, 68, 69, 72, 107
 utility pottery, 47
 See also Chaco Phenomenon
Chaco Corrugated, **50**, **51**, 52
Chaco Phenomenon, 68–69, 71–72, 76, 107, 111
 outliers, 68–69, 76, 107
 roads, 69, 76
Change, 20–21, 22, 136
Chronology (cultural), **11**
Chupadero Black-on-white, **82**, **83**, 111

Chuska Province, 9(map), 47, 49, 65, 106–107
 abandonment of, 111
 pigments, 61, 73, 75, 76, 103, 106–107, 109
Cibola Province, 9(map), 39, 43, 76, 78, 81, 110
Cibola White Ware, 78, 106
Cleneguilla Glaze-on-yellow, **86**, **87**
Classification (pottery), 7–8, 15, 64, 73, 135
 lumpers/splitters, 16
Clays, 48, 64, 136
 Acoma, 123
 See also Color; Firing; Temper
Cliff Palace (Mesa Verde), 6
Coal, 48
Coalition Period (Rio Grande), 11, 112, 114
Cochise Culture, 23, 24, **25**, 27, 44
Cochiti Polychrome, **126**, **127**
Cochiti Pueblo, 88, 89, 90, 91, 116, 122–123
Coil-paddle-and-anvil technique, 27
Coil-scrape technique, 50, 121
Color (pottery), 7, 20, 27
 brown-firing clay, 27–28, 43, 44
 firing and, 45, 58, 125
 fugitive, 32, **48**
 gray-firing clay, 44, 50
 red, 32, 43
 See also Clay; Firing; Pigments; Slip
Colorado Plateau, 23
Conference of Southwestern Anthropologists, 10
Coolidge Corrugated, **50**, **51**
Copper (in pigments), 78, 82
Cordero, Helen, 122
Corrugated pottery, **30**, **31**, 39, 49, **50**, **51**, **52**, 56, 67, **99**
 exuberant, 51
 painted, 31, 50
Crozier Black-on-white, **61**
Cuba (New Mexico), 107
Culinary pottery, 7
Cushing, Frank H., 6
Cuyamungue Black-on-tan, 39, **112**, 113, 116, 125

Dating, 20, 27. See also Dendrochronology
Deadmans Black-on-red, 49

166 INDEX

Dendrochronology, 12, 20, 27, 86
Dippers, 78, **103**, **106**
Double bowl, **58**
Dough bowl, **101**, **122**, **123**
Drought, 86, 89, 108, 111
Duck pots, **49**
Durango (Colorado)
  glaze-paint, 64, 81

Effigy vessels, 64, 76, 81, 102, 108
  handle, 80
El Paso Black-on-brown, 117
El Paso Polychrome, 117, **118**
El Paso series, 117, 118
Escavada Black-on-white, 73, **75**, 76
Escondida Polychrome, **119**
Espinoso Glaze-polychrome, 87

Feathered serpent motif, 115
Fewkes, J. Walter, 6
Field Museum of Natural History, 28
Firing techniques, 28, 121
  fuels, 48, 107, 121, 123
  origins, 24, 25
  oxidation, 45, 58, 131
  reduction, 39, 45, 58, 125, 131
  sites, 28, 47–48, 123
  temperatures, 29, 32
Four Corners area, 7, 49, 58, 125
Frijoles Canyon, 7, 90, 114
Fuels. *See under* Firing techniques
Fugitive color, 32, **48**, **49**, 59
Function. *See under* Pottery

Galisteo Basin, 8, 87, 89, 112, 113
  glaze-paint, 88, 114, 116
Galisteo Black-on-white, 87, **111**, 112
Gallina Banded Utility, 55
Gallina Black-on-white, **107**, 108
Gallina Province, 9(map), 107–108, 109
Gallinas Mountains, 43
Gallup Black-on-white, 37, **72**, 73, **74**, 76, 107
Gila River Valley, 25
Giusewa, 121
Glaze A–F series, 86, 87, 88, 89
Glaze I–VI series, 86
Glaze-Paint Tradition, **18–19**(maps), 64, 81–82, 36, 87, 90, 91, 121, 122
  Durango, 64, 81
  Middle Rio Grande, 88, 114, 116, 121–122, 136
  Pecos, 91, 114, **134**
  silica, 81, 82
Gran Quivira, 43, 121
Grave goods, 38
Gray ware, **17**(map). *See also* Utility Traditions
Great Basin, 24
Guaco (pigment), 102, 123

Hakataya culture, 25, 27
Handles, 50
  effigy, 80
  painted, 77
Haury, Emil W., 87
Hawikuh, 121
Hematite, 39, 47, 49, 86
Heshotauthla Polychrome, 86
Hewett, Edger Lee, 6–7, 8, 13
Historic Period, 11, 43, 51, 81, 121
  pigments, 61, 109
Hohokam culture, 25, 27, 36, 57, 59
Holmes, William H., 6
Hopi villages, 6, 48, 81, 102

Incised decoration, 28, 103, 115, 116, **119**, **132**
Irrigation farming, 115
Isleta Pueblo, 44, 91, 123
Isleta Red-on-tan, 44

Jackson, William H., 6
Jémez Black-on-white, 109
Jémez Mountains, 6, 109, 112
Jémez Plateau, 6, 8
Jémez Province, 9(map), 121, 136
Jémez Pueblo, 91
Jornada Painted Tradition, 117–118
Jornada Province, 9(map), 43, 44, 118
Juniper bark, 24

Kachinas, 87, 90
Kan-a Black-on-white, 107
Kan-a Gray, 48, 67
Kapo (Santa Clara Pueblo), 89
Kapo Black, 116, 125
Kayenta Province, 9(map), 57, 106, 107
Keres peoples, 89, 90, 91, 116
Kiatuthlanna Black-on-white, 33, **62**, **63**, 65, 67
Kidder, Alfred V., 7, 8, 9, 91, 114
"Killing" a pot, 38
Kilns, 47, 123
Kiva, 69, 87, 108, 136
Klagetoh Black-on-white, 79
Kotyiti Glaze-on-yellow, 88
Kotyiti Glaze-polychrome, **89**

La Bajada (New Mexico), 88
Laboratory of Anthropology, 13
Laguna Polychrome, **101**
Language, 12, 47, 58, 113
La Plata Black-on-red, 49
La Plata Black-on-white, 57, **58**, **59**, 61, 64, 106
Las Humanas (Gran Quivira), 121
Lead (in pigments), 81, 82, 86, 121
LeBlanc, Stephen, 12
Limonite, 47, 86
Lino Black-on-gray, 61, **102**, 106, 107

Lino Gray, 45, **46**, 48, 102, 106, 107
  Fugitive Red variant, **48**, 49, 59
Los Padillas Glaze Polychrome, 86

McElmo Black-on-white, **103**, 104, 109, 110
McElmo Style, 109
Magnetite, 39
Maize, 23–24
Majolica, 6
Mancos Black-on-white, **76**
Manganese (in pigments), 58, 78, 82
Mangas Black-on-white, 45, **47**, 51
Martin, Paul S., 28
Martinez, Dominguita, 125
Medicine jars/bowls, 39, **115**, **133**, **134**
Melon bowl, **132**
Mera, Harry P., 13
Mesa Verde Black-on-white, **104**, **105**, 106, 109, 110
Mesa Verde Corrugated, **49**
Mesa Verde Province, 6, 8, 9(map), 15, 47, 49, 58, 81, 110
  pigments, 57, 59, 61, 64, 81, 107, 109, 111
Mexico, 6, 69
  influences, 4, 25, 27, 50, 57, 76, 86, 118–119
Middle Rio Grande Province, 9(map), 61, 73, 79, 86, 88, 90, 111, 121
  glazes, 114, 116, 122, 125, 136
Middle Rio Puerco Province, 9(map), 61, 82, 87, 90
Migration, 112, 136
Mimbres Black-on-white, 33, **36**, **37**, **38**, 39
  pictorials, **40**, **41**, **42**
Mimbres Bold Face Black-on-white, 33
Mimbres Classic Black-on-white, 33
Mimbres Classification, 11
Mimbres Province, 8, 9(map), 15, 36, 43, 118
  "killing" a pot, 38
Mogollon Brown Tradition, **17**(map), 26–31, 43–44, 45, 117
Mogollon Classification, 11
Mogollon Culture, 12, 27, 50, 51, 57, 116, 125
  Jornada Branch, 117–118
  origins, 24
  San Simon Branch, 27
  trade, 36, 39, 78, 79
  utility ware, 27–28
Mogollon Red-on-Brown, 32, **34**, 57
Mogollon Slipped Tradition, 32–39, 44, 91
Mogollon Utility Ware, 27–31, 50
Montezuma Valley, 76, 110
Mugs, **105**
Museum of New Mexico, 7, 13–14

National Park Service, 68
Navajo, 12, 108
Neck Banding, 31, 49, 51, 55, 67
Nelson, Nels C., 8
Northern Rio Grande, 79, 87, 111

INDEX 167

Ogapoge Polychrome, **115**, 125
Ollas, 29, 116, 125
Orange ware, 49, 58
Oshara Tradition, 23, 24, 44, 103
Otowi ruin (Parjarito Plateau), 8

Paint
  brushes, 102
  See also Pigments
Painted pottery, 18–19(maps), 20, 57
  abandonment of, 91
  earliest, 57, 59
  trade, 20, 68, 122. *See also* Trade wares
Pajarito Plateau, 6, 8, 87, 89, 112, 113
Paleoindian period, 23
Paquimé, 43, 119
Peabody Museum (Harvard University), 10
Pecos Classification, 10, **11**, 12
Pecos Glaze Polychrome, **134**
Pecos Pueblo, 7, 8, 86, 87, 88, 91, 114
  glaze ware, 91, **114**, **134**
Pecos River Valley, 113
Pepper, George, 6
Pictorials, 33, 36, **40**, 57
Picuris Province, 87
Piedra Black-on-white, **64**, 65
Piedra Gray, **53**, 54
Piedra Neckbanded, **55**
Pigments, 18–19(maps), 20
  acrylic, 123
  See also Glaze-Paint Tradition; Pigments (mineral); Pigments (vegetal)
Pigments (mineral), 57–59, 61
  characteristics of, 64, 102
  copper, 78, 82
  iron, **19**(map), 57, 58, 64, 65, 86, 102, 106, 107, 109, 122, 125
  lead, 81, 82, 86, 121
  manganese, 58, 78, 82
  See also Anasazi, Mineral-Paint Tradition; Glaze-Paint Tradition
Pigments (vegetal), 18–19(maps), 57, 61, 64, 102–103, 122, 136
  "carbon paint," 102
  characteristics of, 64, 102
  decline of, 86, 88
  preparation, 58, 102
  quaco, 102, 123
  See also Anasazi, Vegetal-Paint Tradition
Pindi Black-on-white, **110**, 112
Pithouses, 12
Playas Red Incised, **119**
Pojoaque Corrugated, **56**
Pojoaque Neckbanded, **55**
Polish, 38, 48, 50
Polished Black Tradition, 39, 44
Polychromes, 116

Pothunting, 7
Potsuvi'i Incised, 115, 116, 119, **131**
Pottery
  function, 1, 6, 7, 20, 22, 38, 50, 135
  origins, 24, 25, 27, 44
Pottery types, 8, 15, 136
  analysis, 16, 20
  meaning of, 15–16, 21–22
  number of, 15
Powhoge Polychrome, **124**, 125
Prayer meal bowl, **130**
Puaray Glaze-polychrome, **87**, **88**, 89
Pueblo Bonito (Chaco Canyon), 6
Pueblo Revolt (1680), 121
Puerco Black-on-red, 78
Puerco Black-on-white, **73**, 75
Puerco Province, 9(map), 81. *See also* Rio Puerco
Puerco-Zuni Province, 9(map), 61, 65, 75, 78, 81
Puki, 50, 89, 116
Puname Polychrome, **101**, 122
Puyé (Parjarito Plateau), 8–9
  Community House, 7, 89

Quarai, 121
Quemado, 24, 39, 44, 61

Radiocarbon dating, 20, 27
Red Mesa Black-on-white, **66**, **67**, **68**, **69**, **70**, **71**, 107
Red Mesa Style, 107
Red Ware, 17(map), 49, 78–79, 81, 86
Reed, E.K., 114
Regressive Pueblo Period, 114
Reserve, 28, 39
Reserve Black-on-white, 39, **77**, 78, 79
Reserve Indented Corrugated, 39
Reserve Plain Corrugated, 39
Reserve Smudged, 39
Rim forms, 33, 86
Rinaldo, John B., 28
Rio Chaco, 106
Rio Chama Valley, 113
Rio Grande Classification, **11**
Rio Grande Province, 9(map), 44, 50, 51, 79, 109, 111
Rio Grande Valley, 6, 10, 13, 15, 49, 82, 89
  Coalition Period, 112, 114
  migrations to, 43, 113, 136
Rio Puerco, 61, 65, 112
Roberts, Frank H.H., Jr., 65, 114
Roberts Classification, 11
Rock House Ruin (Mimbres Valley), 38
Rocky Mountain Beeplant, 102
Rosa Gray, 53
Roybal, Tonita, 125

Sacramento Mountains, 43, 118
St. Johns Polychrome, 79, 82
Sakona Black-on-tan, 125

Sakona Polychrome, 89, **115**, 125
Salinas Province, 8, 9(map), 43, 44, 61, 111, 121
San Cristobal ruin, 8
Sandia Pueblo, 91
San Francisco Red, 32, 49, 78
Sangre de Cristo Mountains, 112, 113
San Ildefonso Black-on-black, **128**
San Ildefonso Black-on-red, **125**
San Ildefonso Polychrome, **129**, **130**
San Ildefonso Pueblo, 39, 113, 125
San Juan Basin, 44, 48, 51, 65, 72, 76, 106, 107, 108, 114
  abandonment of, 86, 107, 110, 111
  pigments, 61, 103, 111
  trade, 49, 79
  Upper, 49, 50, 57, 58, 107, 108, 109
San Juan Incised, **132**
San Juan Polychrome (carved), **133**
San Juan Pueblo, 119, 125
San Juan Red Ware, 81
Sankawi Black-on-cream, 113, 114, **115**, 116
San Lazaro Glaze-Polychrome, 89
San Marcial Black-on-white, **59**, 65
San Simon Branch (Mogollon Culture), 27
Santa Clara Black, **131**, **132**
Santa Clara Polychrome, **134**
Santa Clara Pueblo, 89, 131
  black ware, 39, 125, **131**, **132**
  sgraffito, 131, **133**
Santa Clara Red-on-tan, 125, **131**
Santa Clara Red Sgraffito, **133**
Santa Fe River, 112
Santa Fe Trail, 6
Santo Domingo Black-on-black, 122, **125**
Santo Domingo Polychrome, **120**, 122, **123**, **124**, 125
Santo Domingo Pueblo, 82, 88, 90, 91, 116, 122
Sapawe Micaceous, **49**
School of American Archaeology, 7
School of American Research, 7
Sedentism, 24
Seed jars, 28, **29**, **53**, 58, 71, **72**, **73**, **97**, **98**, **99**, 125, **130**
Series, 15
Service ware, 7, 20, 22, 43, 50, 107, 135
Sgraffito, 131, **133**
Shepard, Anna O., 45, 88
Signatures (by potters), 21
Slip, 20, 32, 39, 45, 50, 65, 78
  fugitive, 32, 49
  micaceous, 49, 119
  red, 32, 44, 49, 57, 78, 81, 89, 90, 102, 110, 116, 125
  white, 33, 36
  yellow, 88
Smithsonian Institution, 6, 65
Smudging, 31, 39
Socorro Black-on-white, **82**, **83**, **84**, 111
Spruce Tree House (Mesa Verde), 6
Stevenson, James, 6

Storage jar, **118**, **126**
Storyteller figures, 122–123
Stratigraphic excavation technique, 8

Tallahogan Red, 49
Tano (Southern Tewa), 88–89, 125
Tansy mustard plant, 102
Taos Province, 9(map), 73, 87, 111
Temper, 45, 47
  analysis, 20, 47
  crushed rock, 47, 82, 86, 117
  fiber, 24, 25
  function of, 45
  quartz, 47
  sand, 45, 47, 65, 103, 106, 107
  sherd, 47, 65, 82, 86
  trachyte, 47, 106–107, 110
  volcanic tuff, 113
Tewa Basin Province, 9(map), 50, 73, 87, 90, 112, 113
  Biscuit Wares, 114–115
Tewa Polychrome, **115**, 125
Tewa Pueblos, 39, 88, 90, 91, 119, 125
  pigments, 102, 122, 136
  polychromes, 89, 116, 122
Theodore Black-on-white, 107
Three-Circle-Neck Corrugated, **30**, 31
Three-Circle Red-on-white, 33
Tiguex, 8
Trade, 20, 27
  historic, 6, 121, 122
  Mexican, 119. *See also* Mexico
  wares, 20, 36, 49, 68, 78, 79, 81, 89, 109
Traditions, 2–4, 13, **17–19**(maps), 20, 21–22, 135–136
  sub-, 22
Tsirege ruin (Pajarito Plateau), 8
Tularosa Basin, 43, 117, 118
Tularosa Black-on-white, **43**, **78**, 79, **80**, **81**
Tularosa Fillet Rim, 33
Tularosa-Patterned Corrugated, 31
Tularosa Style, 79
Tunicha Black-on-white, 107
Tusayan White Ware, 112
Types. *See* Pottery types
Tyuonyi ruin, 7

Utility Traditions, **17**(map), 20, 22, 135
  Anasazi, 45–56, 59, 65, 67, 102, 107, 108
  Historic, 122
  Mogollon, 27–31, 50

Varieties (ceramic), 15
Vigil, Evelyn, 91
Volcanic materials, 43, 44

Walpi (Hopi village), 6
Wares, 15, 136
Wedding vase, **95**

Wendorf, Fred, 114
Wheat, Joe Ben, 12
Wheel (potters'), 50
White Mound Black-on-white, **58**, **59**, **60**, 64, 65, 106
White Mountain Red Ware, 78, 81, 82, 89
White Rock Canyon, 113
Wingate Black-on-red, 78, 79, **85**, 110
Wiyo Black-on-white, **110**, **111**, 112

Yellowjacket (Colorado), 47
Yellow ware, 88–89, 112

X-ray fluorescence (XRF) microscopy, 20

Zia Polychrome, **100**, **101**
Zia Pueblo, 90, 122
Zoomorphic figures, 57. *See also* Pictorials
Zuni, 8, 43, 50, 78, 81, 86
  glaze decoration, 121, 125, 136
  temper, 82
Zuni Polychrome, 91, **92**, **99**